A Few Tricks ꞏꞏꞏ y

DAILY REFLECTIONS ꞏꞏ MEN,
QUEER BOYꞏ,
MAGNIFICENT QUEENS,
AND THE PEOPLE WHO LOVE THEM

Gary J. Stern

The Crossing Press
Freedom, CA 95019

To Baby

Copyright © 1994 Gary J. Stern
Cover art by Jason Weller
Handstand, oil and mixed media on canvas, 60" x 96"
Cover and interior design by Amy Sibiga
Printed in the U.S.A.

Library of Congress Cataloging-in-Publication Data

Stern, Gary J. (Gary Jon), 1953-
    A few tricks along the way: daily reflections for gay men, queer boys, magnificent queens, and the people who love them/Gary J. Stern.
        p.   cm.
    ISBN 0-89594-726-9 (pbk.)
    1. Gays—Psychology—Miscellanea. 2. Affirmations. I. Title.
HQ76.25.S73 1994
305.38'9664—dc20
                                                    94-12505
                                                    CIP

ACKNOWLEDGMENTS

There is a saying, "It takes a village to raise a child," and in my case, at least, it has taken a village to write a book. I wish to thank the following people who each helped make this project possible.

Barbara, for your constancy, your insight, for being available at all hours, and for always calling the work to higher gound.

Zoe and Evan, for patience, reminding me what's most important, and for just being such fabulous kids.

Mom, for your love and lamb chops, and Dad, for keeping an eye on me from that great big golf course in the sky.

Tom, for hilarity after one a.m. and for being the wonderful friend you are.

Ellen Sue, for all the author lessons and encouragement.

Marjorie Shapiro and William Goodman, for invaluable guidance.

Sam Modenstein, for all the years of friendship and for coming up with something gay for me to do in New York.

Beth Fischlowitz, for the perfect week at Coole Park.

Karl Reichert, Curt Peterson, Kel Keller, and Timothy Rose for sharing so much of your lives, for all your support, and for becoming my friends.

Jason Weller, for the cover art and all the research.

Ken Darling, for your work on the manuscript.

Jonathan Lazear and Eric Vrooman for believing in the project from the start and helping make it happen.

John and Elaine Gill and everyone at Crossing Press for wanting the book, for such fine editorial guidance, and for making it beautiful.

Quentin Crisp, Judy Grahn, Mark Thompson, Leigh W. Rutledge, Winston Leyland, and Eric Marcus, for their invaluable collections of quotes and gay source material.

Quatrefoil Library, for making so much so accessible.

The many people who shared stories, books, ideas, and reactions to the endless work in progress: David Ziegenhagen, Bob Dachis, Katherine Mitchell, Rachel Roiblatt, Rita Magnin, Jill and Bob Edelstein, Ralph Rovner, Miriam Seidenfeld, Sue Martin, Menas Zografikis, Tom Palumbo, Jason Weller, Christopher Minarich, Malcolm Fox Linton, George and Evelyn Lonsdorf, Sara Tobias-Reich, Eugene Hoffman, Char Cohodes, Beau Takahara, Joel Hodroff, Steve and Maggie Gray, Jean Anderson, Greg Jones, Terry Anderson, Marty Cushing, Jim Montoya, Pat Peterson, Craig Weitz, Vijit Ramchandani, Audrey Anderson, Emil Angelica, Ms. Andrews, Vince Hyman, Stacy Mills, Jerie Heille, Linda Smith, Carol Lukas, GaVae Pederson, Jill Fixler, Michael Winer, Karen Ray, Raquel Lopez,

David Marty, Mary Beth Koehler, Paul Irving, John Seymour-Anderson, Steve Bonoff, Vivian Jenkins-Nelson, Bob Anderson, John Clark Donahue, Phil Oxman, Michael Lechner, Johnny Sularz, Afzal Shah, Russ King, Joanne Walz, Alexa Oxley, and The Fathers Group. And the following performers, writers, editors, historians, and anthologists without whose particular inspiration and work it would have been impossible for this author to pick up the gay thread and follow it to all the illuminating places it has led: Lev Raphael, Andrew Holleran, Armistead Maupin, Joe Keenan, John Gilgun, Martin Duberman, Harvey Fierstein, Patrick Scully, Jean-Nickolaus Tretter, Myron Johnson, Tony Kushner, Bette Midler, The Flirtations, Rakesh Ratti, Lois Commondenominator, Edward Carpenter, John Addington Symonds, Perry Tilleraas, Andy Rose, Christie Balka, John Preston, Wayne Curtis, Will Roscoe, Jonathan Ned Katz, Randy P. Conner, Rhoda Thomas Tripp, Franklin Abbott, and the International Gay and Lesbian Archives.

ART CREDITS

CONTENTS

October	November	December
1. Lovers	1. Dinner	1. Release
2. Emotional Terrorism	2. Bisexuality	2. Come
3. The Pink Triangle	3. Legs	3. Drag
4. Fights	4. Bad Boys	4. Self-Sufficiency
5. The Heart	5. Outing	5. Ripening
6. The Mahu	6. Bashing	6. Truth
7. Learning	7. Discrimination in	7. The Wizard of Oz
8. Rapture	the Military	8. The Child Within
9. Communion	8. Otherness	9. Allies
10. San Francisco	9. Nourishment	10. Gay Culture
11. World Peace	10. Discretion	11. Divorce
12. The Generation Gap	11. Penetration	12. Heterosexism
13. Separation	12. Size	13. Feet
14. Videos	13. Books	14. The United States
15. Coming Out to	14. Denmark	15. Seasons
Strangers	15. Deepening	16. First Love
16. Foreplay	16. Makeup	17. Self-Pity
17. Hangovers	17. Courage	18. Surrender
18. Asses	18. Legislation	19. Equality
19. Heartbreak	19. Education	20. Depression
20. Healing	20. Thanksgiving	21. Death
21. Maturity	21. Extremism	22. Devotion
22. Straight Guys	22. Marriage	23. Family Events
23. Adventurers	23. Life Partnership	24. Body of Christ
24. Ancestors	24. Phone Sex	25. Gifts
25. Infiltration	25. Straight-Acting/	26. Interior Design
26. Lifelong Coming Out	Straight-Appearing	27. Making Love
27. The Future	26. Real Men	28. Spiritual Union
28. Lust	27. Former Lovers	29. Sweat
29. Puritanism	28. Widowhood	30. Liberation
30. Gay Community	29. Being There	31. The New Year
31. Halloween	30. Authenticity	

January

HAPPINESS

He felt he had been embraced, taken in beneath these warm covers, not by Frankie, but by the world itself, by God, and he lay there, listening to Frankie's heart beat against his ear, afraid to breathe he was so happy...
—Andrew Holleran, Dancer from the Dance

Our images of love and happiness were shaped by an endless stream of silver screen lovers: Lady and that irascible Tramp, Hepburn and Tracy, Bogie and Bacall, Dustin Hoffman and Katherine Ross (Elaine! Elaine!), with the flamelit profiles of Scarlett and Rhett hovering above them all.

Small wonder the idea of happiness in the arms of another man seems impossible. Until you've been there. Then, slowly, flickering movie house images are replaced by something infinitely more compelling.

We don't grow up prepared for happiness, but when it comes, it does what it does for all lovers, moving the very earth beneath our feet.

My happiness is real.

ARCHETYPES

I am distressed for thee, my brother Jonathan;
Very pleasant hast thou been unto me;
Wonderful was thy love to me,
Passing the love of women.

—*Second Samuel, 1:26*

The names of the world's great lovers are glorified in literature, in myth, in prayer, and in song. Our cultures are informed by epic stories of Romeo's abandon, Antony and Cleopatra's perilous bond, the mating of Shiva and Shakti. Our roots run deep into the soil of heterosexual passions.

Cut off from these primal images of male/female love, we may sense ourselves adrift in history, just recently invented, with no birthright and no claim. Homosexual archetypes are fewer and further between, but they are there for us.

David and Jonathan are a beginning. Warriors both, Jonathan loyal and defiant; lyrical David, king to his people. The description of their parting rivals that of any torn lovers, "David arose out of a place toward the South, and fell on his face to the ground, and bowed down three times; and they kissed one another, and wept one with another until David exceeded...And Jonathan said to David...The Lord shall be between me and thee, and between my seed and thy seed, forever."

I am a lover of men, like many before me.

LOOKING

The eye is pleased when nature stoops to art.
—*Richard Wilbur, "A Courtyard Thaw"*

He catches my eye a half block away as he comes rollerblading down Spring Street. He is probably of average height, but the skates make him a head taller than the stream of pedestrians moving in counterpoint on the sidewalk. He takes obvious pleasure in his movements. I stop to watch him approach.

He is wearing khaki shorts, white athletic socks and a shirt of light fabric unbuttoned and billowing around his torso. His hair is chestnut and blunt-cut to his shoulders—a good style for his age, mid-twenties—and it is playing a game with the wind and his shirt and the sun.

Just as he passes me in the intersection, he does a little hop in the air, stretching his arms out for balance. The shirt flies up. He is handsomely proportioned, strong and supple in the way some young men are who don't have to work at it. He smiles, seems to congratulate himself for pulling off the maneuver, and in another instant his blades carry him out of sight.

I turn to resume my walk. I smile, too. I have just seen something beautiful.

My eyes are well pleased.

BEING HIP

You SLEEP on:
a) A futon from Arise.
b) A high-tech sleeping platform upholstered in black leather.
c) Ikea's genius tubular chrome number.
d) The 18th-century sleigh-bed you rescued from that barn sale.
e) A knotty pine colonial from Ethan Allen.
                                —Question from "The Queer Quiz," Out Magazine

There was always a lot of pressure being lesbian or gay—what with everybody so overwrought about who we like to sleep with and all. But things have changed. Now that we're acknowledged as trend-setters, we've got a whole new set of pressures. Like worrying about what we sleep *on.*

The business of being hip was work enough when it was strictly an inside deal. It was no one but ourselves, after all, who set dress codes for the ideal clone, the delectable disco bunny, or the butchest boy toy. Who would have thought there'd be a cool gay/lez magazine "Queer Quiz" that teasingly tested our urban sophisticate hipness quotient? What most of us knew from queer quizzes were wrong answers to junior high school queries about how you're supposed to cross your legs.

Let's not be seduced by our prestige as an up and coming market segment. After all, we didn't get hip in the first place by following the crowd.

It's hippest to ignore the whole thing.

INNUENDO

Why don't you come up and see me sometime?
—Attributed to Mae West

Old friends overheard:

"Well, I would come up and see you, but I really am much too busy."

"Oh? I thought business had been a little *slow* for you lately."

"Uh, huh. Well, God knows you'd be the expert on *slow*."

"Yes, well, slow has its virtues, not that *you*, my dear, would know."

"True, I *was* fast in my day. But never loose."

What is it with gay men? It seems conversation, especially among close friends, often veers on a course that would cause Emily Post to believe she'd entered the seventh ring of hell.

Here, innuendo has risen to an art form. An Olympic sport. Dueling banjos run amuck. A sort of moveable feast of communal foreplay.

Yes, well, it all depends on how you slice it. Some jokes go too far. Others, alas, not far enough.

I'll take my licks.

THE BIBLE

Thou shalt not lie with mankind, as with womankind; it is abomination.
—Leviticus, 18:22

Twelve words that have formed the basis for untold alienation and violence loosed on homosexual people over centuries. For those of us raised in Christian or Jewish traditions, Leviticus swims through the deep of our subconscious like a moral Loch Ness Monster.

With her forceful essay, "In God's Image: Coming to Terms with Leviticus," Rebecca T. Alpert makes it safe to go back in the water. Alpert offers three approaches—all within traditions of biblical scholarship—to deal with the passage.

The *Interpretive Approach* draws out alternative meanings. For example, the text may tell us to recognize and respect differences; one should not make love to a male as if he were a woman.

The *Critical Approach* makes the case for overriding some injunctions based on historic perspective. After all, the Bible also condoned slavery and second-class status for people with disabilities.

Finally, Alpert suggests *Encountering the Text* in order to go through, then beyond, our anger. We can use Leviticus positively: as a doorway to dialogue, an opportunity to engage our contemporary congregations with the facts of our experience and the reality of our holiness as human beings.

Ignorance is the true abomination.

ASKING

I got as far as, "Hi. I'm....." and stopped. I couldn't remember my name.
—Rolf R.

It's so scary to put ourselves on the line! Time comes, though, when nothing ventured clearly boils down to nothing gained. So what's the worst that can happen when we ask someone out?

Well, we can forget our own names, for one thing. But so what. The attractive and agreeable young man embarrassed by a sudden onset of amnesia still succeeded in his venture. Boy gets boy anyway.

Or he doesn't. The heartthrob we've been eying for weeks in aerobics class says he's busy. Or he's straight. Or get lost. *Fine.* One less fantasy cluttering up our libido. And one more pat on the back for being the kind of person who's willing to take a chance on getting what he wants.

I'll ask.

FAMILY

A Family: Two or more persons who share resources, share responsibility for decisions, share values and goals, and have commitments to one another over a period of time. The family is that climate that one comes home to; and it is that network of sharing and commitments that most accurately describes the family unit, regardless of blood, legalities, or adoption or marriage.

—*American Home Economics Association*

Myth: *Gays are a threat to the family.*
Reality: Some families are a threat to gays.

This potent little piece of propaganda is a handy weapon in the ongoing battle against us. The logic has always escaped me. Is it that we threaten the families we grew up in because they can't tolerate the truth? Or is it that we threaten *the basic building block of society*? Really, is somebody seriously worried that straight people will all decide homosexuality is the superior option, quit getting married and having kids, and the human race will become extinct? (And the Oscar goes to...*Planet of the Gays!*)

Myth: *Homosexuals are incapable of forming families.*
Reality: Homosexuals are incapable of forming families—legally by marriage—almost everywhere in the world. We just manage on our own.

A fascinating Catch 22. On the one hand we're attacked for a "lifestyle" incompatible with (hold your nose) *family values*, but it's the same Neanderthals who complain about us that freak out at the idea of domestic partnerships and gay marriage. What to do?

Do as we have done for some time. Keep choosing our own families, the networks of sharing and commitments that, regardless of blood, legalities, or adoption or marriage, are the people we come home to, the people we trust and love.

I'm a family man.

HUMAN RIGHTS

We ask for all that you have asked for yourselves in the progress of your development; and simply on the ground that the rights of every human being are the same and identical.
—*Elizabeth Cady Stanton*

The fight for human dignity has been waged on countless fronts throughout history. Looking back, it is almost inconceivable that slavery in America ended just over 100 years ago and that one decade prior to that Elizabeth Cady Stanton first brought her challenge to the New York Legislature to stop classing women with "idiots and lunatics."

The lesson here is not to wait patiently for the basic rights of gay and lesbian people to be recognized, but to realize we stand in a long line of courageous men and women who committed themselves to the overturning of inherent injustice. They, like us, knew the ugliness of entrenched discrimination and hate, felt the backlash that is the evil twin of progress. And we, like them, will fight for what is right.

One hundred years from now, a new generation will admire how we changed the world.

My rights are inalienable.

DREAMS

I surfaced out of that dream like a diver who knows, as he slides like a knife to the bottom of the pool, that he's just experienced the most perfect dive of his life. In my dream, I'd been down on one knee, lacing up my boot. I'd looked up suddenly and seen a naked man standing in front of me. This was no ordinary man. You might almost say this was some kind of spirit. He had a glow to him. He said, "Why be afraid, Stevie? It's all right." That's all there had been to it.

—John Gilgun, Music I Never Dreamed Of

Our dreams are full of messengers. They come to us across space and time, do and say the impossible, leave us haunted by nightmare dread and grace us with perfect dream peace.

Some cultures believe we enter a spirit world while we slumber. Among Native Americans, children sleep protected by woven "dreamcatchers" hung over them to ferret out interlopers with evil intent. Jungian theory says dreams are the realm of symbol. We can learn the language of the subconscious and unlock a storehouse of age-old experience and knowing. The gestalt approach is inner conversation. You are you. You are the boot being laced. You are the naked man with a glow to him. What is each part of you saying?

Our dreams lead us and follow us. At the bottom of the dream pool are the prisms and currents of our lives. Our deepest fears, deepest longings, deepest knowledge lie shimmering in the water.

I dive deep.

FINDING OURSELVES

The journey of a thousand miles begins with a single step.
—Chinese Proverb

Being gay is an uncharted destination. Whether we ran from it for years or knew our direction early on, there came a time when each of us took the critical first step of acknowledging to ourselves where we were headed.

I was on a work retreat, but the strategic planning questions struck me at a much more personal level. "What is your vision for the future? What will you have to give up in order to move from here to there?"

I began to see my future and drifted into an image of life with a man. We smiled at each other as I entered the room. I felt my life energy rise, slowly uncoiling from the base of my spine. Then I imagined another room. In it was my wife of ten years. I knew I loved her, but a deadness arose. I opened my eyes and knew something had shifted, an inner struggle finally resolved. In a quiet, simple, and suddenly undeniable way, my life was demanding to be lived differently.

I mustered myself, went into the bathroom, looked at myself in the mirror and said aloud, for the very first time, "I'm gay."

My gayness is a life force.

CONDOMS

Let a little something come between you and a close friend.
—Safe Sex Ad

A lovely American woman, out to make a good impression on her French dinner hosts, is engaged in spirited discussion on the superiority of French bread over its poor transatlantic relation. "It's better," she exclaims in her best Berlitz *Français*, "because it doesn't have any *préservatifs*! American bread is just full of them!"

Unfortunately, her point is lost in translation. *Préservatif* is French for condom.

It seems the French, always a step ahead on minting words pertaining to *l'amour*, have done it again. But whether we're shacked up in Paris, France, or Paris, Texas, the reality is, we have no more business jumping into bed without our trusty condom than we do jumping overboard without a life preserver.

So between us, let's not kid around on this one. There's no two ways about it.

I'll bake mine with préservatifs.

LONELINESS

Besides, all the people who are as alone as I am will one day gather at the river. We will watch the evening sun go down. And in the darkness maybe we will know the truth.

—Alice Walker, Meridian

We run from our loneliness as from a ball of fire. To bars. To movies. To sex. To drugs. Why is it we are afraid to be overtaken? What do we believe will happen to us?

When we stop long enough, when we just sit with it, we begin to understand. Loneliness has a vastness full of whispers and pleas: to be held, to be rocked, to be wanted, to be loved. It does indeed cause us to tremble. And to weep.

Little by little we learn more. We hold and rock ourselves. We say, "I want you." We find we have the capacity to be our own comfort and are not so alone after all. We see the last rays of the blazing sun and they warm us to the quick.

The antidote to loneliness is intimacy. It begins by getting close to ourselves.

I am not alone. I have myself.

COUPLISM

There are days when solitude is a heady wine that intoxicates you with freedom.

—*Colette*

Contrary to much popular thinking, the primary aim of daily life is not, for many people, to be part of a couple. Now pairing off has enjoyed a significant boost among gay men since the advent of AIDS, but this should not be construed as a vote *for* monogamy so much as a vote *against* the now obvious risks of promiscuity.

Nonetheless, a new "ism" is rearing its ugly head in our midst: the presumption that people who are not currently part of a twosome spend their honest moments wishing they were. With coupling elevated to a superior lifestyle, the hapless uncoupled must be *relationship-impaired.*

There are other ways of looking at it. As Baba Ram Dass so succinctly put it back in the '60s, the boiled-down secret to life is to "be here now." Many gay men do not covet their neighbor's husband. We are actually happy being alone, whether temporarily or permanently, and find our solitude to be heady enough.

There is value and richness in being alone.

SELF-WORTH

Our parents said they loved us, but they didn't act that way. They broke our hearts and stole our worth, with the things that they would say.

—*Elia Wise, For Children Who Were Broken*

It was thoughtless, for the most part, our parents simply aping prevailing sex role stereotypes and a heterosexist notion of the world. But their words did hurt us and most of us live on with broken-hearted little boys buried inside.

So what's a big boy to do? The process of reclaiming what they stole is difficult and painful. As children, we constructed whatever defenses—and pretenses—necessary to gain the love we could. Ironically, what we used in childhood to protect us from the thievery of our parents now robs us of the ability to honor ourselves in the present.

Recovering our essential self-worth means going back, often with skilled professional guidance, and opening the wounds of the past. When we get through the rage and the tears, we find treasures long buried that can be returned to their rightful owners. Us.

I'm worth the trip.

COMING OUT

And when he held my head up to kiss me, I felt like a straggling desert caravan, savaged by bandits, swept up in a sandstorm, that had suddenly emerged near an oasis—still devastated, but humbled by relief.
—Lev Raphael, Dancing on Tisha B'Av

Our stories of coming out are as varied as the stories of our lives. Whether we first tasted the nature of our thirst on the lips of another man, saw what was true after long and labored soul-searching, or acknowledged our gayness pleasingly as one does a warm gust of wind, we each had our moment of arrival.

Coming out is a beginning. From that time, we can begin to nourish what has often been a starved and shunned aspect of our being. We find others like us to share the details of our journey. We sample the local fare.

There is still a long route to travel. An oasis is merely a stopping point where we replenish ourselves and gain essential strength. Then we go on.

I am glad to have arrived.

DATING

Dating is a relationship for practicing intimate relationships.
—Stephen Wade and Craig Anderson

When I first started dating guys, I was Woody Allen on speed. If I was the least attracted to him (and, God help me, even when I *wasn't*), I would divulge, within the first 15 minutes, a panorama of intimate details about my past, at least two soaring dreams for the future, and still manage to pepper the conversation with probing questions usually reserved for hostile cross-examination. In the nonverbal part of my mind I was constructing our idyllic relationship while remodelling him as necessary to suit my specifications.

Then, I had all I could do to resist calling "time out" to ask my hapless victim how he was *really* feeling about how things were going so far. Needless to say, I got some feedback to the effect I came on a bit *intense*.

I can't claim that practice has led to perfect—and intense is part of my nature—but over time I've managed to settle down a lot. Dating *is* practice. We experience ourselves in a range of settings, discover what we really want (and don't) and eventually find the balance of openness and restraint necessary to carry on the quest.

I can practice as long and as often as I need to.

MULTI-CULTURALISM

And maybe I'm now injecting some of my prejudice by saying that "even a homosexual can be a revolutionary." Quite on the contrary, maybe a homosexual could be the most revolutionary.
                    —*Huey Newton on Gay Liberation, Gay Roots*

Black and white, elite and working-class, Mexican-American, Puerto Rican, Cherokee drag queen, Laotian leather man—the diversity of the gay community is an enhanced image of America itself.

In Minneapolis, where I live, you can traipse through hundreds of nightspots for some inkling of our varied population—and not find it—until you drop by the Gay 90's nightclub. Suddenly you're at a Rainbow Coalition convention. But is our multi-culturalism more than skin-deep?

Poured together by our way of loving, stirred by the challenge of liberation, we are a proving ground of the multi-cultural revolution. Breaking the bonds of all forms of prejudice is a crucial imperative to be taken on by every one of us.

Outside, on the street and beyond, the country is playing out a momentous class and racial struggle. Inside, our dance floor is an American cauldron.

Every barrier I break down is a revolution.

SEX

For me, being fucked is very physically stimulating and tremendously psychologically satisfying. But, the sensations are even more intense when I'm fucking. And, the only experience more supreme than either alone, are both with the same lover. The experience of wholeness and refreshment are unequalled by anything else I know about.

—Richard Nash, *Gay Love, Gay Roots*

Our eyes burn into one another, we stand inches apart, loosen buttons one by one, trade butterfly kisses and kisses that bruise, our hands up and down and across and inside. We press closer, hard together, chests opening and reaching like the uppermost leaves of great trees.

There is more and more and not enough. We are hot, wet, provocative, rude. We make soft tracks and lay down shimmering ecstatic trails. We fuck and fulfill each other, drink of each other, put out everything we've got and seize what comes back.

We've known sex quick and dirty and sex that gives us seconds, minutes, hours beyond time. Sex takes us apart at the seams. Sex makes us whole.

Sex is a glorious gift.

CHIVALRY

In feudal times nearly every [Japanese] knight had as his favorite a young man with whom he entertained relations of the most intimate kind, and on behalf of whom he was always ready to fight a duel when occasion occurred.

—*Edward Westermarck*

Happily, modern-day chivalry seldom requires us to sharpen our lance in time for sunrise dueling, but the underlying principles of loyalty and self-sacrifice remain as noble as in days of yore.

Fencing for one another might mean taking over a tiring hassle with the airlines: we're better at strong-arming so we graciously step in. Action on others' behalf could be lobbying for domestic partner benefits at work or raising hell about AIDS policy at the health department. It may be simple: "Let's trade seats, you'll never see over that *hat*"; helping each other on with our coats; dropping him off at the door and making the frigid hike from the parking lot alone.

Being chivalrous is wonderful. We feel good about ourselves when we go out of our way for others. We don't do it for applause, we do it for honor. And for love.

I'm a knight in shining armor.

COMING OUT STAGES

This model postulates that five stages describe many of the patterns seen in individuals with a predominantly same-sex sexual orientation. The stages are: pre-coming out, coming out, exploration, first relationships, and identity integration.
—Eli Coleman, Developmental Stages of the Coming Out Process,
Homosexuality & Psychotherapy

Coleman is quick to point out this is a road map, not a set of train tracks. There are alternate routes, side trips, and the need to circle back and revisit parts of the journey. There is a destination, a goal that seemingly can only be reached by completing the growth steps of each stage. So let's go.

Stage 1: "I'm different from other kids." We may not actually think this at the time, but plenty of other people do. Here's where we learn being a fag is not exactly desirable. We might despair and even try to kill ourselves. *Growth steps:* get open enough to find the truth, with tenderness for the child within, go back and rebuild self-esteem.

Stage 2: "I'm gay." We say it to ourselves and to at least one other person. Sometimes we get nervous and shake. We start to experience the consequences, both hurtful and helpful. Somewhere inside we're greatly relieved. *Growth steps:* think it, write it, say it, read about it. Find as many encouraging and sympathetic ears as possible.

Stage 3: "I think I'll give it a try." Sweaty palms, strangers, and six scotch and sodas. Thrills, chills, and spills. Sorry, guys, it's back to adolescence with all its maddening ups and downs. Also known as "the candy store phase" and remember: eat them with the wrapper on. *Growth steps:* do a lot of things that make good stories later. Make gay friends or get involved in the community. Go to a homoerotic film festival. Wake up each morning alive.

Stage 4: "Let's get an apartment." We bring enormous expectations and precious little skill to our first serious flings. Some last, but many fall apart bitterly. If we find ourselves repeating bad patterns, counseling is a wise choice. *Growth steps:* buy a scrapbook and next time be careful how you sign the lease.

Stage 5: "It's good to be me." Looking back, we've come a long way from Sheboygan. That's okay. Maybe we decide to buy a farmhouse at the edge of town and open a Bed and Breakfast. At this point, being gay is just one part of who we are. We're in the driver's seat now and the rest of the trip is up to us. *Growth step:* find happiness on our own terms.

I can get there.

REDEMPTION

I took her hand in mine, and we went out of the ruined place; and as the morning mists had risen long ago when I first left the forge, so the evening mists were rising now, and in all the broad expanse of tranquil light they showed to me, I saw no shadow of another parting from her.

—*Charles Dickens, Great Expectations*

For centuries, great powers of the world have arrayed themselves against us. The Church burned us. Governments banned and gassed us. Historians negated our very existence.

In the late 1800s, homosexuals in the Western world began, out of a terrified silence, to make claims to our legitimacy, our need for acceptance and love, our innate virtue. And now, on the cusp of the 21st century, mists are rising all around us.

Ultimately, each individual must redeem himself from whatever ruined place he has known. And we may clasp hands across time with those who never lived as we can and walk together into the light now breaking, finally, just ahead.

I will never part with my nobility as a human being.

January 23

THE WORKPLACE

EAGLE exists as an effort to establish Gay and Lesbian people as valuable and worthy members of the corporation and society and to create a working environment of mutual respect...We will seek opportunities for our members to improve their careers and their personal lives and to do so with pride in who they are.
—Purpose Statement, Twin City Chapter of U S West EAGLE

The rush to embrace diversity in the workplace is an enterprise of mixed motives. While the customer is always right, 20 million of us aren't straight: market share to the rescue. But never mind bottom line motives; there is profit sharing. For U S West to succeed, the workforce itself has to reflect—and respect—diversity. Into this rarefied air flies the EAGLE. Little by little, chapters grow, hard work is done, safety and acceptance increase, and the unthinkable—a picture of our lover on our desk—becomes commonplace.

A win-win deal all around. The company wins. The customer wins. Our fellow employees win. And we win big. Homophobia-reduction in the workplace improves our own lives, and makes an important and permanent difference for plenty of others.

I work with pride in who I am.

MEN

I followed the other Experiment around, yesterday afternoon, at a distance, to see what it might be for, if I could. But I was not able to make out. I think it is a man.

—Mark Twain, The Diary of Adam and Eve

When I first came out, my forays into the world of men were a hot topic of conversation between me and some of my women friends. One day, while licking my wounds after an earnest fellow who all but pledged eternal fidelity over a second glass of wine informed me three days later that the whole thing was "too much trouble," I suddenly got this cosmic insight into what kind of battlefield my female comrades-in-arms had been trudging through.

Still smarting from rejection (the kindest term I had for him was *emotional slug*), I called a veteran of many years' experience to commiserate. Laughing uproariously at my naivete, she saw this as my big comeuppance: I was now consigned to dating the male of the species. Years of Cosmopolitan Magazine's sage advice on *"How to Get and Keep Your Man"* flashed before my eyes.

Then a comforting thought hit. If all those legions of women had managed to keep their eye on the prize, so could I. And the nature of the prize? A grand experiment. Crown of creation. Strength, passion, poetry: I think it is a man.

I want one.

ATTENTION

"What're you doing?"
"Looking at the stars," I say.
"I'm looking at you."

—*Gary Glickman, Magic*

When we're taken with someone, he glitters like the night sky. We notice how he walks, eats, kicks off his shoes, the funny way his forehead wrinkles when he's thinking, the sexy bit of hair above the collar of his t-shirt. We see it all, but do we say it?

In the cagey first days of relationship, we fear overacting will cost us the audition: "Too gooey...*Next!*" Further on, we hold back because adoration makes us appear vulnerable, too invested. Still later, familiarity may breed neglect. "I'm here, aren't I? Doesn't that show how I feel?"

Come *on,* guys! We're missing out all over the place! We need to name what we see; say the words and learn to hear them. The loving attention of another man is a sweet little slice of heaven.

Let's dazzle each other.

SHAME

Shame...is crippling because it contains not just the derisive accusation that one is a wimp, a bully, a runt, or a fag but the further implication that one is at core a deformed being, fundamentally unlovable and unworthy...And most people are unable to face it. It is too annihilating.

—*Robert Karen, Shame*

Shame comes over us like a wall of blinding rain. In a split second, we are drenched with it, and much as we try, we cannot wipe it from our eyes, our mouths, our souls.

The power of shame is meant to prevent human beings from committing acts of violence or abuse. It is instilled in us as children by whatever forces sought to shape and control us in their image. As adults, shame signals transgression: we have betrayed a covenant engraved on our psyche without our knowing and without our consent.

To live as free men, we must violate the core of our shame and bring it to light. We must face the holy terror of it. This is not a journey to take alone. It should be done under the wise care of a good therapist.

To the extent that shame governs our inner selves, we are already annihilated. Clouds are everywhere and we cannot stop the rain. But there is in our world a safe haven. It is us. And it is ours.

My gayness holds not a trace of shame.

FOOD

I have friends who begin with pasta, and friends who begin with rice, but whenever I fall in love, I begin with potatoes. Sometimes meat and potatoes and sometimes fish and potatoes, but always potatoes. I have made a lot of mistakes falling in love, and regretted most of them, but never the potatoes that went with them.

—Nora Ephron, Heartburn

Food—and the rituals that surround it—play a significant part in relationships. There's the seduction scenario: appetizers, a delectable main course, accompaniments, the ideal beverage. It's all deliciously calculated. First we stimulate the taste buds. Later we stimulate the rest.

There are compatibility indicators: can we agree on a restaurant? How about grocery shopping? Is meandering down the aisles something we both enjoy? Or does he hope you'll just run off with a list like his mother did?

There's a cornucopia of possibility: take dieting together. There are serious possiblities for bonding around a mutual commitment to cholesterol counts. Or consider that venerable institution, the dinner date. Swept him off his feet lately? And hey, real men eat chocolate. Which is a pretty cheap way to a guy's heart.

Yes, food and relationships have a lot in common. Both go sour if not properly cared for, most anything will do when you're hungry, and many items are best heated up.

I'm delicious.

HISTORY

We have been the silent minority, the silenced minority—invisible women, invisible men...we were outlaws against the universe...long we were a people perceived out of time and out of place—socially unsituated, without a history—the mutant progeny of some heterosexual union, freaks...That time is over...Knowledge of gay history helps restore a people to its past, to itself; it extends the range of human possibility, suggests new ways of living, new ways of loving.
—*Jonathan Ned Katz, Gay American History*

There is a hunger in human nature for knowledge of the past. We place ourselves backward in time to regain connection with origin, where our people came from, what they believed and how they lived, what arrangement of biology and time produced these living, conscious beings. We study the past to understand the present, to prepare ourselves for our role as co-creators of the future.

We now know we were present from the start. The mystery of our existence stems from the same deep sources as that of all things. We have been celebrated, brought our wisdom to clans and kingdoms. We have been marginalized and hated as threats to tribal survival, social order, power-thirsty regimes. We carry the instincts of the outsider, the creative force of that which insists it *is* and therefore has a right to be.

We appear now in the pages of history as if a brush stroke has finally rendered to sight what waited, indelible, recorded with invisible ink. We can now do as others have long done, restore to this people its past, and extend the range of human possibility into new ways of living.

We have a voice, a history, a place in the universe.

KVETCHING

I personally think we developed language because of our deep inner need to complain.

—*Jane Wagner,*
The Search for Signs of Intelligent Life in the Universe

The Yiddish word *kvetch* is both a verb and a noun. To kvetch means to gripe, to sigh, to rant and rave periodically about life's burdens and frustrations. A certain amount of kvetching is healthy—and fun. After all, life is no bowl of cherries and girls who come on like Rebecca of Sunnybrook Farm are seldom named life of the party.

It's different when someone's deep inner need to complain stops being a weekend interest and flowers into a career. Then we're talking about a full-blown *kvetch:* someone who lives to piss and moan.

Naming what hurts or confuses us is important. Once we know what's wrong we can do something about it. But if we see being gay—or life in general—as some big affliction, we start taking victim status for granted and we're stuck.

What to aim for is a happy medium. Remember: misery loves company, but company only loves misery so long.

It ain't all good, but it ain't all bad either.

WAITING

Sometimes, when one person is missing, the whole world seems depopulated.
—*Lamartine, Premières méditations poétiques*

In *The Music Man*, stiff-backboned Marion-the-Librarian leans wistfully against the porch railing and sings "Goodnight My Someone" into the empty night air. Our heart goes out to her as her invitation to sweet dreams tucks in the world.

Then Robert Preston rolls into town and Marion's real troubles begin.

When our own missing person turns up we can count on a roller-coaster ride unlike any other. One night we're the last cowboy in a ghost town and the next we're at a carnival. Lights blaze, we've got cotton candy sticking in our hair, and we'll be dizzy, thrilled, and through a house of mirrors before we're taken home to bed.

It's hard, when we're waiting, to keep faith that he's out there, searching and longing for us just as we are for him. He is the only person we really want.

We will find each other.

EYES

*But the top of the list were his eyes...Every moment or two I had to
come back from where I was to look at them, drink their gaze, their
longing for more, their joy over what was happening, their questioning
of the consequences.*

—*Gerrit Jan Van Der Duim,*
Roger and Me, The James White Review

When I fell in love with Jon, it was his eyes more than anything else that entranced me. They are blue, of the sparkling variety, but also touched with suffering and a depth that made me
want to just keep on looking into them to what was inside them
and to what was beyond them for a very long time.

Eyes being windows of the soul, we sometimes see more than
we should. It is, perhaps, the soul that is drawing us. Staring into
a thing so wildly beautiful we easily miss more up-front messages: the warnings, the fear, the questioning.

In the end, it proved I fell in love with something much
deeper than what was actually available and it was my eyes that
had been too open, too penetrating, too blind.

Men's eyes. We look into them: clear, smokey, transported
by pleasure and longing. And they look into us. When we're in
love, when we're making love, we see forever.

I want to see and be seen.

February

NAKEDNESS

Crucifixes are sexy because there's a naked man on them.
—Madonna

Hmmmm. Kind of puts those Calvin Klein ads in perspective. And opens startling vistas within the framework of Religious Experience.

Nakedness is fascinating. While there are plenty of bodies we're disinclined to give a second glance, we respond to others like an archaeologist who just discovered a lost civilization: the complexity, layers, clues on a scavenger hunt leading us in expanding roving circles.

Some naked men pull our hearts into our throats, arouse us totally, brutally. We would carry them, worship them, nail our hands to them. It is a fearful, awesome thing full of power and danger and full of God.

Let's take off our clothes.

DARING

Life is either a daring adventure or nothing. To keep our faces toward change and behave like free spirits in the presence of fate is strength undefeatable.

—Helen Keller, Let Us Have Faith

Fate dictates much, but not all. Where we are born, who parents us, our race, gender, sexual orientation, and natural abilities are all laid out before we get here. The rest is up to us.

Some people are defeated by life. Others survive and flourish against all odds. What tips the balance is the drive to change our circumstances, to take fate on a dare and make of our lives what we want them to be.

Onward to high adventure: an unguided tour through the exotic terrain of gay life. We slip into after hours bars, sojourn with Radical Faeries, enlist with Act Up, wear our Pride button to work, love perfect strangers, create our own rituals, and march down Main Street.

It takes guts to keep exploring, keep trying it all until we hit what's exactly for us—a way of being that's like coming home, a place where our spirits are free.

I dare to find my own way.

SEXUAL ORIENTATION

Many individuals are not exclusively heterosexual or homosexual: Kinsey, Pomeroy and Martin (1948) found that sexual orientation is best described on a continuum. Sexual orientation can be described even better on [three] continua of behavior, fantasy, and emotional attachments.

—Eli Coleman, Ph.D.,
Developmental Stages of the Coming Out Process,
Homosexuality & Psychotherapy

Ever been in a group where people are discussing their sexual orientation? It sounds a lot like Astrological Signs: "I'm a three." "I'm on the cusp between a one and a two." "I used to be a four-and-a-half, but now I'm a six." Just as with Signs, it's hard to get what it all means.

For a long time, I thought I got it, but I didn't. I now define myself as gay, but having been in a marriage with a woman for eleven years, the question I'm most often asked is, "Did you know you were gay all along?" The answer is no. It was damn confusing when I concluded being gay was a deeper vein and I was desperate to understand what made it imperative for me to leave a woman I loved and live a different life.

The light bulb came via Coleman's three parallel lines. I'm at different places on each, but the numbers only add up at the homosexual end of the spectrum. Earlier in life it didn't seem to matter, but to move into all of my sexual and emotional being, I could no longer live so divided. What finally made a heterosexual life unlivable was the driving need for integration.

To live fully in myself is a blessing.

HOMOPHOBIA

Patriarchy is threatened by men who bend over for men, which reveals that men are vulnerable; and by women who don't, which shows that they aren't.

—*Adrienne Leban, Sexual Beggars*

Let's say human nature has two sides: the little devil on one shoulder and the little angel on the other. The angel counsels patience, love, and generosity. The devil is forever making big promises with fat payoffs and it seems he has been winning over a lot of men for a very long time.

Here's his pitch: "Stick with me, buddy, and we'll have it all. Money, women, wine...you'll rule the roost, you'll call the shots, nobody's gonna be bigger than you 'cause you're the best, baby. You're in the club. You're on top. You deserve to stay there and if anybody tells you to bend over, you just blast 'em out of the water."

"What's the catch?" some guys might ask. "No catch," he soothes. "What's yours is yours and if other people get out of line you might have to teach 'em a lesson. Just keep your guard up. Nothin' to it."

Enter religion. Enter class divisions and caste systems. Enter property ownership and rights of the first son and wife-beating as an expected part of life. Enter all manner of natural law and divine revelation sounding suspiciously like the small fellow in the red outfit with the silver tongue. Enter silken priests and paunchy patriarchs who teach lessons and amply reward the million minions who learn them well.

Enter faggots and dykes. Enter witch burnings and inquisitions. Enter gay men and lesbians and assorted renegades from the club. Enter vulnerability. Enter a threatened, frightened, overfed little devil who hates people that don't play by his rules.

I'm a threat.

THE GREEKS

We are stardust, we are golden, and we've got to get ourselves back to the garden.

—*Joni Mitchell, Woodstock*

The Golden Age of Homosexuality. In ancient Greece the love of men for one another was considered given of the gods; as were lesbian affections, both special and distinct from union between the sexes and all three secured in the pantheon of wondrous and necessary love.

Attraction among men is described eloquently in Plato's Symposium. Aristophanes says, "...they are valiant and manly, and have a manly countenance, and they embrace that which is like them...when one of them meets with his other half...the pair are lost in an amazement of love and friendship and intimacy."

Male beauty was extolled in the arts and was part of the humor of the day. A lyricist writes,

> *You recline that magnificent pair of buttocks*
> *Against the wall...why tempt*
> *The stone, which is incapable?*

But we are off base should our garden images be of free and wanton sexuality. It was common then, as it is now. The philosophers, however, delved into love's essence and imbued what they found with high morality. "Thus noble...is the acceptance of another for the sake of virtue. This is that love which is the love of the heavenly goddess...making the lover and the beloved alike eager in the work of their own improvement."

The Greeks call out our devotion to timeless ideals, the pursuit of which brings honor to any man and any culture that embraces them.

My love was known by ancients. And gods.

ANDROGYNY

He who, being a man, remains a woman, will become a universal channel.
—Lao-Tzu

Among the barbaric treatments of prisoners of war is the practice of confining men in small square cages scarcely bigger than their doubled-up bodies. If they emerge at all, these men may remain stunted for life, forever caught in a freeze-frame of torture.

Raised as American men, the woman inside most of us suffered a similarly hideous imprisonment. Nothing in our childhood evoked quite the cruel reprisals as did betrayal of a streak of femininity. What strength, what grace and courage she has to have withstood this onslaught. Through it all, she spoke to us, brought us messages of fullness and roundness, whispered of instinct and her pleasures.

We are lucky, those of us who can now give voice to this woman. We have escaped a narrowly prescribed world and are in touch with much more. We are both man and woman, and so can live out the deepest, most universal truths of creation.

She is free.

SHOWING LOVE

There are never enough "I love you"s.
—Lenny Bruce

A callow youth with romantic ideals thought he had the situation aced when he arranged a standing weekly order of a dozen long-stemmed roses to be delivered to his sweetheart. The first time they came, she was properly thrilled. By the fourth week, she hated them.

One could judge the little lady as ungrateful, but no, she had a right to be pissed. He wasn't showing love, he was showing he didn't want to be bothered with details. Now some boys just don't get this right at all. Saying, *"I haven't left, have I?"* is not a particularly stunning gesture of affection and regard. Neither is a system of automated gifts. What places these acts in the far-from-enough category is the absence of love's essence: in the moment attention.

Entries in the good-stab-at-enough category: remembering what's important to him, learning his emotional language and speaking it, most anything unplanned and spontaneous, running to the store for the one ingredient he forgot to pick up for dinner, saying, "I love you," just because we do.

I love you.

BELONGING

I feel curiously ill at ease when I have been away from gay people too long; it's a feeling almost like a lack of oxygen.

—Christopher Isherwood

One of my strongest experiences of longing-for-kind came over me at a four-year-old's birthday party. Of the 15 or so families there, we were the only Jews. It was perfectly nice in every respect. We chimed smiling goodbyes, strapped our daughter in her car-seat, and in unison, our voices edged with desperation, my wife and I said, *"Let's go to the Del."* There, comfortably ensconced between the Shapiros and the Kaplans, we inhaled heaping portions of corned beef, chicken soup, and bagel-lox-and-cream-cheese. Our equilibrium returned. We belonged.

Gay men, like Jews, live dispersed among a sometimes perfectly nice, sometimes perfectly hostile majority. When we get together, our sense of safety and bonds of shared history change the air. We relax, let down our guard, and cruise the refreshments.

Belonging means being a necessary part of something. As Jews, we are taught at the tenderest of ages that each of us is a vital link between past and future, a crucial actor in the drama of our people. As gay men, we are often taught we belong nowhere.

It's a lie. We belong everywhere. We belong to ourselves. We belong to each other.

I have a rightful place.

LIPS

Spanish sailors with bearded lips,
And the beauty and mystery of the ships,
And the magic of the sea.

—Longfellow, *My Lost Youth*

The first touch of his lips to ours sends a shudder and a calm deep inside. There will be more. They have a peculiar weight, gentle and rough at once, heavy on our mouths, against our neck, on our fingertips.

They are of distinct color and shape. Rich. Thin. Blonde. Sometimes painted violet. They break open into smile, press together in determination, mouth words, sighs, move silently and speak of desire.

They open to a soft wet world; taste of salt and of chocolate. There are waves as they move against us, lower onto us, take us beneath their surface.

Our own lips ripen and open, become sore from passion, make magic of their own. Later, when we are alone, perhaps weeks, months later, our lips burn at the memory of him, and we hunger for return to the waves, his depths, the sea.

Kiss me again.

GOALS

Raise your sail one foot and you get ten feet of wind.
—*Chinese Proverb*

A bright, attractive, and still-on-the-market young man recently said to me, "I've set a new standard for myself. What I do from now on is going to be about love—all the time and nothing else." He immediately blushed, self-conscious about being too grandiose or having ridiculous expectations. But he meant it. And it will happen.

Well, maybe not *all* the time and *nothing* else, but I would bet my favorite shirt that little by little, day by day, his life will have more love in it. He will have to respect himself greatly and honor his own truths—which will make him increasingly attractive. He will have to learn to be uncompromising about not settling for less as he dates and finds lovers; that love comes not so much from an exchange of affections as from a disciplined heart.

I don't know him well, but it's thrilling to watch him raise his sail. He has invoked the power of the wind.

I can achieve my goals.

CRUSHES

He's a hook, a sweet hook you've swallowed that tears at your inner flesh. Such pain, O, Lord, and how you love it!
—*Anonymous, from the Greek Anthology, translated by John Gill*

It's the best of times and the worst of times. There's no telling what will come of it, but we've lost our ability for rational thought so what's the difference. He is *perfect*. Makes us tremble. You'd think a fishing line was connected from his eyes to our pants. He looks. We get a pull.

So many gifts and so little time. We must shower him with frankincense, myrrh, and compact discs. Our VISA card has lived for this moment. Oh well, we're saving money on groceries since eating is out of the question. And who needs sleep? Oh this is sweet, we feel like we're going to burst, split open. It's the most peculiar, delicious, suspenseful pain.

Truly we *are* going to burst if this continues. A man will do this, rip the covering off what normally holds such passion in check. Crushes are beyond sense. They begin in sweet pain and may result in bitter agony. In the meantime, O, Lord, let him reel us dripping wet out of the water and into his luscious net.

Every so often, we get hooked by a big one.

February 12

LOVE AND AIDS

How could anyone ever, ever not want the kind of love I have to offer? It's preposterous.
                    —*Robert Keene, person with AIDS, The Color of Light*

If my lover was diagnosed HIV+ would I leave him? Not in a million years. Would I enter into a love affair with a man I already knew had AIDS? I'm not sure I could knowingly say yes to the short-term risk or the long-term loss.

One of the lessons I have learned from long study of the Holocaust is this: if we tolerate dehumanization of ourselves or those around us, we are all in a train car to hell. Failing to recognize a man who is HIV+ as a full human being with whom I might give and receive love amounts to failing this test.

Where then is my first responsibility? To myself? And, in my case, to my young children who need their father very badly? How responsible am I to a man with AIDS I might love—to protect him from isolation, from dehumanizaton, from pariah status perhaps worse than the disease itself? How much do I owe all of us, that no life might ever be viewed as less precious than another?

No easy answers. No easy questions. At the very, very least, we must all keep asking.

In Hillel's words: If I am not for myself, who will be for me? If I am only for myself, what am I? If not now, when?

URNINGS

He pointed out that there were people born...on the dividing line between the sexes—that while belonging distinctly to one sex as far as their bodies are concerned they may be said to belong mentally and emotionally to the other...this doubleness of nature was to a great extent proved by the special direction of their love sentiment. People of this kind he called Urnings.

—Edward Carpenter on theories espoused by Austrian writer Karl H. Ulrichs in 1864

Karl Ulrichs' voice was among the first in modern history to break silence on the subject of homosexuality. For this we owe a debt of gratitude; however, many of us are probably quite relieved *urning* didn't stick. ("Mom, I don't know how to tell you, but I'm an...*urning.*" "Bobby, I'm not really surprised. Your father and I always thought there was something, well, alien about you...)

The name was inspired by Plato's Symposium in which men's love of one another is credited to the influence of Heavenly Aphrodite, daughter of the God Uranus. Ulrichs' connection began the process of reclaiming the natural and important status of our love sentiment as intertwined with the roots of serious Western philosophy.

Was he right? Do we live straddling the line between the sexes? No. We now understand all people are born with a mysterious mixture of sexual and gender traits, that some of these evolve over a lifetime, and that each individual's nature is singular, undivided, and in every case unique.

I live outside the lines.

VALENTINE'S DAY

"What you do in your own bedroom is your own business. I don't care what you do there as long as you don't parade it in public."

That is a put-down, because heterosexuals feel perfectly free to parade their sexuality in public.

—Richard Nash, Gay Love, Gay Roots

From a gay perspective, Valentine's Day seems less a parade than a stampede. We hear the approaching drum corps pound its relentless heterosexual beat and then the bugle and harp brigades are all over us. Flower shop windows, drug store card sections, hotels, and tables-for-two blare their romance of exclusion. Forget the bedroom, we're not even in the house.

We've got two options here. Ignore it or claim it for our own. Ignoring something so pervasive is tough—and takes a toll. The message is, "You don't exist." Claiming it is also tough, but action is empowering. So pick and choose from the following V.D. to-do list:

1. Buy gifts at gay card and book shops.
2. Spend romance dollars at other "out" gay businesses.
3. Challenge advertising imagery at mainstream establishments.
4. Tell purveyors of heterosexism we're 10% of the market and resent being defined outside the customer base.
5. Kiss in public.
6. Send him flowers at work.
7. Tell the immediate world we love each other.

I can join this parade if I choose to.

BALANCE

On one end of the spectrum is passion; on the other safety. People tend to either have passionate but unsafe relationships or safe relationships without passion.

—*Terence Gorski*

Scenario one: We're in. Sparks fly on both sides. He stops asking *if* he should come over and starts asking *when*. We're willing to trust it a little and as we do, something weird happens. We find ourselves pulling back, unsure. It doesn't feel safe.

Scenario two: We're in. Sparks fly on both sides. We want to be with him every minute. We buy him a pair of red silk boxer shorts, leave passionate little notes in the morning. He puts on the brakes, has a sudden need for "space."

Scenario three: We're in. Sparks fly on both sides. We go to a cabin for the weekend. It's fabulous. We come back and don't see each other for two days. It's fine. He says, "I think I'm falling in love and I'm scared." We say, "Me, too." He says, "It's hard for me to let go." We say, "That's good. I have trouble getting a grip."

It's all risky business. Every time we're *in*, we might be in over our heads. Too safe and there's no chance. Too passionate and we scare the living daylights out of him. The secret is balance. Drawing from both ends of the spectrum, we create safety in ourselves and steadily fan the flames between us.

I can hang on and let go at the same time.

PASSING

And then you get to hang out with everyone who hates you and feel really, really good that the people who hate you now like you. Instead of hanging out with the people who love you and saying "fuck you" to those who hate you. And I think that's a big difference between me and everybody else here. I don't try to please people who hate me. I mean, fuck them.

—Roseanne Arnold, *Christopher Street Magazine*

Many of us go through life disguising our gayness, doing everything from a classic closet act to withholding information on our plans to participate in a Miss Muscle contest to wincing through homophobic remarks we overhear on the job. This is *passing,* allowing the world to define us as heterosexual or as a nice gay person who doesn't flaunt it or as someone who doesn't let being a faggot interfere with just being one of the guys.

There are plenty of rewards for this behavior. Sometimes it's essential: we do it to keep a job, a job that feeds not only us, but momma and our sister's kids. Sometimes it's not so essential: we do it to keep the peace, a peace that puts food on the table, but leaves us starving.

In the beginning, we feel we've beaten the system. We're getting where we want to go, we know who we are, and so what if there's games to play, we can handle it. Beside, they like us and it feels good. For a while. As time goes by, the little costs add up. The system is beating us.

I can make it based on who I truly am.

SUPPORT GROUPS

Let's begin by introducing ourselves. Please share your name, and if you were a fruit, what kind of fruit would you be?
        —Facilitator of a Coming Out Support Group

Six incredibly tense guys in the room and no one laughs. I can't believe it! Either A) The facilitator is too young to know what "fruit" means and it is an honest mistake; or B) Nobody but me "gets it" and the others just get busy imaging orchards of apples, oranges, and kiwi; or C) It is all a very very bad dream and I'll soon wake up on vacation in Jamaica.

Turns out it is simply support group amateur night and the callow fellow in charge has badly misjudged the ability of his audience to take a joke.

Things get better. Life stories are shared. Tears and laughter flow, and the leader figures out how to shut up. Most important, we all get the juicy stuff we came for: support.

Such groups—often led by real pros—abound. They are all valuable. We get out of isolation with our questions and concerns, learn from the experience of others, make friends (and sometimes lovers), and, no matter what kind of fruit we are, find we ourselves have something to teach.

Support is all around me.

FATHERHOOD

"And you love other men, too, don't you?"
"Yes, I do. It seems to me loving men is a thing I do especially well."
"Well, that's okay if we have enough for us."

> —*Jack Latham in conversation with his*
> *almost 4-year-old daughter, Charlotte*
> *A Faggot Father Speaks Out, Gay Roots*

Many gay men are fathers. We co-parent our biological and adoptive children in various combinations—with our partners, our ex-wives, our children's lesbian mothers, and sometimes all alone.

Gay parenting has special challenges. Our young children wonder, "If being gay is OK, why does it matter who I tell?" Our teenagers, bravely battling the-pimple-that-ruined-my-life, aren't thrilled about a significant fact that separates them from their peers. Our grown children, while sometimes our staunchest advocates, are still coming to terms with all of what we gave them.

Us? We're just typical parents. Fiercely protective of our kids. Trying to help them understand things we barely understand ourselves. Laughing, hugging, yelling at them to clean up their rooms, worrying, counseling, shelling out enormous sums of cash for Nintendo, camp, proms, parking tickets, and college.

We're devoted to them. They love us. We're their fathers.

I love my children beyond measure.

WALT WHITMAN

When you read these, I, that was visible, am become invisible,
Now it is you, compact, visible, realizing my poems, seeking me,
Fancying how happy you were, if I could be with you,
  and become your lover;
Be it as if I were with you. Be not too certain but I am now with you.
                    —Walt Whitman, Calamus No. 45

Somehow I got through public school with Walt Whitman, Walt Disney, and The Shaggy Dog all mixed up as one person. It's not so strange, really. The two Walts gave us expansive, fantastic visions of America. Disney bombards us with modern marketing. Whitman secretly blesses us.

Take even a little time with his writing and Walt Whitman emerges visible and distinct from the un-televised past. The man's eyes, they say, were uncommonly arresting and magnetic—you were drawn out of yourself and into a greater sphere. His manner of dress was a scandal, showing off that chest hair as he did. His words are a pathway to a place where the rustle of grass is a joy to the senses and the whole of our being is known, and touched, and made love to by the invisible fingers and mouth of the poet.

This laureate, this lover who could have lain luminous against us, created a language that calls clearly from the deeps of time. I am certain he is with me now, we are *dear comrades*—one of his names for us, this part of creation he saw and lived, this glory among the leaves of grass, this love among men.

My love is visible, beautiful, a connection to all things.

ACCEPTANCE

One of the real tests of morality and Jewish ethics today is not how gays and lesbians act, but how we do. The judgment is on us, not them. We are being measured for our fairness, for our compassion, and yes, for our love and respect for all people created in the image of God—and that is all of us.

—*Rabbi Bernard S. Raskas*

Acceptance is nothing more than a beginning. We accept the terms of peace treaties, but that in itself is not peace. We accept apologies, but forgiveness takes more time. We accept a range of conditions as the best possible for now, but sculpt out of them much grander visions of the future.

Acceptance of gay and lesbian people is no ultimate goal. Those who meet this minimal test cross the threshold to a place of more profound moral challenges. Fairness, compassion, love, and respect are essential standards of ethical communities. Live and let live is far from enough.

The judgment is on all of us: to love one another exceedingly well; to measure up to the highest calls of our duty and our faith; to be what we all are—reflections of a creator who sowed seeds of infinite variety.

God planted me.

COUNTERCULTURE

Where we're coming from is anti-establishment, and if being gay is being anti-establishment, then our crowd is going to do things like shout, "I'm a homosexual," and just not give a fuck.
—Jennifer Finch, bass player with L7, The Advocate

When I get to heaven, I'm going to lobby hard for a seat on the Jesse Helms Purgatory Board. Once installed, my idea is to send him to an endless series of L7 concerts. There he'll be, front row center, the pulsing soles of Jennifer Finch's black bomber boots looming over his head, mobbed on all sides by delirious fans chanting, "I'M A HOMOSEXUAL!!! I'M A HOMOSEXUAL!!!" During intermission he'll sell Robert Mapplethorpe prints and donate the proceeds to ACT UP.

In the '60s, counterculturalists placed daisies into rifle barrels of the National Guard, took a match to our draft cards, and slipped hits of LSD under our tongues. It added up to a movement: a new national mindset that helped stop a war and open up a whole new way of looking at things.

In radical counterpoint to today's conservatism, we have L7 and a host of other sexual revolutionaries putting it in the face of the immoral minority, a crowd apparently devoted to hating everything that isn't just like them.

A thrilling phenomenon of social physics: for every controlling, repressive move the establishment makes, an equal and opposite movement arises to shout back we just don't give a fuck.

I'M A HOMOSEXUAL!!!

PUPPY LOVE

It was seven o'clock, supper over, and the boys gathering one by one from the sound of their house doors slammed and their parents crying to them not to slam the doors. Douglas and Tom and Charlie and John stood among half a dozen others and it was time for hide-and-seek and Statues.

—*Ray Bradbury, Dandelion Wine*

We knew, but we didn't know. We certainly didn't call it love. But the sweet, mysterious, and quietly disturbing sensations were all there: hiding breathlessly side by side in the bushes, praying we would never be found; standing stock still in the chill evening air, matching wills with a glowing boy trying everything possible to make us move; sleeping over at our best friend's, lying in bed talking for hours, wrapped together in a soft cocoon.

Looking back, these were our experiences of puppy love. Not, after all, our first slow dance at the sock hop, our awkward efforts at joining the make-out crowd, not the famed kiss we delivered as Prince Charming in the sixth-grade production of Sleeping Beauty.

Today, if we love Douglas or Tom or Charlie or John, we can bring it all back—the good parts, that is. Seeking sweetness, yes; standing like statues before the mystery, absolutely; but we needn't hide any more.

I've got a puppy inside.

NEUROSIS

Let you homosexuals face it therefore; all of you, every mother's son of you who is exclusively desirous of homosexual relations, is indubitably neurotic.

—*Albert Ellis, 1955*

So much for the '50s. Ellis, who was somewhat liberal on homosexuality and spoke strongly against discrimination, based his argument on the "problem of exclusivity." He meant to offer hope to those plagued by the idea they could only be truly and permanently fulfilled through same-sex relationships. A cure was possible! Get thee to a therapist and get to the root of neurotic refusal to admit more possibilities.

Ellis applied the same standard (sort of) to devout heterosexuals. If a straight guy marooned on a desert island wouldn't eventually make it with the other sailors, Ellis figured he, too, was a bit crazy.

I could go along with this idea if gay and straight sexuality were on equal footing...just imagine the headlines if sexual open season became the psychological norm:

PROM PSYCHOSIS! BOYS ONLY DANCED WITH GIRLS! COUNSELORS MOBBED!

MINISTERS INSIST ON OPTION PERIOD BEFORE MEN AND WOMEN MARRY!

COSBY ADVISES TV SON TO "TRY A GUY" BEFORE THROWING LIFE AWAY!

But back to planet earth, it's time us homosexuals faced the indubitable facts: we're fine just the way we are.

The possibilities are limitless: I'm living proof.

GRIEF

The ancient guardians of our self-image, the blockages of the heart, become uniquely evident...arise from just beneath the surface to present themselves in a blaze of anguished feelings. In intense grief of loss we rediscover, unmistakably this time, the grief we have always carried, the ordinary grief that inhabits and inhibits our life.
—Stephen Levine, Healing into Life and Death

A rabbi once told me grief is the great teacher. He was right. I have been overcome with grief twice in my life. First when my father died. Second, and much more powerfully, when I came out and left my wife and home.

Elisabeth Kubler-Ross charted the recurring spirals of this force of nature: denial, bargaining, anger, depression, acceptance. Grief for my father was simple and pure: he was there, then he was gone. My other loss cut deeper: I was there, then I was gone.

The process of grieving spins out in slow gut-churning swirls broken by sudden intense squalls. The winds, if we allow ourselves to be carried, take us back in time, to storms of grief long stored, to wordless cyclone pain over what life has ripped from us.

The acceptance stage is extraordinary, like arriving at another shore. We have been taught what emptying and release really mean. Then life—and grief—go on. Tears for what we want and can't have, joy at the smallest provocation. Compassion for the suffering of others, wonder at every juncture. Driving winds as loved ones pass and we slowly turn toward our own dying, with passion for living in our last breath.

My grief is my treasure.

FIRST NIGHTS

He was quiet at bedtime. I could picture him tossing all night. I set the night-lamp in its place, and knelt down by him. "I would follow you to the last shores of the world, if it were a thousand miles."
He said, "Stay with me here instead."
He was readier for love than he had known, but I had known it. I used up some of the fire within him, that would have stayed sealed in its furnace, scorching his heart.

—Mary Renault, The Persian Boy

We don't forget first nights with men we have loved. There is freshness to the fire that can never be duplicated. Time is altered, moves with strange slowness and yet in a rush. Much passes between us and much more remains.

Sometimes there are words, sometimes not. Always there are moments of anticipation, signs to be read. We wonder not so much if he will follow us to the last shores of the world as if he will join us in the bedroom. Or on the floor of the living room. Or against the wall in the hallway. We gauge his readiness and the rate of our own pulse.

Then, for the first time, we are naked in each other's arms. Smells, strange and familiar, fill our heads. His warm body fills our hands, our legs, our belly. We learn all at once the texture of his hair and skin, the weight of his lips, his proportions, his touch, how he takes and what he gives.

We use up some of each other's fire and are reminded what this feeling is about, this newness and greatness of first loving, this unsealing of what scorches us inside.

I like playing with fire.

HEROES

Reversing a long-standing policy that effectively barred openly gay men and lesbians from its ranks, the FBI pledged not to discriminate on the basis of their sexual orientation or conduct. The change in policy was announced as part of an agreement to settle a class action lawsuit brought by former FBI agent Frank Buttino, who was fired after his supervisors got an anonymous letter informing them that he is gay.

—*Los Angeles Times*

In a unanimous decision, a three-judge panel of the U.S. Court of Appeals ordered that Joseph Steffan be graduated from the Naval Academy and promptly commissioned as a lieutenant. The panel found that Steffan's expulsion was "not rationally related to any legitimate goal" and violated the Constitution.

—*From News Services*

Everywhere around the world men and women put their livelihood, security, their very lives on the line for the cause of human rights. Failure is common. Success is usually unnoticed. The limelight reaches only a small handful who by happenstance or superior public relations instinct or by the enormity of their victory are dubbed heroes.

Here then, riding on the shoulders of unsung scores, are Joseph Steffan and Frank Buttino, who brought the U.S. Navy and the FBI to their knees. (J. Edgar Hoover must be rimming, er, that is, *spinning* in his grave.) If there is a gay hall of fame, Steffan and Buttino should be inducted.

So let's do it.

Herewith, conferring the highest esteem for resolute, out, and uncompromising acts of heroism in the cause of human rights, for giving hope to the many gays who contacted them and shared their stories of fear and discrimination, on behalf of the countless men and women who have fought and lost or fought and won invisibly, and on behalf of future generations who will be spared similar ordeals, Lt. Joseph Steffan and 20-year FBI veteran Frank Buttino are forever noted in history as heroes, role models, and men of distinction.

To those sung and unsung, our gratitude and respect.

CONFORMITY

Success, recognition, and conformity are the bywords of the modern world where everyone seems to crave the anesthetizing security of being identified with the majority.

—*Dr. Martin Luther King, Jr.*

The price of conformity is high. To buy success on others' terms, a man sells his soul.

Many of us legitimately craved relief from being different. Especially as kids subjected to "femme tests," getting left out, beat up, and enduring a hundred other humiliations. Some of us learned to pass. Some of us still do. But just as the blackness of African-Americans says *other* in white eyes, so our gayness sets us apart.

The hyped American Dream is seductive, the security of fitting in anesthetic. It dulls us, puts us to sleep, makes us painfully removed from ourselves. As gay men, we need to step back and wake up. We need to own our souls, dream our dreams, and reject the poverty of conformity. When we do, we find out how rich and right we are.

No price on my soul.

SURVIVOR'S SYNDROME

Sharp nostalgia, infinite and terrible, for what I already possess.
—*Juan Ramón Jiménez*

It is wholly unreasonable that such a stark and empty place has taken up where once there was abundant life. In war, towns and villages are wiped out, scores executed, roots and hopes erased. So with massive deaths in an epidemic. So with AIDS.

Those who survive—by luck, by grace, by reasons we will never know—have every reason to be numbed and to be frightened by the weight our living has now acquired. Survivors are prone to depression, to anger at being left behind, to envy of the dead, to shame for such feelings and thoughts.

Those who witness the passing of so many possess more than their share of life. To keep life, to hold to it, to ride out the terrible grief: this honors the dead, this allows time to make meaning of the terrible and precious gift of living that all survivors bear.

It is good and right that I am alive.

LEAPS

One doesn't discover new lands without consenting to lose sight of the shore for a very long time.

—André Gide, The Counterfeiters

A wanderlust lay in each of us, part and parcel of our inner being, fixing our direction differently from other men. We have all struggled, had no sight of shore, been utterly unsure why we were chosen for our singular journey on such rough and uncharted seas.

But we are not, after all, so different from the others. Every individual, to live in accord with his true nature, must at some time cast off the bounds of convention and enter a starless region which, for a very long time, gives neither comfort nor assurance. We consent only to movement. Purpose and destination are unknown.

Our restless sea voyage at last yields sight of a lone swallow, at first so faint that its silhouette is barely distinguishable from blank sky. Soon we see a greater play of birds and finally the slim wavering line of approaching land. Once we reach it, discoverers all, we know we were right to embark, that our route was true and safe and ours alone.

At one moment, *we leapt*; eyes closed, hearts pounding, with some kind of crazy faith we would come to life on the other shore.

I live in a new land.

March

FALLING IN LOVE

When you fall in love, you feel you've discovered the bird of paradise, the magic person from the Other Land. You suddenly see a human being in all his magic extraordinariness. And you know that you can never understand him, never take him for granted. He's eternally unpredictable—and so are you to him, if he loves you.

—*Christopher Isherwood*

Once you've fallen in love for real you understand what the fuss is about. Those Persian poems, D. H. Lawrence, Patsy Cline—it all finally makes sense. Still, you are aware your experience is touching something new, something epic in its own right.

There is a moment we feel our balance going. "It was something in that story you were telling, suddenly I..." The normal edges of what separates us from others dissolve and all the sweetness of the world rushes in.

Whether we look back ruefully or look back in awe, the immediacy and enormity stay fixed in time like a sunset that somehow took us over the horizon with it. Magically, we have been to the Other Land and there encountered *him*, so dazzling, so comforting, so unbelievably magnetic—oh yes, sometimes we have to pull back, sometimes we're just not ready—that we want to sign on right there for a long course in *getting to know this man*.

No wonder poets praise falling in love, yet never capture it completely. There is too much there. We fall in slow motion to the depths of our soul's desire.

This is worth longing for.

BASICS

Since when do you have to agree with people to defend them from injustice?

—Lillian Hellman

Sometimes we fight the wrong battles. A great number of people will never accept homosexuality as the natural phenomenon that it is. First of all, too bad for them. Second, what difference does it make if we don't have everybody on our side?

What we must have are the basics. We are created equal and entitled to life, liberty, and the pursuit of happiness. People don't need to adore us in order to agree that any infringement on civic freedoms presents a danger to society as a whole. Injustice injures not only particular individuals, but eats at the broad protective foundation on which democracies and inclusive communities are built.

We needn't let ourselves get dragged into every debate about the propriety of who we sleep with, whether God intended us, or if it's really overbearing mothers who are "to blame." No, the issue for the body politic is simple equality: access to jobs, housing, opportunities, and the perks of freedom due all human beings.

Let's nail the basics.

NEW YORK

Nothing is "normal" here. So everything is normal.
—Native New Yorker

If you're looking for "gay" to define your identity in New York City, look for something else. While shouting it from the rooftops might get a rise out of Dubuque, Manhattan won't stifle a yawn. This is odd at first. Something is amiss, like the absence of traffic noise when you first arrive in the country. We're used to the static, used to the dull pain of worry we're about to be found out, about to stand up to a round of jeers as if our adolescent dream of arriving in school with no pants on has come true.

Amazingly, in New York, we're normal. Or normally abnormal. Or anyway, who gives a damn. New York is the great equalizer. No matter your station in life, national origin, or t-shirt advertising a favored sex act, it's all the same when trying to get a taxi in the rain. And no sense trying to conform to a common standard when there isn't one. In New York, it's every man for himself. On his own terms. Up against the same wild odds. Refreshing, isn't it?

I'm normal as normal can be.

MASTURBATION

The debating society at my school was discussing the motion "That the present generation has lost the ability to entertain itself." Rising to make my maiden speech, I said with shaky aplomb, "Mr. Chairman —as long as masturbation exists, no one can seriously maintain that we have lost the ability to entertain ourselves."

—Kenneth Tynan

Truly, masturbation has gotten a bad rap. After all, it is here, in the privacy of our own time and space, that we can fully—if single-handedly—experience The Life of the Imagination.

On this joyride, fantasies get full rein. Say hello to the men of your dreams: no cock too large, no limit to the number of room-service waiters arriving simultaneously (and, strangely, in no rush to get back to the galley), no airplane bathroom too small or ill-appointed. Let it rip, boys! *No one is watching.*

Greatly underrated as well is the sheer sensuality of it. Soaped up in the shower, well-oiled in front of the mirror, laid back in bed with our favorite erotic literature—and we set the pace—tame or tortured, furious to luxurious.

Second best? Not always.

I am well entertained.

ANGER

I'm not from the school which says "We mustn't fight back and be just like they are." I'd like to kill somebody. I really would.
—Daniel Curzon

Long before we came to understand our difference, the world was punishing us for it. Nearly every gay man has stories of being excluded, shunned, teased, verbally or physically assaulted. Degrading stereotypes abound. Fag jokes still go over well in many circles. We turn on TV, see some jerk spouting homophobic nonsense, and we'd like to go after him with a club. The injustice is overwhelming.

Our anger is real. Absolutely legitimate. And ultimately self-destructive if we don't acknowledge it, channel it, and heal whatever personal wounds have caused it. By all means fight violence and prejudice. By all means act up and speak out. By all means pound a pillow to vent the rage. But anger as a way of life is a cancer. "Just like they are" is bigoted and riddled with fear. Being different means not eating ourselves alive.

I will not be destroyed by anger.

CATEGORIES

People invent categories in order to feel safe. White people invented black people to give white people identity...Straight cats invent faggots so they can sleep with them without becoming faggots themselves.
—James Baldwin

We limit and deny ourselves whenever we accept placement in a category. The world seeks to define us—and not just us. The label "other" has long played to the tortured fears and false self-confidence of Aryan supremacists, fanatic religionists, and fascists of all stripes.

Fact is, the invention of blackness as the shadow of whiteness and the invention of faggots as insurance against gayness are convenient ways for a bunch of threatened people to hang on to their power and avoid the truth: which is that they really aren't that different—and certainly no more entitled —than anyone else.

In the meantime, we're left with their mess. Cleaning it up requires exploring the edges, fending off the many gay versions of knee-jerk categorization, taking the heat, and making the world safer for everything that ventures off the beaten path.

I defy all categories.

DENIAL

If you bring forth what is within you, what is within you will save you. If you do not bring forth what is within you, what is within you will destroy you.

—*Jesus, The Gnostic Gospels*

There it is, straight from the horse's mouth, a ringing endorsement of coming out if I ever heard one. Now some in the religious community would rush to label such interpretation heresy. But here's the problem with them: these people are middle management. Me, I want vision from the top.

What The Man is saying is borne out in the stories of denial and liberation we so often hear from gay men. Many of us lived for years troubled by something we dared not name. Some had a notion, but became immersed in a formula life that finally fell apart. Others intentionally led double lives, running and lying and telling ourselves that our ulcers and nightmares and DWIs were just a string of bad luck.

When we deny our gayness, we destroy ourselves. A gay child, a gay boy, a gay man has always waited within each of us: to be free, to know love, to know joy. Bringing him forth saves us, brings us fully to life, to the real life we were meant to live.

I will bring forth what is within me.

INVISIBILITY

Never have I tuned in to Jeopardy *to find them competing for an "Answers" category of "Famous Faggots for $10."*

—Anonymous

As the saying goes, "Sometimes history has set the record a little too straight." It's galling that the lives of historical figures are routinely taught—Achilles, Alexander the Great, Walt Whitman—with no mention of their intimate love of men. It's a sort of conspiracy: everyone can safely assume everyone else is, and was, heterosexual.

The average person hasn't the vaguest idea if their mail carrier, electrician, butcher, landlord, choir leader, car salesman, boss, tax accountant, welfare worker, or airplane pilot is gay. The vast majority of us are invisible. Which is safe. Which keeps us invisible. Which is unsafe: no matter how out we are, somehow we can still be *exposed.*

We need all those gay guys from history out front with us. And we need to let our own real histories speak for themselves. When Stonewall Day becomes a national holiday, candidates for office routinely campaign with their same-sex lovers, and Famous Faggots makes it to *Jeopardy*, visibility will finally be routine. Until then...

It's up to me to make a little history.

JAPAN

On a summer's night in his fourteenth year, like the long-awaited song of the nightingale, Jinnosuke first made love to Gonkuro. They met in strictest secrecy, fearful lest news of their love become known. Except for the moon, not a soul knew what was going on through the autumn of his fifteenth and sixteenth years.

—Ihara Saikaku, *The Great Mirror of Male Love,*
translated by Paul Gordon Schalow

The highly ritualized and ordered nature of traditional Japanese society did not exclude homosexual love relations. Ihara Saikaku's tales of seventeenth century Samurai and Kabuki worlds reveal the intricate customs of *wakashudo*, the way of loving boys. Far from the European norm that relegated male love to a perverse sexual tangent, a cult of connoisseurship arose in Japan.

Relationships of great formality took place between men and much younger boys. In the Samurai class, these associations were within strict codes of loyalty which, if violated by either party, resulted in suicide or vengeful killing, the only possible resolutions to restore honor. True love was valued above all and, as in the story of Jinnosuke and Gonkuro, the risk of death meant nothing by comparison.

Young Kabuki actors were idealized..."In his youth, his beauty could kill birds on the wing..." Theatre artists supplemented their meager wages by prostitution. Contrary to Western understanding, genuine romance, loyalty, and loving were played out in these relationships as well.

While never actually describing a sexual act, Saikaku's accounts are suffused with a sensuality that draws on Japan's natural beauty, the intricate detail of embroidered kimonos, symbolic hair styles, and passionate pledges of lovers. The result is an eroticism at once bearing the heady scent of cherry blossoms in spring, a sip of warm sake, and the promise of artful devotion to pleasures between men.

I am a connoisseur of men.

PARENTS

I have found the best way to give advice to your children is to find out what they want and then advise them to do it.

—Harry Truman

My first therapist made a practice of pushing his clients to bring their parents to a family meeting within the first few scheduled sessions. The idea scared the shit out of me and my parents weren't too happy about it either, but they came. It was different than I thought it would be. Jerry basically interviewed them about their own lives—their childhood, parents and grandparents, thoughts on their failures and success. I didn't say a thing.

My mom found Jerry "sweet," my dad dubbed him "a helluva guy," and I thought he was a genius. Inside of an hour, my view of my parents fundamentally changed. I realized they have life stories of their own. Their drives, limitations, self-concepts and values were laid down long before I entered the scene.

It took six months to get straight what's what between my dad and me. About ten years to stop getting hooked by my mother.

It finally came down to something simple. They're them and I'm me. I cherish what's valuable in my inheritance and reject what holds me down. I am extremely fortunate that neither abuse nor serious neglect is part of my history, things extraordinarily more difficult to heal.

What advice would I give them? Do what you want. Their advice for me? I don't much need it any more.

My life is my own.

THE BOY SCOUTS

A scout is trustworthy, loyal, helpful, friendly, courteous, kind, obedient, cheerful, thrifty, brave, clean, and reverent.
—*The Boy Scout Law*

And straight. The Boy Scouts' insulting policy and court battles on behalf of bigotry are objectionable on so many levels one barely knows where to begin. There's a temptation to write this tawdry business off as kid stuff. But we can't. We obey the law.

★ We are obligated by the trust of future generations and our loyalty to higher ideals.

★ We are helping rid the world of discrimination.

★ We are slavishly obedient to the Bill of Rights. (Okay, we have some other ideas about obedience, too.)

★ Friendly, courteous, and kind is the norm—unless dropped by a lover.

★ Cheerful is our very name.

★ Thrifty? Well, we may fall down a bit in that department, but no one is perfect.

★ And no one is braver. We walk, live, and work under threat of danger and regularly take on big ignoramuses like the Boy Scouts of America.

★ Now what do they mean by clean? God knows we bathe regularly.

★ Which brings us to reverent. Lesser men would fold up their tents and take a hike. Not us. In pursuing justice, we put reverence into action.

I deserve a merit badge.

BREAKING UP

Just remember, we're all in this alone.
—Lily Tomlin

For a while there it seemed like we were in it together. But what was magic and promising isn't any more. If negotiations have come to naught, if we just can't get what we need, if patience has been thoroughly tried, then chances are it's time to go.

Breaking up, so the lyric goes, is hard to do. No shit. But staying together when it should be over is worse.

Intimacy has to be about growth. When conditions are right, we can grow together, taking turns as each other's sunlight and rain. But no matter the cause, be it cheap betrayal or some inexplicable mismatch of the soul, when mutual growth stops, then staying is slow death.

Breaking up is wrenching, painful, and sometimes absolutely necessary. In the long run, it's not a matter of being alone, but of being alive.

I have the strength to leave.

GUILT

Our mission is much bigger than we could ever have imagined. Our ministry is one of public manifestation and habitual penetration. Our motto is "Give up the guilt."

—Statement by the Sisters of Perpetual Indulgence

Please complete this simple test. Give yourself 10 points for each "no" answer, then check your results below.

1. In the midst of steamy sex, do you hear a little voice saying, "You know, it's wrong for you to enjoy this so much."
2. Do you regret coming out to someone because it turned out to be really hard for them to handle?
3. If you disappointed your parents by being queer, do you feel badly about that?
4. Do you ever just sort of feel guilty for being gay?

Your results:

40 points: Congratulations! You are entirely guilt-free. You may proceed to the next reflection if you like.

30 points: Guilt is not an overbearing problem for you. You might practice by taking a "mental health day" from work...and not feeling guilty about it.

20 points: You are verging on a guilt problem. See if you can spend the better part of the weekend in bed with a lover and enjoy every minute of it. If not, try again each weekend until you succeed.

10 points: Guilt is a potentially serious problem in your life. Counseling or a gay support group might be great for you to try.

0 points: The good Sisters' prayers have gone out for you. You are the victim of a homophobic, co-dependent society. You could almost certainly benefit from seeing a gay-sensitive therapist. You'd be amazed at how much better you can feel!

My gayness is nothing to feel guilty about.

NATURE

One day toward the end of summer—on the kind of day when the light is hazy and diffused and the air is barely moving and heavy to breathe—my friend and I decided to have an impromptu swim before returning home... The water was clear and cool as we dove in...He came up right behind me and reached around and into my shorts...I noticed that he was hard, as he rubbed against my backside. As his hands reached around me...I became aroused and hard, too. It felt good and right, like something that was supposed to be. I knew then that this is what I had been waiting for...
   —M. Owlfeather, *Children of Grandmother Moon, Living the Spirit*

There is a day, at least one, that captures the essence of each season. Shimmering and crystalline winter; pungent, promising spring; summer, scorching or lush; crisp, blustery autumn with a hint of rotted leaves and fruit. One may look skyward, shield the eyes from sun or wind, breathe, and open the senses. Asking why these things are so is a matter of wonder and a form of prayer.

There is a day—a distinct memory or a day yet to come—when he is behind us and reaches around and into our shorts and we grow hard and push back against him and it feels good and right and like something that is supposed to be. And when he has gone, we turn our faces toward the stars or into the darkness of our room and we feel inside something that is good and right and supposed to be.

We have asked why these things are so, some as a matter of wonder, many as a challenge to nature, few as a form of prayer. We can gentle the mind, sweep away distortion and pollution, and break the surface into a clear cool depth where our nature is interwoven in the actual basis of things. And as we grow aroused, we experience something pungent and promising which has the potential to both nourish and scorch, which is a part of the cycle of life, which is what we have been waiting for.

I am beautifully and rightly made.

NECKS

Return often and take me at night
when the lips and the skin remember...

—C.P. Cavafy

My eyes return to my lover's neck. He lies down, his head tilted back and slightly to the side, looks at me, asks me to come to him. His neck holds a fine shadow and compels me with its mix of muscle and throat. I remember sculpture. The neck is sturdy, elegant. I look up to his face, I look down to the whole of his body.

My fingertips return to my lover's neck. I nearly encircle it, feel his blood beating inside of it. My fingers interpret the mixed messages his skin sends, the neck so vulnerable in its corded strength. I remember the contradictions, the pulse, the extraordinary softness just below the line of his beard.

My lips return to my lover's neck. Young men have worn their marks like trophies, saying to the world, "I have been loved." It is often the first taste of him, wet and dry meeting, so many senses all at once. He smells of sandalwood and I am always awed by how much I love this. My lips take me back and forth and my own neck weaves over him in a slow memory just beginning to be made.

I take, and I give, and I remember.

CONNECTION

It finds a home in Alpine valleys, Albanian ravines, Californian canyons, and gorges of Caucasian mountains. The royal palaces of Madrid and Aranjuez could tell their tales of it. Endowed with inextinguishable life, in spite of all that has been done to suppress it, this passion survives at large and penetrates society, makes itself felt in every quarter of the globe where men are brought into communion with men.
—John Addington Symonds, A Problem in Modern Ethics

"*I thought I was the only one.*" This has been the experience of countless young men as the knowledge of our gayness stole over us. We felt we were in an unknown ravine, a place overlooked by neighbor and faraway map-maker alike. We could spin a globe of the earth, watch it go round and round, and think there was nowhere to be welcome, certainly no palace guards to announce our arrival as royal guests.

In 1873, when John Addington Symonds wrote the above words in regard to "sexual inversion," he was among the handful of Englishmen confronting contemporary legal and medical practices as based solely on bigotry and misunderstanding. He led a conflicted life, worked to influence lawmakers and theorists of the day, and eventually settled in Switzerland with his wife and daughters where, in a more liberal atmosphere, he was able to achieve some balance between outward appearances and his acute desire for communion with men.

His work, though suppressed in its time, survived and helped to penetrate the veil of historical silence that left so many for so long wondering where we connect. Now we know. The connections stretch everywhere across the globe and lace backward and forward throughout the time men will inhabit the earth.

I am connected.

BREAKFAST

The morning shone clear and calm as one always imagines tomorrow will shine.

—*Dylan Thomas*

We stir from the warmth of sleep, our lover nestled beside us. Our eyes turn from the morning sun and turn instead to him. His skin is moist and luminous. His chest rises and falls softly. Opening, his eyes meet ours. We make love. Then, we make coffee.

People usually consider dinner the most romantic meal of the day, but it's not. Breakfast is. Longtime bedfellows settle in with caramel rolls and the Sunday paper. Newer lovers can't quite believe he's actually still there—at *our* kitchen table, drinking from our grandmother's china cups we've reserved for just such a moment.

Morning is the shiny, fresh time of day. In clear light, we look at him, feel our gratitude for his presence, and pass the Wheaties. It's all so extraordinarily down to earth.

I'll put on some coffee.

FAMILY REJECTION

The rest of the family ostracized me. I was no longer welcome in their homes or around their children. They feared that my gayness was contagious. My cousins were told that I was "sick" and they should stay away from me. It hurt.

—*Vernon Maulsby,*
Nightwings, Revelations: A collection of gay male coming out stories

The price for coming out can be high. People we have known all our lives, people we thought cherished us, might instead reject us icily. Exile from the family is raw pain, even when it wasn't such a hot family to be part of in the first place.

When rejection of this magnitude is our experience, we must be very careful not to minimize its impact. Betrayal by our families hurts us deeply. If we take the time, we can move through it.

Time does heal wounds, but only if they are opened and cleaned. Cynically dismissing "those assholes" won't work. Pretending it doesn't matter will cause an infection. We need to rage; we may cry and scream to the heavens. One day we will come to accept what has happened. Amazingly (because it seemed so dark and endless at first), the pain runs its course. We find we're okay. Intact. A survivor.

Then comes a bonus. If we have truly grieved our loss, we have gotten free. The coming out story that started this page ends with these words:

"I have my wings...and Now...I can Fly."

INTIMACY

Your hearts know in silence the secrets of the days and the nights.
But your ears thirst for the sound of your heart's knowledge.
You would know in words that which you have always known
  in thought.
You would touch with your fingers the naked body of your dreams.
                                    —*Kahlil Gibran, The Prophet*

We are born with a thirst for intimacy. The degree varies, but we all have it. It may be some animal holdover thing. It may be that we're all one in spirit. It is a mystery that at first is so silent and so secret and so big that all we can do is thrash around looking to be satisfied and generally won't get too far at all.

The drive for intimacy brings us close to others and shows us ourselves. Our lovers hold up a mirror in which we see our shortcomings; also our sweetness, terror of being wronged, the nature of what we desire. He does this, too; our loving makes us both more real.

It's a messy business and it doesn't always work out. We want to move past the bullshit. We find that getting intimate means getting honest. We learn to put the words of our heart on the table.

Truth and trust are the wellsprings that will quench our thirst. This is where we touch the naked body of our dreams.

I seek the knowledge of my heart.

JERKS

I never hated a man enough to give him diamonds back.
—Zsa Zsa Gabor

In retrospect it always seems so obvious. *He must have planned to steal my stereo all along!...If he was actually going to call he would have written down my phone number..."God, I forgot," isn't quite apologizing for no birthday present. Not wanting to use a condom at the last minute really did break our agreement.*

The problem is we're not sure who to blame: "How could I have been so *stupid?*" vs. "How could he have been such a *jerk!*" Let's work on the stupidity first. Undoubtedly he had a number of redeeming qualities which led us to be blinded by love, lust, or an appreciation of expensive gifts. So okay, we made him a set of keys for the apartment on the second date and maybe that was a little rash. Live and learn.

Now then. About *him*. There's three types:

1. *They don't mean to be jerks*, they were just brought up badly. These boys are educable. Enduring a few hard knocks might be worth it.

2. *They've had it too good*—too charming or too cute—and they think they're God's gift to homosexuals. Two options: they wise up or you do.

3. *They're **Real** jerks*. Masters of deceit. Creeps. Wash those men out of your hair and by all means keep the diamonds.

No need to subject myself to jerks.

GIRL TALK

Bring me your tired old queens, your poor drags,
Your horny masses yearning to be free,
The disco bunnies of this teeming land,
Send me these tempest-toss'd homos,
And I will lift my skirts and take them in.

—*Greg Jackson*

While out for a chat with a new friend during the I-don't-see-anything-funny-about-this stage of my coming out process, the friend being a man who liberally and consistently applies the female pronouns (she, her, hers) to persons of the male gender, I allow as how I really dislike all this girl talk and isn't it disrespectful to women and I've never felt more male in all my life and doesn't this reinforce negative stereotypes and he interrupts me, saying, *"Oh, honey, lighten up."*

One could say I've come a long way into a much more Holly Golightly sort of appreciation for the delights of genderfuck. It's double your pleasure, double your fun; secret passwords into a club for the broad-minded. To outside detractors we had to (prepare for worst insult possible) *be like girls* to get in. Since living well is the best revenge, I enjoy being a girl.

Now serious put-downs of women are not OK and not funny, but that's not what 99% of this is about. It's one of the great parts of being a sexual outlaw. Here beneath these skirts there's a brave new frontier where the men are men and the men are women. And if that's a little much for anyone, she can just step out on the veranda and fan herself a bit until she feels better.

Thank you, June, I will talk how I like to.

STARTING

In real love you want the other person's good. In romantic love, you want the other person.

—Margaret Anderson

"Real" and "romantic" love are not, in the long run, mutually exclusive. Let's face it, though, when we're just starting out ("Hey, look over there. No, the little one. I *want* him.") we usually just *want* him....and sometimes we mostly just want his *body*. This makes sense. How are we supposed to know what the other person's good might entail without starting *somewhere?*

There is the "science lab" scenario. You know, you work together for years cracking the genetic code of the fruit fly. You learn each other's tastes in take-out food, medieval music, allergy medications and the like. Then, one day when you bump heads both rushing to pick up a dropped test tube you discover how much you really do care for one another and pretty soon you're swinging from chandeliers.

It doesn't matter where we start. Wanting the other person is delicious, inspiring; it's like junior high—your mind wanders a bit and you're crossing your legs to disguise a hard-on. Or caring about the other person's good may be what first captures your heart; it's weird, but you just never wanted so much for someone *else* to be happy.

If you're into the idea of the long run, the secret is putting the two types of love together. Tender spiced by hot—hot tempered with tender. Either way makes a stunning combination.

Let's get started.

RULES

All I thought of was making my colors sing, without paying any heed to rules and regulations.

—*Henri Matisse*

Each of us is entrusted with palette and brush at birth. At life's end, the canvas is finished. Early on we are instructed, often rigidly, in how our colors are to be used. Red goes here, blue there. Don't stray outside the lines.

We can do as we're told, fill in the boxes, make sure our work conforms to regulations. But if we do, we have wasted our paints. Listening too well to our teachers and critics, we will think too much of their thoughts and too little of our own. In order for our colors to sing to us, we have to block out the interference.

There is an enormous difference, a flush of power and pride that rushes up inside us when we make our first tentative brush strokes that are original. The colors may clash, but no matter. We can say, "They're my *colors* and they sing to *me*." This is where genius begins.

I have complete artistic freedom.

SELF-ACTUALIZATION

Sooner or later, you start taking yourself seriously.
You know when you need a break. You know
when you need a rest. You know what to get worked
up about, and what to get rid of.
And you know when it's time to take care
of yourself, for yourself. To do something that makes
you stronger, faster, more complete.
Because you know it's never too late to have a life.
And never too late to change one.
Just do it.
—Nike Ad

Not so long ago, sneaker ads promised running faster and jumping higher. Now we can self-actualize through footwear. Give advertising another decade and it'll be hop, skip and jump to Enlightenment. Nike's aren't cheap, but really, they're a bargain if you buy the whole program.

It should be so easy. Running around dressed up in our *actual self* is a high demand sport. Top performance takes conditioning, constant practice, and the willingness to comb ourselves for flaws and weaknesses in our moves.

Self-actualization is a process. First we get our feet on the ground, then we learn to take off. The result is grace under pressure. Personal best: the constant pleasure of knowing who we are, what we need, and making the most of what we've got. After a while, you just do it.

I'm a natural.

THE PERSONALS

CUTE cybernetic-Homo, 24, 5' 6", 130#, seeking friendship, possible relationship. Looking for OUT hunky, sensitive, intelligent, funny, romantic, sexy guy 24-29. Me: above description plus quirky sensibilities. No assimilationists. Reply to RELATIONSHIP Box #3199 ☎
—Personal Ad

Cruising the personals is intense, even if you're not in the market to buy. Merely flipping through can produce anything from love-at-first-sight to an identity crisis.

"LOVES RUGBY sounds *incredible*. God, I wish I was 10 years younger," or "This one is so much like me I can't believe it," or "Maybe I'm just in a rut. Maybe I should answer one of the ones I'm *not* attracted to."

It's much less complex in the "initials" sections—the "BBM into grp JO some SM"—crowd. That's much like catalogue shopping except the item you order delivers itself in person. As for the ones you actually call—or the ones who call you—the general report on the experience over time is that it gets very tiring. *"So many men and so much coffee. Is this really how I wanted to live when I grew up?"*

There *are* stories of Personals Ads True Love as there are winners of the New Jersey State Lottery. And some memorable one-night stands as well. There is also, it's worth noting, a potential addiction issue here. When taken too seriously, this whole thing can make us think we have a life. When taken in stride, well...if I was 15 years younger I'd give CUTE cybernetic-Homo a call.

When the going gets tough, the tough go shopping.

THE INTERMEDIATE SEX

It is hard to imagine human beings more skilled in these matters [affairs of the heart] than are the intermediates. For indeed, no one else can possibly respond to and understand, as they do, all the fluctuations and interactions of the masculine and feminine in human life.
—Edward Carpenter, The Intermediate Sex, 1908

In his pioneering effort to understand and define what we are, Edward Carpenter gave us the name "intermediates." He comes across well today, though perhaps idyllic and naive, given his life early in the century at Millthorpe, a small English farm where he wrote and lived openly with male lovers.

It isn't fashionable just now to forward utopian ideas. We're more sophisticated. We've got hip hop and HIV, we've got categories for everything, we're tired of new age crap, and many argue we're the same as other guys except for who we sleep with.

"Quite so," Carpenter might say if he popped up in a time machine. "I can see how your sensitive natures are positively overwhelmed by the assault you are under night and day. Called this and that on the daily news. The subject of ludicrous inquiries in your parliament. Who would have time to consider the gentler side of one's nature and the broader questions these great struggles pose?"

Flying back ninety years with him to Millthorpe, he might enlighten us, as he did other foreign visitors, as to the creative role of intermediates in countless cultures and the exquisite fine-tuning we are capable of. Over afternoon tea, he might share his theory that the meeting of masculine and feminine inside us gives an extraordinary humanity and sympathy and a remarkable power in dealing with our fellow human beings.

My nature holds many gifts.

DANCERS

The raw vigor of his flamboyant leaps, the animal rapture that pro-
pelled him in huge turns around the stage, the passion that smoldered
as he bent over his partner—it was all excess and it was all gorgeous.
People screamed in their seats.
                        —Time Magazine eulogy for Rudolf Nureyev

What a thrill to watch male beauty showcased this way—and
it's considered quite polite to stare. A strange paradox that society says men aren't supposed to love men. Seeing them like this,
who can resist?

In our case, no need to. What dancers display on stage is animal prowess refined through the most arduous training imaginable. Except when eroticism is an intentional theme, dance tends
not to convey it. Dance is, however, smolderingly sensual. We
see and are caught up in the strain, the control, the abandon, the
flat-out beauty.

Dancers' bodies—to most people's taste—are breathtaking.
And the effect of look-but-don't-touch can be strangely satisfying. We walk away like dancers ourselves, aware we are cut from
the same cloth, related. Aware of how perfectly natural and noble
it is to be awestruck by the body and movements of a man.

I love to see them dance.

GENETICS

Gorski believes that when the hormones that normally cause the development of male traits don't function properly, the result can be either a feminized brain in men, or a masculinized brain in women. The result, he said, is often homosexuality.

—*Minneapolis Star Tribune citing opinion of University of California geneticist Roger Gorski*

Science is hard at work isolating the "gay gene" so we can all know what causes us. Frankly, I hope that microscopic little queen keeps eluding them. Note Gorski's language, "hormones...don't function properly." It may be scientific jargon but it comes off arrogant as hell. Those little hormones are doing *just exactly what they're supposed to do* and at a very predictable rate. The patterns vary regularly to produce an important and necessary variation in the species. Mother Nature wants it that way.

But this is more than a case of scientific bad manners. This is scary. If research can identify *the problem*, won't the next step be figuring out how to correct it? We could nip this homo thing in the bud! It'll rank right up there with the polio vaccine.

Paranoid? The human race isn't exactly famous for letting scientific knowledge that can be put to good use just lie around in some lab. Witness the nuclear bomb.

But let's say the idea of genetic cleansing is too far-fetched. I'm still torn. No question that proof we're *legitimate* products of nature might help dispel homophobia, but that lets everyone off the hook too easily. If it becomes biologically incorrect to pick on gays and lesbians, the bullies of the world will just find someone else.

Let's eradicate the hate gene.

SPIRITUALITY

*...sexuality is profoundly connected to spirituality, indeed is insepara-
ble from it...we touch our wholeness and the fullness of our power, and
at the same time our connection with a power larger than ourselves.*
—*Judith Plaskow,*
Toward a New Theology of Sexuality, Twice Blessed

I will never forget what it was like to first feel this connection. I got home after a date with a guy I had a terrific crush on
and while standing alone contemplating the matter in my
kitchen I felt something surge through me like a furnace roaring
to life. I was, for the first time, fully experiencing—and welcoming—a simultaneous sexual, emotional, and intellectual attraction. *I wept.*

Most mainstream religious traditions downplay the importance of sexuality in general and reject homosexuality in particular. Most spiritual teachings, however—even those underlying
the mainstream—emphasize *wholeness*. When we embrace and
engage distinct aspects of ourselves—our intellect, our emotions,
our sexuality—the whole is greater than the sum of its parts. We
somehow create an opening that allows what many call a greater
or higher or brighter power to enter our lives.

Since that night in my kitchen, the connection has never
broken for me. It stays on behind everything like a thin blue pilot
light. Often it flares brighter, warming me with joy and insight
and strength. It is a sense of spirituality that connects through
me as a gay man—and yet reaches far beyond.

My sexuality is whole, good, and vital.

LONG-DISTANCE RELATIONSHIPS

I diligently obey the training by which I was very early accustomed to be separated from my mother—which nonetheless remained, at its source, a matter of suffering (not to say hysteria).

—*Roland Barthes*

This is one of those good news/bad news stories. The good news is we're in love. The bad news is he lives in El Paso. Not that there's anything wrong with El Paso, in fact the whole state of Texas is suddenly very alluring, but there's this little problem of 1500 miles.

There are many ways these stories start, all happy. From The Unexpected Meeting: *I couldn't believe it. The last place I thought I'd meet a lover was at Regional Shop Steward Training...*to The Once in a Lifetime Opportunity: *Of course you have to take the job. You've always wanted to be in L.A. and we're solid enough for a long-distance thing.*

There are many ways these stories end, many unhappily.

Long-distance relationships are a delicious torment while they last. Falling into bed with him after the always too long separation is exquisite release. We ravage each other like teenagers.

Getting on the airplane we're a little numb (and probably sore) but within a few days the suffering hits home. Each time we leave we have to give him up and become single again. There is no rationalizing it, the loss is real every time.

This is tough and very grown-up stuff. We have to be careful that out of sight doesn't drive us out of our minds. Can love endure?

Where there's a will there's a way.

EXILE

How did I get here? Somebody pushed me. Somebody must have set me off in this direction and clusters of other hands must have touched themselves to the controls at various times, for I would not have picked this way for the world.

—*Joseph Heller*

Not at the outset. Not when we left the note on the kitchen table explaining where we had gone and why. Not when we felt ripped out at the roots. Not when we felt the weight of an angel's body on top of us and we wrestled against him for our lives, and lost, and were sent off by him in a direction we knew not of, and slept spent and alone and unsure why the memory of white wing feathers between our fingers forced this journey into exile.

Lesson in the meaning of higher power: we do not hold the controls. Lesson in being cast out: the strong man thus finds a home within himself. Lesson in bitterness: when those who reared us as their own will not have us back. Lesson in humility: what we did not pick is the gateway to our heart's desire.

You can never, ever go back. A choice was made for you. Hands unseen pushed, tore out other dreams, imprisoned you on a barren island. You railed and wore torn clothing. You wept in the dark. You woke on the shore of a new land, entered a society of foreign custom and speech. You restored yourself. You began a new life, could never have known what adventure and rightness and bounty lay in wait for you in what you now love fiercely as your homeland.

God pushed me.

April

FOOLS

To never see a fool you lock yourself in your room and smash the looking-glass.

—*Carl Sandburg*

We all make fools of ourselves at some point or another. It's an occupational hazard that comes with venturing out of our rooms.

The motto of the wise fool is "nothing ventured, nothing gained." We can refuse an invitation to dance—painfully aware of our body's unique anti-rhythm defense system—and miss a chance to charm Mr. Hunky who doesn't dance so well either. We can refrain from writing a sincere message that exposes our feelings and end up nowhere because neither of us knew how to make the next move. We can ignore the sparkle in the dandy's eye at the art gallery and miss the love affair of a lifetime.

No question locked rooms lead to locked lives. And no question the fear of appearing foolish is the greatest foolishness of all.

Some chances are worth taking.

LIMITS

I like being choked. Is there any way I can put my partner at ease about my particular needs?

—Question in the Advocate Adviser

To be whole, emotionally healthy gay men we have to make it our business to challenge the many limits society has imposed on us. Our rejection of restraint is displayed through the exciting extravagance of gay subculture, be it Bette Midler's early act at the Continental Baths, San Francisco's famous Cockettes, the Broadway production of La Cage aux Folles, or the hottest, nastiest after-hours dance floor in town.

It is tempting to decide there are *no* limits, that any suggestion we not do something is another manifestation of massively fucked-up mainstream values. As tempting as this notion of total freedom may be, it confuses the basic difference between freedom and license and has led, on more than one tragic occasion, to a license that killed.

It is vital we know where to draw the line, that we *not* feel at ease about specific acts that are inherently dangerous. From my personal vantage point as a parent, this is the first and, perhaps, the *only* limit I pray my children will accept.

It's important to have our limits.

FRIENDS

It is the friends you can call up at 4 AM that matter.
—Marlene Dietrich

It is a great compliment to receive such a call. Unless, of course, we've got a pal on the other end of the line who ought to have his dialing privileges cut off. But assuming the call is legit—there is trouble, illness, heartbreak, young love, a dark night of the soul, an overflowing case of the sweet mystery of life—the steadfast friend is honored to be roused in the middle of the night.

For many of us, a close circle of friends is our chosen family. Whether separated by distance or by dissonance, we just don't count on mom or dad or sis or bro the way we count on our friends. And they on us. These affinities of the spirit are vital to our well-being. We provide each other the necessities of life, everything from hot tips to hot meals to hot gossip.

Real friendship is not easy. It requires patience, generosity, and the kind of loyalty that means biting our tongues one day and caring enough to tell a hard truth the next. Nothing matters so much as a friend when we need one. And little tells us how much *we* matter as being needed by a friend.

Call me any time.

GAY SPIRIT

For at the heart of our vision is a vital spirit-force, bringing a revolutionary change in how we see ourselves and other people and the goals toward which we strive.

—*Mitch Walker, Visionary Love:*
The Magickal Gay Spirit-Power, Gay Spirit

Gayness takes us many places one might not otherwise go. Because conventional forms don't provide for us, we must create and recreate a vision of our own.

At the heart of our quest is a restless vitality, the birthright of our coming out. Every thinking man asks the meaning of his existence. Every thinking gay man also asks the meaning of his gayness. It is tempting to resolve the questions solely on sexual terms: *I sleep with men;* on psychological terms: *My love for men is healthy;* or on political terms: *I am equal.* The greatest mystery lies with the spirit.

Is our spirit gay? Pre-Judeo-Christian traditions worldwide say yes. Our spiritual history is with shamans, healers, witch doctors, mad dancers, keepers of sacred rites of unity and balance. The world is in desperate need of ancient magic, but there are no longer elders to anoint us in these roles. If it is this that resides in our spirits, then it is long past time we again bring it forth.

My gayness is a gift to the world.

GETTING ATTENTION

The childhood trauma is repeated: he is always the child whom his mother admires, but at the same time he senses that so long as it is his qualities that are being admired, he is not loved for the person he really is at any given time.

—*Alice Miller,* The Drama of the Gifted Child

Patterns laid down in childhood are difficult to break. Children crave attention and will go to considerable lengths to get it. We scope out what the grown-ups like and try to deliver. Our parents' disapproval is devastating. If they withdraw their love we are in a panic to restore it.

Unfortunately we repeat the trauma. We scope out what *he* likes, then try to deliver. There's nothing wrong with wanting to please our lover, but it's easy to overemphasize the qualities he admires. Once we fall into this pattern, he can begin to loom Svengali-like before us. Despite a sinking feeling in the pit of our stomach, we're not sure how to break the spell.

The good news is, we're not children, he's not our parent, and once we see what's going on, we can get things back on an even keel. Saying we *don't* want a particular type of attention or admiration may frighten us—it's like *asking* him to withdraw his love. When we do, we make a confident adult statement that allows the potential of attentiveness to who we really are.

I want to be loved for who I am.

THE CHICAGO SOCIETY FOR HUMAN RIGHTS

...to promote and to protect the interests of people who by reasons of mental and physical abnormalities are abused and hindered in the legal pursuit of happiness which is guaranteed them by the Declaration of Independence, and to combat the public prejudices against them by dissemination of facts according to modern science among intellectuals of mature age.

—From the charter of The Chicago Society for Human Rights, 1924

Returning from service in the Army of Occupation following World War I, Henry Gerber brought home the inspiration he had gained from forward-thinking German homophile groups and publications and determined to start a society to advance homosexual rights in America.

No one of reputation or means would support him, but willing to "slave and suffer and risk losing my job and savings and even my liberty for the ideal," he managed to pull together the $10.00 cost of incorporation, a preacher of brotherly love, a railroad man, and an "indigent laundry queen" as national officers, and wrote and published two issues of *Friendship and Freedom*, the Society's modest journal.

By the end of 1925, the first known homosexual organization in the United States was out of business. Henry and his friends had their heads above ground just long enough to have an article titled "Strange Sex Cult Exposed" on the front page of the newspaper, to be jailed without charges, to have the postal service accuse them of sending obscene matter though the mails, to spend all they had on their legal defense, and, in at least Henry's case, to lose his job.

One might say they failed, but they did not. The Society's existence set a precedent, sent powerful reverberations though the homosexual underground, and broke permanently the belief that gay people in the United States were unable or unwilling to organize on our own behalf.

From tiny acorns, mighty oak trees grow.

NONPOSSESSIVE LOVE

We must learn to respect the humanity of our fellow-man, not to invade him or coerce him, to consider his liberty as sacred as our own; to respect his freedom and his personality, to foreswear compulsion in any form: to understand that the cure for the evils of liberty is more liberty...

—*Alexander Berkman*

Loving without possession honors our essentially separate journeys through life. We have no absolute claim on another's heart. This doesn't suggest cool detachment, an inability to commit, or that spiritual union with another human being does not or cannot occur. It does suggest a calibre of loving that allows the potential of more than one intimate connection in our lives at one time.

Nonpossessive love is not what you'd call a mainstream idea (it appears infrequently on TV, rarely in religious imagery, and almost never in country western songs). So naturally it raises an eyebrow or two when we first hear about the guy with two lovers who both know about and like each other, toward whom he feels equal affection, loyalty, and commitment, and neither of whom does he plan to give up or invite to move in.

However we link our lives—from harem to holy matrimony—it's not the form that matters. It's the content. Love without possession holds no compulsion to control. There is respect for the intimate contours of each other's needs. There is tender care that grows and grows in this sweet fertile soil called liberty.

What is freely given is the greatest treasure.

CALLING

Oh God, in the name of Thine only beloved Son, Jesus Christ, Our Lord, let him phone me now.

—Dorothy Parker

Okay, let's come clean: who among us has not prayed over the phone, commanded it out loud to ring, or, at the very very least, sat through at least one drag performer's rendition of *"It Must Be Him?"*

Anyone answering "Not me," to the above question has either never had an amazing first date, never been to a drag show, or never had a phone. The rest of us have laid ourselves at the altar of the celestial ring, our achy breaky hearts beating against our breasts, our lives and dreams and hopes for Saturday night flashing before our eyes.

Yes, nearly every mortal man knows the phone as an instrument of torture, but can the cycle be broken? Absolutely. For starters, we can blow off playing it cool and just call the guy. If he doesn't answer or doesn't call back then this is a case of what-you-hear-is-what-you-get. The deadlines are up to you. If he calls within them, your prayers have been answered. No call? Could be the Good Lord is trying to tell us something.

If he's the right number, he'll call.

ADOLESCENCE

If I had knocked up the school's star cheerleader, it would have appeared only as a desperate effort to camouflage the queerness that differentiated me from regular people. For the issue was not really who was having what kind of sex with whom. As rural high school sopho-mores, almost none of us were having sex with anybody.

—Frank Browning, *Culture of Desire*

There are exceptions to every rule and so goes the story of the defiantly self-confident sixteen-year-old whose response to his uncle poking an elbow in his ribs and asking if he has a girlfriend is, "No. Am I *supposed* to?" Highly aware of his advantages, the same doe-eyed boy is quick to remind a too-hungry trick of just how much trouble he can get in for consorting with a minor. Miraculously, and with few regrets, this fellow lives to tell his tales.

Adolescence has been likened by experts to temporary insan-ity. The hormones do it. Even the most popular, the most engaged, even those who actually *were* having sex, report a des-perate effort to camouflage themselves. It is queer indeed, wet dreams, growth, hair, wanting to *be* a cheerleader (before they took boys), wanting to linger in the shower room and knowing there is something terribly unsafe in this desire.

It was, for many, a period of acute pain. Terrible isolation. Attempted and successful suicides. And, for many, a period of thrilling exploration, delicious innocence, devilish deeds. Nowadays almost everybody is having sex with somebody; we're quite sanely differentiated in our queerness and, if we've brought everybody up to date and into the brave new world, we've got this uncle who sticks his elbow in our ribs and says, "So, do you have a boyfriend?"

It's my show now.

COMING OUT TO PARENTS

*When our daughter came to us and told us she was a lesbian, I did
something for which I will never forgive myself. I hesitated a moment
before I took her in my arms and told her I loved her.*

—*Hinda Kibort*

The drama of claiming our authenticity plays out with singular meaning and intensity in the relationship with our parents.
Coming out to our mother and father is critical.

In rare cases, the best choice is *not* to come out: we know we
would suffer abuse and the measure of our independence is our
refusal to be victimized. In other cases, we need to take a deep
breath and make sure we proceed with realistic expectations.

We have to expect that pride and delight in who we are
come first and always from ourselves, not from mom, dad, or
anyone else. We have to expect them to react—both initially and
down the line—on the basis of who *they* are, not who we are. We
have to expect their process to take time, just as ours did—perhaps only a moment, perhaps months or years, perhaps some
other lifetime.

The woman quoted above—who could surely be elected
Mother Of Us All—is at one end of the spectrum. Parents-from-
hell inhabit the other. No matter where they fall, this coming out
is for their good. They deserve to know the truth and have the
opportunity to grow from it.

Most important, this coming out is for us. Because we
deserve to tell the truth and experience the power of it.

Mom, dad...I'm gay.

SHOULDERS

Oh, but a man's reach must exceed his grasp, or what's a heaven for?
—Robert Browning

Standing face to face, hands reach across to shoulders. Coming into contact with the marbled strength that flows across them, we may have the impulse to find a handhold and climb, to press our bodies up and against and into this man.

Our grasp goes deep here. We cling and hold and dig down hard, inflicting pleasure with our fingertips and hands. But this is not a place of lingering long, the shoulders, there is too much gravity in them, pulling us down the length of arms, down the expanse of back and chest, down to the darker, more complex center of the body. The shoulders are a crossroads that also lead us up; to dramatic contrast of soft hair, the delicacy of neck and face.

Later, pressed naked together, sweating, after a climax that flashes through us like a lick of heaven, we come to, slowly, aware the whole of our flexed arms are wrapped around and around his shoulders, and as we uncoil we stop reaching for something we just before, just for an instant, could grasp.

How beautiful to see, to touch, to hold onto.

NEGOTIATION

If you want it bad, you get it bad.
—*Anonymous*

Ever notice how, if you're really craving some affection, casually say, "I think I'll just lay down and read for a while," and saunter off to the bedroom that within minutes he shows up acting like he just got back from six months at sea? Or how much better it feels to have his drinking problem—and him—out of your life? Or when you screwed up the courage to say you had this gut feeling you weren't ready to move in together, he turned out to be relieved because he felt the same way?

The principles of win/win negotiation are proven in business, in diplomacy, and in love. We're talking daily reality here. Sometimes you take a stand on your bottom line and don't back down. Other times it's best to give his ego a break and let him make the next move. Here are some tips:

1. **Appear strong.** If you do, you attract strength.
2. **Know the true value of what you've got.** Everybody's worth having it good. That includes him...and you.
3. **Walk away if you don't get what you need.** Chances are, you'll be pursued. If not, *ciao baby*. There's greener pastures somewhere else.

If it isn't good, I don't want it.

BIRTHDAYS

Being gay has taught me tolerance, compassion, and humility. It has shown me the limitless possibilities of living. It has given me people whose passion and kindness and sensitivity have provided a constant source of strength.
It has brought me into the family of man, Mama, and I like it here. I like it.

> —*Michael Tolliver in a letter to his mother,*
> *Armistead Maupin, More Tales of the City*

Thirteen days before I turned 38, I packed my clothes, cassette player and a few tapes, left the house I had planned to grow old in, and temporarily moved in with my mother. I was a pretty sad gay boy on my birthday. My kids gave me a funny little golf toy. My best friend made me dinner.

On an especially dark night soon after, I had the sensation of wrestling with an angel. At one in the morning I called a Rabbi friend long distance. He reminded me of the meaning of the story of Jacob who wrestled with God's messenger and woke up with a wound in his thigh. Jacob learned humility. He came away with a hidden reminder of the fact that every man feels pain. He was renamed Israel and promised the legacy of a great nation.

On my 40th birthday I had a whole new life. My boyfriend gave me a Tiffany key ring with two charms. One has my first initial engraved on a small round piece of silver. The other is a tiny replica of the Ace of Hearts.

At the risk of proclaiming myself a born-again homo, I have to say I now enter the world much differently than I used to. Obviously I've been lucky. I take a little credit for working hard at working things through, but I give more credit to what my gayness brought me.

There are plenty of ways to come to life, but this is how it happened for me. Coming out and being gay brought me to myself. And thereby into the family of man.

Happy Birthday.

INTERNALIZED HOMOPHOBIA

To heal is to touch with love that which we previously touched with fear.
—*Stephen Levine*

Like slow unseen poison, the forces of fear pump out their lies. It is a heterosexual world. Gay feelings are aberrations. Gays are perverts. Anal intercourse is disgusting. Homosexuality is a crime against nature. AIDS is God's punishment. Queers and faggots deserve to be beaten up. Real men don't blow each other. You're a sissy. Homosexuals are dangerous to children. What could be more lonely and bereft than the life of an aging queen?

The indoctrination is so pervasive that homophobia exists in many of us at a cellular level. Our coming out stories are heroes' journeys, victories over vast forces arrayed against us. But the damage done by entrenched fear is not healed all at once. We feel it when we're self-conscious about coming off "too gay," in our embarrassment at some in-your-face group's latest tactic, anytime we don't believe we're entitled to first-rate public treatment and first-class intimate love.

There's a shitload to undo here. We know we're getting free when we can look ourselves in the mirror and say the words out loud—gay, faggot, cocksucker, queer—and have them bring a slow smile to our faces. Not anger. Not undue pride. Just *yes*. Yes, this is me. This is what I want. This is what I now touch with love.

I love being what I am.

MANNERS

For Christ's sake, open your mouths; don't you people get tired of being stepped on?

—Bette Midler, Gay Magazine

Bar scene: the friend of a friend asks me to dance. I'm always intimidated to dance with black guys, but delighted to be asked and readily agree. I'm actually quite a good dancer and after a bit he tells me so. I'm flattered. I put on my best moves. He takes off his blazer. We dance twice. Three times. I buy him a drink. We touch each other—chest, thighs, that sort of thing. We flirt. Then, he disappears for a napkin to wipe the sweat off his face. And doesn't come back.

I'm pissed! And a bit humiliated. I don't know *what* he is. And I could give a damn what bar customs are. In my book he was rude. Needlessly.

So I decide to find him. In part to restore my dignity by speaking up, in part to teach him some manners.

He sees me coming in another part of the bar and makes for the john like someone about to throw up. I follow him. "Hey, you were *rude*, man." I don't exist. "You could have just said you needed to go. Or thanks, goodbye." I'm invisible. "You hurt my feelings. It doesn't have to mean anything. It can just be for fun." He looks at me. "I'm not myself tonight, not myself lately," he says. I smile a little, "That's okay. Thank you for asking me to dance. I had a really good time." I pat him on the shoulder and walk away.

Living as we do in close quarters, manners are all the more important. *Please. Thank you.* Saying excuse me if you step on somebody. Or taking care not to step on them in the first place.

I give great manners.

BEAUTY

What a piece of work is man.
—Shakespeare

The male form is exquisite. Whether we admire Baryshnikov's grace, the earthy power of Kirby Puckett, or the sculpted fingers of a stranger punching his floor in an elevator, men captivate us.

Being fixated on the perfect body has its downside. Since few of us were blessed with one —either ourselves or in the person of our lovers.

But every gay man knows, up close, the sinews, the muscle mass, the delicate mystery of the collarbone, the subtle turn of biceps where they melt into the chest and shoulders. And we all know well, from afar, the phenomenal beauty of men who, by how they have been worked by God, simply take our breath away.

I love to look.

TOUCHING

He dared to look into Crunch's eyes. Crunch's eyes were wet and deep deep like a river, and Arthur found that he was smiling peace like a river.
Arthur asked Crunch, "All right? Do you feel all right?"
Crunch put Arthur's head on his chest, ran one long hand up and down Arthur.
"You're the most beautiful thing ever happened to me, baby," he said. "That's how I feel."

—*James Baldwin, Just Above My Head*

He is the most beautiful thing that ever happened. And so am I. There is wonder, always, in this. We have touched and been touched before, but in the moment, as we shiver slightly in anticipation and the soft hairs rise from our arms to meet his fingertips and the warm contact spreads a message out to every region of the body, in the moment, it is like first water to thirst, which is only ever temporarily slaked, and the first touch is both small and deep, *deep like a river.*

We touch each other to say and ask for many things. This can be a challenge: gentle and soothing may not yet be part of the vocabulary: *Come on, aren't appreciation and a rough fuck the same thing?* No. The skin invites something more; slip down into a world of dark wet eyes, not manly, no control in a river, *not in a deep river.*

"All right? Do you feel all right?" Much more right when I have been touched. Most right when I have been held, when long hands have run up and down me, when I have been made love to; open everywhere, deep and wild and wide and peaceful.

Touch me, baby, touch me.

BOUNDARIES

Love, although not a discipline of fear, is also a discipline.
—Stephen Spender

This week on "The Big Boundary," we'll look in on the saga of Mike and Mario, two dashing '90s homos having a go at a long-term relationship.

Scene: The bedroom   *Time:* Tuesday, 12:22 AM

Mike: God damn it, Mario, I've got to be in court at 8:00 and I cannot get into this whole thing about whether we buy a house or not right now. I love you. I want to talk about it. But not now. *OK?*

Mario: Oh, wait a minute, I get it. This is a *boundary* issue. I've got a house-beautiful thing and you've got a sleep thing. We can't have this conversation because it's just a bad time for you—it's not that you don't care, right?

Mike: Oh, baby, there is hope for you yet. Now come over here and kiss me goodnight.
(Music up, fade to black.)

It is a sign of loving ourselves when we say, "Crossing this line will violate me. You may not do it." It is a sign of loving another when we say, "I understand this is your boundary. I will not cross it." Negotiating bedtime can be a boundary issue—a simple one. More complex give and take is tougher. This is a discipline of confidence, love, and care, one essential to the foundation of respect on which enduring relationships are built.

A sign of true love is respect for boundaries.

ARROGANCE

He has the greatest blind side who thinks he has none.
—*Dutch Proverb*

It was almost immediately following lunch with a friend, wherein I listened in a most judgmental fashion to his exploits and confusions, secretly congratulating myself for being above such nonsense, that I proceeded to violate a principal rule of self-respect in my most intimate relationship and collide head-on with a bout of shame from which it took three full days to recover.

Once I could stand to look myself in the mirror, I realized I'd had a rough trip on the predictable byways of arrogance. It's like this: the moment we think we're one up on the other guy—whether a friend or the teeming hordes—we become an accident waiting to happen. Cause and effect is clear: arrogance equals blind spots and blind spots equal trouble.

When we slip into arrogance we're really just frightened—or tired. It takes a lot to develop our own standards and even more to meet them. If we learn to read the signs—judgment, self-satisfaction, superiority—we can prevent ourselves from falling asleep at the wheel.

I've got my eyes on the road.

THE MIDDLE EAST

When the Arabs established themselves in the Mesopotamian plain,
they found there a homosexual love which had flourished from time
immemorial, connected to the most ancient cultural and religious
traditions...

—*Marc Daniel, translation by Winston Leyland,*
Arab Civilization and Male Love, Gay Roots

Today's Middle Eastern antagonists capture headline news, the region's history and traditional sensuality disappearing behind a veil of modern extremism.

The Koran itself is modest in its condemnation of homosexuality. Muhammad excluded it from the list of grave sins which offend God. Islam thus pays tribute to the region's significant Greco-Roman influences as well as religious and mythological roots that embraced gay love from remotest antiquity.

From the Tigris and Euphrates basin come five-thousand-year-old epics of love between men. From ancient Syria, Goddess cults of Astarte with gay rites celebrated in temples. From the Nile Valley come stories of gay love between Gods. And from the ninth century A.D., two hundred years *after* the establishment of the Islamic Empire, Hamzah ibn Abi Daigham gives us this poetry steeped in the eroticism of the Middle East:

We stayed tonight, you and I,
    far behind camp.
We stayed without overtaking the tents
    or following the enemy.
We stayed motionless in shadow
    and in the cold of the night,
entwined and covered with a mantle from Yemen,
    full of intoxicating scents.

I was rocked in the cradle of civilizations.

THE DISEASE CONCEPT

Just as in malacia and pica the patient eats coal, gravel and earth with an infinite relish, so in psychic pederasty does man love the male! Sodomy, studied with the pitying and forgiving eye of the physician and psychologist, is accordingly a disease which ought to be curable, and which many times is cured.

—Paolo Mantegazza, The Perversions of Love

Looking back, the disease concept almost seems quaint, in the same league of debunked ideas as bleeding patients into anemia, scientific "proofs" of racial superiority, and masturbation causing warts.

Not that being a healthy homo is an easy thing. Decent doctors and psychologists may have crossed sodomy off their list of diagnoses, but this has not stopped the coarse and gravelly notions of sickness, perversity, and heresy from being shoved down our throats. It's a wonder we don't spend most of our time throwing up.

Except for a small hard-core fringe still claiming they can straighten us out, the disease idea has bit the dust. Still, we've got some recuperating to do. Whether under the care of skilled therapists, with the aid of good books, in groups, with friends, mentors, lovers, or all alone, every queer man must cure himself of the self-doubt and self-hate that stand between his love of the male and the infinite relish with which he should rightfully enjoy it.

I've taken the cure.

LONGING

The heart is a fountain of weeping water which makes no noise in the world.

—*Edward Dahlberg*

The voice of longing calls from subterranean places, ancient pools and cisterns where the tears of the ages are stored. Strange that something so demanding, something that surges with such vivid imagery and physical force, should be silent to the outside world. At its most intense, longing wails all through us. Our hearts are awash in it and we feel it down to our bones.

The source is the pain of separation; from the embrace of our beloved, from the safety of the womb, from the bosom of God. We long so for love's promise of reunion. We are drawn to the company of men, to the wells of nakedness where we drink of each other's passions and bodies and souls.

The longing of the heart is pure. If we honor it, stay with it, let its weeping be a fountain within us, then it may also be heard in the world. And its call returned.

I hear the longing of my heart.

SELF-ACCEPTANCE

One must finally take one's life into one's arms.
                                    —Arthur Miller

We can accept ourselves reluctantly, grudgingly, *Well, I'd better make the best of it*...or we can go a big step further and accept our nature as a gift.

At the advanced age of 37 with a lot of therapy under my belt, the act of coming out was a big statement of self-acceptance. Still, it felt second best, a booby prize for my valiant effort at heterosexuality.

It had been 15 years since my bisexual days, at the end of which I regarded sex with men as a compulsion and always endured an aftermath of shame. I chose a wonderfully sensitive older man named David as my first "new era" lover. I made love to him passionately and as I came I cried in his arms. "Welcome home," he whispered. I felt no shame, but I wasn't quite home yet.

Some months later, I finally fall for a guy in a big way. It is truly different from the mixture of infatuation (he didn't look so hot in the morning) and out-of-control hormones (he didn't look so hot in the first place) I mostly experienced to that point.

Somewhere between our second and third date, it comes to me in a flash. *There is nothing second-rate about this.* I am on Cloud Nine, feeling every kind of attraction all at once, I want to give to him in the worst way...this is love and it's great. I write it down to make it official. With these plain words I take my life into my arms:

I accept my gayness. It is my way of loving.

INSECURITY

My photographs do me an injustice. They look just like me.
—Phyllis Diller

The voice of insecurity has only one thing to say: *you're not good enough.* This unreality gets dumped on us early and its impact grows as we struggle to find our place in this big bizarre world.

It seems the answer to insecurity is fitting in, a touch-up of our self-portrait so it works well with the others. There are lots of goodies out there and if we look just right, talk just so, and don't rock the boat we can get our share. But it's all someone else's idea. Conforming to standards other than our own will never truly make us secure. We're just a bit too queer.

The only way out of this fun house is to smash the mirrors, to find the unwavering image of who we are that shines back from the bottom of our own souls. There is where security begins.

I have always been good enough.

LOVE'S TORMENTS (PART I)

Make 'em laugh; make 'em cry; make 'em wait.
    —*Charles Reade*

"He loves me. He loves me not. Oh God, he says he loves me...but *wait a minute*, he hasn't said it since *Thursday*. He did buy that card...but he couldn't *really* love me. I'll call and ask him. No! *Christ*, how stupid can you get. I'm starting to feel like fucking *Patty Duke*. I'm losing my mind. *He loves me.* He..."

Have a familiar ring to it? This little torment goes around in our heads until we think we're stuck in the grooves of an old 45 spinning at warp speed. A very good friend might shake us by the shoulders, *"Come on now, snap out of it."* A cold shower can help. Or HE might arrive and somehow, with just the right warmth in his smile and depth in his gaze, make it all drift off like petals in the wind.

It's a torment. He makes us laugh. He makes us cry. He makes us wait. We want to *know*, god damn it! We're dying to know. *Am I finally safe?*

Time calms and time tells.

LOVE'S TORMENTS (PART II)

And in fact artistic experience lies so incredibly close to that of sex, to its pain and its ecstasy, that the two manifestations are indeed but different forms of one and the same yearning delight.

—*Rainer Maria Rilke*

In the open undesigned place that is love, in the strong and varied light, we are touched by pains and ecstacies known to artists and to lovers. Sex is the medium. It is there we experience most directly the breaking down of barriers, the yearning moments in which our lungs gulp air and we ache desperately for release.

This is not lust. Lust is centered, driven. Love is dispersed, open. The soft skin on the underside of our arms cries out as loudly as what pushes smooth and insistent between our legs. *Oh, we want him.* We want to create something between us. We want this hot ecstasy that so delights and burns our bodies.

And when we are spent, before we begin again, during this period of time when we are in love with him and in love with sex as much as we will ever be in love with anything, we feel an ache that runs everywhere. There is only one thing for it and not enough of that.

This is a torment I can endure.

OVER-RESPONSIBILITY

When your mother or father got drunk or abusive, you wondered what you had done to set them off. When they fought about money, infidelity or anything else—even when they were depressed or irritable — you knew it was somehow your fault. If they separated or divorced, you felt completely responsible.

—A Time to Be Free, Anonymous

It doesn't take alcoholism, abuse, or divorce to produce an over-responsible child. The messages can be much subtler: "Be a good little boy for mommy." "C'mon, son, do your ole man proud." Way down deep, most of us learned it was Job One to satisfy our parents' demands.

It may have been a matter of survival. Being a "good boy" wasn't just about extra ice cream and pats on the head, it was a set of critical strategies to get love and avoid abuse. In adult life we can change the rules. We can figure out what works for *us*, then negotiate, knowing the choices include walking away from people and situations that ultimately take more than they give.

This is a huge difference from childhood. Walking out at age five isn't an option. But is it now? Do we know we're entitled to quit when we've given a guy or a group or a job our very best shot and we're still not getting what we need? Over-responsibility is deeply tricky. Even considering the possibilities can feel like betrayal.

I am responsible for my own well-being.

GRATITUDE

If we let it, gratitude will leaven the whole of our life and, like a magnet, attract infinite blessings. It's a promise.

—*Charles Pounders*

Being gay may seem a mixed blessing. There is, after all, a fair amount to put up with and, as human beings, we are endowed above all God's creatures with a singular capacity to complain. So getting to the point of saying—no strings attached—"*I am grateful to be gay*" may be tough.

Here are some gratitude list-starters:

1. There are no sex role stereotypes to overcome in relationships.
2. Gay bars have the best dance music.
3. There's nothing like being kissed by a man.
4. There's nothing like kissing a man—everywhere we want to.
5. We can share clothes and after shave.
6. We hear lots of fascinating coming out stories.
7. Liberation isn't just a concept in history books.
8. We know what it's like to be brave.
9. We get to wear all kinds of things made out of leather.
10. Being queer is really fun because the rules are up to us.

It's amazing what happens to us and around us when we truly come from a place of gratitude. Unmixed blessings show up every day.

Thank you.

SHARING

Two can live as cheaply as one—if they both have good jobs.
—Sigmund Freud

One of the clearest signs of love is the impulse to share. At the beginning of romance, boundaries dissolve. We are open, want to know and touch everything; his history, his body, his way of being.

This comes to an end. Little by little, our fences reassert themselves. We descend into the valley of *the-little-things-that-drive-us-crazy*. He leaves empty toilet paper rolls, you wage the famous battle of the toothpaste tube, it was definitely *his* neglect that caused your ten-year-old philodendron to bite the dust.

Then a crisis hits. You get laid off. Your sister gets engaged to a homophobe, you don't know if you can handle the wedding, and your parents yell at *you* not to spoil things. His car throws a rod and the only available $1500 for repairs seems to reside in *your* savings account. Now the real sharing starts. Or stops. The tests are pass/fail. They're popped on us without warning and show just how well we know how to give.

Assuming we pass, relationships ultimately hit new crossroads with serious questions about shared vision, shared spirituality, shared commitment to places of honor in each other's lives. Tutored by love, we may learn, over years, a depth of trust that enables us to open our hands and hearts completely.

What's mine is yours.

MORALITY

The moral inhibition of the child's natural sexuality...has a crippling effect on man's rebellious forces because every vital life impulse is now burdened with severe fear...morality's aim is to produce acquiescent subjects who, despite distress and humiliation, are adjusted to the authoritarian order...

—*Wilhelm Reich*

Behind the facade of society's smug defenders of morality is the stink of greed. These people have The Golden Rule confused with a preemptive strike. They figure the best strategy is to "do unto others *before* they can do unto you."

Little wonder queer folks in general and gay pride parades in particular get a lot of hackles up. The guys in leather jock straps and majorette boots strike deep into enemy camp. If the outraged moral crowd knew how to tell the truth, they'd say, "Look, you faggots. What really pisses us off is you messing with the basics of sexual inhibition. Do you think we're going to stand around and watch while you trash our structure of power and control? *No way*. Now get the fuck back in your closets."

This is the real deal. This is the voice of the authoritarian order. It has nothing to do with care, respect, honesty, or fighting oppression—the things true morality is all about. The minute we come out as gay men, we've enlisted in the rebellion. Now *that* is a moral act.

My vital life impulses are strong and free.

May

HOPE

Only you and I can help the sun rise each coming morning. If we don't it may drench itself out in sorrow.

—Joan Baez

What do we hang on to in our darkest nights and days? A memory? A glimmer? We all face such times, when sorrow is like a tidal wave threatening to drown us out. We must have hope. We cannot live long without it. From where does hope arise when the waters swirl around?

From deep in the heart. To find hope we must yield to sorrow, but never give in to despair. The heart bears enormous pain, but only if we open it, only if we allow a mighty crashing of waves within. Then, from under the darkest water, a shoreline emerges tinged with light. Within seas of sorrow lies a light as bright as the sun.

Hope shines deep inside my heart.

LEATHER

Thus, by being initiated into his own mysteries after enduring the trial of mania, Dionysos becomes what he is...a Dionysos whose divine history incorporates the essential elements of the religious experience that he introduces into the world of men under the sign of Strangeness...
—*Marcel Detienne, Dionysos at Large*

Well, which is it? Dionysos making a comeback in a black bomber jacket, a cult of abuse, or just a bunch of regular guys who like dog collars and clothespins?

Depends on who you know.

Let's clear up any misconceptions about this Dionysos fellow. Like most Gods, he had his good and his bad side. He'd show up when things needed to be shook up. He was also the God of sensuality. The Greeks built controlled ecstatic ritual around him because they thought it was good for the masses. Dionysos was also known to get carried away with drink. Some rituals got out of hand and led to a regrettable run of human sacrifice.

The Gods had their mysteries and their fun. We've got leather. It has all the right qualities: allure, danger, ritual, worship, the promise of total submission. Every one of us has endured the trial of mania, being a Strangeness in this world, and hey, we deserve a long hot initiation.

There is something about leather. How it's cold and hot and rough and creamy all at the same time. Religious experience? Can be. If you know how to work it right.

I am heir to ancient ecstacies.

CHANGING HISTORY

I was about 14. We were riding along in the car. I can remember exactly the corner we were turning. Inside I was dying to talk to someone about it so I asked my father, "What do you think about homosexuality?" He said, "They're all going to hell." And that was the end of the conversation.

—Russ B.

Few of us grew up affirmed for our emerging difference; our histories of isolation and abuse are there inside us, locked in perfectly remembered moments.

Yet it is possible—and necessary—to change history. Otherwise we are forever 14 and turning that corner, always hearing our father say we are going to hell.

Here is how history is changed: first, we give the memory its due. We tell everything about it, to others if we wish, but most important to ourselves, out loud, with *feeling*: anger, outrage, fear, sadness, confusion—whatever is there. Then, we tell the 14-year-old inside us what he most needed to hear: that dad was stupid and wrong; that the right answer to the question is, "I think homosexuality is fine. I'll be proud of you no matter what you are and if you're confused or worried about anything, you come to me."

There is one more change we can make. We can alter history for someone else, for a boy turning a corner in a car with his father today. Or years from now. Coming out and making ourselves whole replaces a historic wrong with a present right. On such healing the history of the future is built.

I am changing history.

CLOSENESS

...unless he can overcome his early training about not expressing his feelings, not asking for help, having to take care of himself, and the larger than life self-importance that most men are taught, Joe is going to have trouble with closeness and relationships.
> —*Jeff Beane, Choiceful Sex, Intimacy and Relationships for Gay and Bisexual Men, Men & Intimacy*

Sounds like Joe has a lot of troubles. And an awful lot of work if he's going to overcome all that bad stuff. So let's give him a break. First of all, he's just an average guy and it's not his fault. Really, it's not. Early training is intense. And it's not just a home study course. This "behave like a man" thing is mercilessly pounded into adolescent boys by roving packs of peers.

Keep your distance, Joe. Feelings are a sign of weakness. Show nothing. Betray nothing. Give nothing.

We all got the message. And we do have a lot of troubles, especially as gay men. We don't have women to teach us about intimacy. We're just plain stymied unless we break through the terror and figure it out ourselves.

Joe gets a little close and then he runs like hell in the opposite direction. Our fear is larger than life. Our closeness is critically important. We need contact, companionship. We need sex. We feel things, need to be known. We need love.

Break out, Joe. Feelings are a sign of strength. Show yourself. Betray your captors, Joe. Give of yourself.

Intimacy is freedom.

LABELS

You and your definitions! I really don't think about my sex life in such a black-or-white way. Like I said, it's very American of you to try to make me pin these things down. We don't do this in France. We know a lot of things about everybody, but we don't have to say everything out loud.

—Thierry Mugler, The Advocate

Having come out at 37, I am leery of labels. The conventional wisdom is that before I came out I was living a lie. Not so. I was living the truth of a man whose complex sexuality evolved to a point where "gay" is the best available label—for now. Having come this far this way, I'm not about to predict where it goes in the long run.

American culture is cool on ambiguity: witness our most popular art form, the sitcom. We expect complex things packaged and resolved within 30 minutes and so it goes with sexual orientation. Most people, gay, straight, and otherwise, would prefer we neatly claim where we stand and promise to stay in one camp.

We can't. What we can do is stop betraying ourselves, our sexuality, and our promises. All labels belie the truth. We're not gays or breeders or tops or slaves. We're sexual beings alive with mystery and change, charges and attractions, drives that need to be held in check, drives that need to be let loose. Some sexual promises last a decade, a lifetime. Some last a night. Or an hour.

To ourselves and our lovers we owe the whole truth as we know it. To a craven world eager to label, box, and shelve us, we owe no explanation at all.

It's just not a black-or-white thing.

EVIL

Homosexuals, you know what the reasons and motives of your opponents amount to; you know, too, that your leaders and advisers have for decades been tirelessly working to destroy prejudices, spread truth, and achieve justice; but in the last analysis, you must carry on the fight yourselves.

—The Action Committee, Germany, 1920s

From before the turn of the century until the Nazis came to power, there was a thriving homosexual rights movement in Germany. International activists lent their names to the cause, numerous publications and cultural activities dealt openly with homosexuality, a scientific institute on sexology was established, and a petition with thousands of signatures against anti-homosexual laws was presented to the Reichstag.

Germany's descent into madness dragged nearly a half-century of progress into the ashes. By 1935, the Nazis outlawed kisses between men, embraces, and even gay fantasies. Homosexuals were later gassed and burned along with Jews, gypsies, the handicapped, and all perceived enemies of the Reich.

The rhetoric of today's radical "Christian" right could be read from the pages of any Nazi tract. Among the lessons of the Holocaust is the fact that organized intolerance and hate cannot moderate itself. Any such ideology is nothing more than politics fronting for evil.

The words of the German Action Committee—its leaders surely later arrested and killed—must remind us that our enemies today are real and serious and ruthless. They are the born-again army of the age-old struggle against authenticity and freedom. The battle we are fighting is a battle for our lives, for life itself.

This time, we will win.

BETRAYAL

And the trouble is, if you don't risk anything, you risk even more.
—Erica Jong

We are outraged when our trust is betrayed. We feel burned. We believed in a guy who deceived us about who he was. He lied about his whereabouts or he fucked our best friend (double betrayal!) or he stole things from our home and from our lives.

The trouble is, we played a part. We overlooked things or misread signs. Okay. Now it's time to face facts. Theft: pretty obvious. Lies: when exposed, they speak for themselves. Fucking around if that wasn't the deal: beware any sort of explanation. The lesson is once burned, twice foolish; not to stop trusting altogether.

Betrayal is a third-degree burn. It hurts like hell and may scar as it heals. This doesn't mean we should pull back altogether. It just means we should approach with caution, remember what can happen if we're careless, take a little longer to scope out a situation. If we stop taking risks altogether, we leave ourselves out in the cold.

I can trust a little bit at a time.

CHANGE

There are only two mistakes you can make. One is to rush it. The other is to ignore it.

—*Dr. William Goodman*

"It" in this case was the simultaneous process of coming out and grieving for the marriage and life I was leaving behind. The whole thing just felt like too much. I had no desire to go through all kinds of *stages* in the coming out process. I didn't *want* to feel 16 again. I didn't like being attracted to practically every guy I met. And I didn't like being compelled to retreat to my shower and cry and howl for what I had left behind.

And so it went. I slowly realized that every part and every day of this process made sense. I learned lessons, I got used to myself, and eventually I came to terms with being alone. Nothing made it faster. Nothing about it would go away. And after some months, I actually didn't want it to.

Dr. Goodman's advice turns out to be about living. We go through stages and have experiences and need to let go of what we leave behind. This is daily practice to keep us fresh, clean, and alive.

I can't rush it and I won't ignore it.

FUNCTION

These people who seem to spring from between the cracks, these androgynous alchemists, have a certain and necessary function for life on this planet.

—Mark Thompson, *Gay Spirit*

Alchemists turn base metal into gold. In this we are no different than other men. We are all given the raw stuff of our lives and time on this planet to work it into refined and precious things. Yet, as gay men, we differ from the majority in our combination of chemicals and complex compounds.

We are more likely to encounter and act on the androgynous elements in our mix. We experience the female principle, the receptive. We allow ourselves to be entered and become more knowing. We invoke the masculine principle, the assertive. We move toward what we want and become more visionary.

As androgynous alchemists, consider our gifts to the planet. First function: to be different among people and thereby teach respect for difference, for the necessity of all created things, for balance. Second function: to be ourselves, to enjoin complex forces and show the world how each of us glitters in his own right.

I am necessary.

HANDS

Then, in the blazon of sweet beauty's best,
Of hand, of foot, of lip, of eye, of brow,
I see their antique pen would have expressed
Even such a beauty as you master now.

—*Shakespeare*

It is our own hands we can speak of best. We know of his: where they have been, where we want them to go, perhaps not so well what they look like as how they feel. Our own hands we know more completely: their shape, the length of the fingers, whether they are hairy, where they are smooth, where rough, the length of our lifeline.

With our own hands we seek to know his beauty. They take on a quality of movement all their own, like the pointer on a Ouija Board moving across letters on its route to spelling out answers to questions silently asked. Our hands want to know, have a right to know.

We touch sweet beauty's best. Our fingers move across the nap of his head or between silken strands. Our palms are enthralled by flank of his back, by the turn of his ass, by the heat where his thighs meet, by the sleek length of his legs. Our hands ask to know everything, to touch everything, to be inside him. Our hand circles around his hardness and we seek to master him there, to own his beauty and his pleasure and our own. We master all of this, hold it in the palm of our hand.

My hands are ablaze with beauty.

INCLUSIVENESS

I don't believe that gay people have the role of shamans or priests or artists. There have been times when gay people were honored, when difference and otherness was sacred rather than satanic. That's an important thing. But are we really less well represented in the banking community than in the arts community?

—Tony Kushner, The New York Times

How terribly ironic when it is the gay community making us feel sharply "in" or "out." With being gay so trendy and all, next thing you know we'll have to present our credentials and apply for membership.

Screening Committee: And tell us, Mr. Dover, why is it that you wish to be accepted into our community?

Applicant: Oh, please call me Ben. Well, ever since I was a little boy I've just had this thing about other boys. You know, I wanted to be with the other boys, like there was this kid next door, very blond, very Scandinavian, and we used to like to play World War II and...

Screening Committee: Yes, we understand, thank you. Now according to your application you are a member of the Republican Party. We find this rather, well, incredible. Can you explain?

Applicant: It could date back to my childhood. General Eisenhower was my hero. Loved that jacket he wore. And he was the first one to put the finger on the whole military-industrial complex. Anyway, what's the point of your question?

Screening Committee: Well, there are certain expectations, certain roles. The privileges of membership are reserved only for those who...

Cut! Cut! Enough. We, of all people, should know better. Gayness is a matter of self-definition. Banker, Artist, Indian Chief...to each the fulfillment of his own ambition, his own dream, his own sacred difference.

Everyone is included.

REMEMBERING

In remembrance lies the secret of redemption.
—Baal Shem-Tov

I remember everything. I remember walking along the sidewalk in summer at dusk, barefoot, bare-chested, six years old. The most delicious feeling, almost like flying, was in my body. I wanted to be naked, to feel the air.

I remember being in bed with my brother and playing guessing games in the dark, drawing with our fingers on each other's backs. "It's a B... No, an R...Now it's an M..." Everything secure and warm and right.

I remember sleeping over in 9th grade on the pull-out couch in the basement, giving back rubs, then front rubs, then his hand just grazing across my hard penis in my white underwear, our bodies moist, our skin still soft, just in the flush of puberty. I was timid. I thought he might be queer. He is. I am, too.

I remember now so much more. My body knows and tells. I have all of it with me. Panthers, satyrs, wild horses, wicked fairies, a little boy flying on summer's warm wind.

I have not forgotten.

COMMUNICATION

Everyone's quick to blame the alien.
—Aeschylus, The Suppliant Maidens

Sooner or later, every exploration outside our solitary orbit arrives at a cosmic crossroads. Sooner (as in the next morning) may put an end to the launch right quick. Later, we're better able to throttle back and consider alternate routes. No matter when it happens, it seriously cools our jets: that blank look of incomprehension followed by a narrowing of the eyes and then, accusingly, "What are you, from another *planet??*"

The heart leaps to the throat, "Oh God," we fear, "I've blown my cover." Our nearly perfected imitation of an Earthling is severely at risk. We backpedal, we sweat, we explain, we apologize, and because there is still sufficient stardust in the air, we try again.

We offer lessons in our native tongue or work harder at understanding the complex construction of his. This effort (mutual commitment is required) is crucial to the ultimate success of the mission. Unless respect and understanding develop, fascination with alien culture wears thin. Any breakthrough helps and no one is at fault; there's just been a failure to communicate.

The goal is an interplanetary federation. Fluency in each other's languages. The ability to make ourselves known.

Take me to your leader.

HAVING CHILDREN

When he realized that he would never marry, he grieved over the children he would not have.

—*Seymour Kleinberg*

How ridiculous to assume heterosexuality is a prerequisite for having children. Granted, raising a child is a daunting task and the seriousness of this enterprise requires deep commitment. But the desire and drive to be a father is the only really essential element. If we have this, most any obstacle can be overcome.

Raising children ranks among the most challenging and rewarding of human experiences. It isn't right for everyone, but its rightness is not related to gayness. This is new thinking for many. Exclusion from child-rearing has been a built-in assumption, an accepted punishment, and a myth perpetuated as much by gay men as anyone else.

Let's wipe the slate clean and start over. Imagine a world where wise elders size us up as children and mentor us in all our native inclinations, parenting included; a world where many varieties of love and nurturing are compatible and society's arrangements follow suit. Let's imagine none of us is forced to grieve over what he rightfully and naturally should have.

I can be a father.

PRETTY BOYS

I want more in life than meeting a pretty face and sitting down on it.
—Harvey Fierstein, Torch Song Trilogy

It's gotta be tough, looking so pretty. You need those beautiful broad shoulders to carry around everyone's watery gazes and even wetter thoughts. Surely it's fun at times, looking in the mirror and seeing something so gorgeous smiling back (though I am told it's all relative and even the prettiest suffer from zits and general bouts of insecurity).

The sadness and difficulty is isolation. The great attractiveness of some men leaves a gulf of falseness all around them. At the center of all that attention one must wonder, "Does he care for me? Really? *Me?* Or does he just want to park his ass on my face?"

Relating on the basis of physical beauty only goes so far, which is not to demean the aesthetic rush of laying eyes (or more) on the astounding accomplishments of nature that roam among us. But whether the object of wonder is oneself or the heart-stopping specimen across the room, getting more out of life means getting past the surface, no matter how pretty, or comfortable, or captivating it appears.

I feel pretty.

CURES

I'm still attracted to men. There's still things that trigger me, but not so much as I used to be. I find myself less and less looking and wanting. It's becoming a pretty numb state I would say, a state of where the Lord has changed that...

—*Participant in* Freedom at Last Ministries,
a one-year live-in program for changing the "homosexual lifestyle"

I'm still attracted to men. And thank God for it. I suppose I could have stopped these attractions somehow. Electrodes on the penis, nausea-inducing drugs, frontal lobotomy, that sort of thing. But wait a minute. I *like* being attracted to men. It's this warm delicious thing. There just used to be these demon wishes it wouldn't interfere with my life. Thank God for no more demons.

Still, there's things that trigger me. Really beautiful, confident, out there women. I notice them totally and feel slightly deficient I can't come up with the "total" response. And from time to time I get sucked in by endless hype that makes the good life and a het life appear to be one and the same thing. But most of the time—and every minute I'm with my lover—I don't feel the slightest bit deprived of anything.

As far as numb states are concerned, those of us who pray might send up a word or two for those who have entered them. This scares the hell out of me. This is the program that has brought us child-abusing priests, suicides, trick-murdering consumers of the sex trade. Such "cures," at their *least* destructive, are a repressive hell on earth.

I'm cured of any notion I need a cure.

SEPARATION

There is the Hindu story of the child in the womb who sang, "Let me remember who I am." And his first cry after birth was, "Oh, I have forgotten."

—Source Unknown

My lover comes back to me in dreams like a lost part of myself. There is peace. Then the scene shifts and we run breathless in a nightmare drama. I fall through trap doors into dark mist. There is a brief sunlit scene where, for a moment, I can see him and we are safe, but Devious Forces close in and I am off.

My lover lives a thousand miles away. These dreams are not just of him, but of remembering who I am with him, the immense satisfacton of what he calls forth.

The mornings after an airplane separates us I awake and the dull reality of my sole self tangled in the bed strikes body and mind simultaneously. There is the familiar ache. I grasp the spare pillow (smelling of him) to my body and close my eyes. The dream has already slipped away, but I can still feel the encompassing warmth of his body. He surrounds me from behind or presses face to face against me. With my arms, my chest, my stirring cock, my heart, I remember. I am adrift in this womb, my bed, our dreamscape. My body cries, "Where is he? *Where?*"

Hot coffee and a shower work wonders.

MOTHERS

"But where are your wings?"
—Gene Kelley upon meeting my mother,
circa 1938, after my father's frequent descriptions of her charms

Given our experience of her, it may seem extraordinary that anyone ever saw our mother as an angel. *"But where is your broom?"* is what many would consider the better question.

Regardless of where she falls on the scale of supernatural qualities, there comes a point when our job is to get our heads out of the clouds and just get on with it. Ironically, angel-moms hold us back as much as wicked-moms-of-the-west. We loathe to disappoint the former and need to stop having our strings pulled by the latter. The trick is to invite mother back where she belongs: inside the borders of her own psyche and firmly outside of ours.

Gayness puts this relationship stringently to the test. Some mothers pass, some don't. Same goes for the sons. Today, what's important is our ability to live our own lives by our own standards. It doesn't really matter any more whether she's got wings, but whether *we* do.

Look, ma, I can fly!

AFRICA

In order to become a kimbanda, *one has to be chosen by a spirit, following which one undergoes a kind of shamanic transformation. Frequently, divine choosing of a* kimbanda-*to-be manifests as an illness that cannot be healed by way of herbs or sacrifices alone. The sick person becomes well again only when he or she recognizes and accepts the destiny of spiritual service.*

—Randy P. Conner, Blossom of Bone

Contrary to some schools of Afrocentric thought, homosexuality was not introduced to the continent in the unwelcome baggage of colonizers, missionaries, and slavers. Its presence among native African peoples is documented by carvings dating back at least 5000 years.

The Kwanyama, Yoruba, Azande, Nama, Lango, and Zulu are among numerous tribes known to recognize and, in many instances, honor their gender-variant and gay members. The link with homosexuality and spiritual service is common. Among the *Kwanyama*, only the *omasenge*—transgender gay man—and female *kimbanda* are allowed to possess or play the *omakola*, a musical instrument used to summon divine beings during initiation rites and other ceremonies.

Young men weren't born full-fledged shamans, diviners, or healers, though female spirits were known to visit male children in the womb and signs of their special nature were evident early in life. The later stages of initiation differed tribe to tribe. A chosen one might journey alone into the jungle to capture a river snake and wear it as a neck ornament; eat only herbs until a state of grave weakness allowed him to be possessed and instructed by spirits; spend months isolated in the healer's hut as apprentice to ancient practices; fall ill and become well again only by accepting his destiny.

Gay men and women who descended from the tribes of Africa may hear voices in their dreams, *"We are your ancestors...We have long tried to make your people understand that we want you to be our house—to speak for us."* And these men and women may learn of their connection to past generations, to a home within, to the mystical importance of their being.

We are chosen people.

LETTING IT BE

Don't threaten me with love, baby. Let's just go walking in the rain.
—*Billie Holiday*

Sometimes we want everything. Now. "Hey, baby, I'm not asking for a lot. Just make a lifetime commitment tonight and we'll work out the details later." We mistake to push: love sets its own pace. Maybe it *is* the Minute Waltz. Or just a bad case of Saturday Night Fever. And suppose you draw tickets to a full-length production of Sleeping Beauty: what kind of impatient prince walks out before she wakes up?

The problem comes when we're moving to a different beat than our partner. Our heated come-ons are deeply sincere. He's it, we know it, *let's dance.* He's there, he's interested, and he's threatened. The solution? Slow it down. If it's love, it won't go away. If it's not, at least we'll know it wasn't a matter of the wrong rhythm. In the meantime, hold to the moment. Savor any sweetness, no matter how fleeting. Sing the blues. Walk in the rain.

I can let it be.

TRICKING

"I'm tired of going to bed with people and being just the same afterward as I was before," Malone sighed. "How do all these men survive with all this perfectly meaningless sex?"

***

"What were you doing, darling?" said Sutherland.
"Looking for love," said Malone in a quiet voice.

—Andrew Holleran, *Dancer from the Dance*

Tricking is a lot like life. Opportunity knocks—sometimes through our own effort, sometimes not. It can be a lot of fun and we get to see the inside of other people's homes and hotel rooms. It gets boring sometimes, but then we might fall in love. Or get knifed by a stranger.

This is a land of diverse drives, some healthy, some not so. Men seek adventure, danger, relief, intimacy, sweat, affection or any combination thereof. Like in other pursuits, success means keeping out of harm's way—and getting what you want.

The practice does require mastery of some skills. Number one is eye contact. First, it has to be made, then correctly deciphered. Next comes small talk. It's not so much what is said, but the level of interest in the delivery. Third is negotiation: knowing our bottom line, testing for his, cutting a deal.

Some people think this is only about sex. But tricks are also about *connection.* Some one-night stands are incredibly sweet, phenomenally intense. Unless we're completely jaded, we cannot help but take in something essential of another man when we make love with him. It may be short, it may be "meaningless," it may be drug-induced. It is still and always both risky and real.

The choices are mine.

DISCRIMINATION

When General Eisenhower...asked her to ferret out the lesbians in her WAC battalion, [Sergeant Johnnie Phelps] replied:
"Sir, I'll be happy to do this investigation for you but you'll have to know that the first name on the list will be mine...I think the General should be aware that among those women are the most highly decorated women in the war...no cases of illegal pregnancies...no cases of AWOL...no cases of misconduct...every six months the General has awarded us a commendation for meritorious service."
Eisenhower, knowing better than to look a gift horse in the mouth, simply said, "Forget the order."
—Andrea Weiss & Greta Schiller, Before Stonewall

The intention to discriminate is rarely so overt and, unlike this World War II scenario, seldom so easy to deflect. Discrimination surrenders about as graciously as well-armed troops dug into a beach. It takes the collective courage of more than one generation of path-breakers and activists to get to higher ground.

A truly useful aspect of the I-pay-taxes-for-*this*?? 1993 gays-in-the-military spectacle was the language and awareness it created around discrimination. One after another, distinguished professionals made the simple point, "I am perfectly capable of doing the job." Which is something we all need to hear, all need to be reminded of, and may need to repeat like a mantra if we find ourselves under the gun.

There is a predictable and noxious "prove it" phase that victims of discrimination have to endure once in the door. Our performance is scrutinized. We are likely to be sabotaged and targeted for all kinds of crap. Some of us will "fail" at being supermen and bow out. Some will win grudging respect, even inspire allies who emerge from the woodwork to fight alongside us for truth, justice, and something other than the historic American Way.

Confronting discrimination is heroic work. In our case, it takes coming out, holding ground, an occasional wise retreat, and knowing that every single stand we make deserves a medal.

I am perfectly capable of doing the job.

CREATIVITY

I work, I love, I rest, I see and learn. And I report.
—Audre Lorde

Toward the end of her life, Audre Lorde, much acclaimed black feminist lesbian New York poet, took the African name *Gamba Adisa*, meaning "Warrior: She Who Makes Her Meaning Known." What a fine prescription she gives for living creatively.

Gay people are noted for creativity. We are over represented in the arts and infamous for our flair. Some say it comes with the territory; a certain something in the genetic mix. Others say creativity is demanded of us—we are forced to invent our own way of life, each blazing an original trail.

To some, this whole creativity business is yet another limiting expectation. "It isn't enough that I'm queer? I have to design clothes and compose opera to round myself out?" Ahh, but this misses the point. Don't we all work? Love? Rest, see and learn? All that's left is to report. Whether it be celebrated sculpture or a whisper in the dark, when we pass on what we know, we create immortal testimony to the bit of life we have lived and informed and will one day leave.

In my own way, I make my meaning known.

THE CHURCH

The Church has generally been an alien environment for gay people. "Tell a lie for Christ" has sadly been a requirement that not only killed much of gay spirituality, but seriously maimed any kind of spirituality.
—Episcopal Priest Malcolm Boyd,
Telling a Lie for Christ? Gay Spirit

The institutions devoted to the message of Jesus Christ so often practice contrary to the essence of what he preached. If Christ himself appeared in the courtyards of these temples, he would surely busy himself turning over the tables, shouting, "Tell no lies for *me!*"

No, Christ demands not of those who draw life through his that this intimate spiritual relationship be sullied with lies. This is the business of worldly priests and popes. The demand to deny our essential nature injures us as individuals and stunts our religious communities as well. Our own health often dictates we run from this death trap, but sadly, for many it has meant running from Christ as well.

Gay men who have grown up citizens of Christendom may choose to fight their church, reform it, or leave it. There is significant reason to choose any of these paths. But what is most critical is the relationship with Christ, the ability to take communion with his body in a world of false forms. This life-giving connection awaits any man who comes to his God, heart open, asking forgiveness for lies, ready to speak his truth.

God loves truth.

TENDERNESS

This was ours. There would be other love songs, other lovers, other days that I could not know. I knew only that I would associate and remember always Tom's faint smell of musk, this night, this moment, as "My Foolish Heart" beat next to him, hushed in his arms.
> —Wayland Harper, My Foolish Heart, Revelations:
> A collection of gay male coming out stories

This is ours. This love song that harmonizes with our bodies, keeping time with the beating of our hearts. This is tenderness. It is conveyed through a subtle realm of breath and silence and direct looks and soft caresses. Its sweetness cannot be measured.

Tenderness is drowned out in the onslaught of hyper-sex that flexes its muscles from videos and gay newsracks and falsely advertises itself in everything from vitamin regimes to waiting-dripping-call-1-800-HOT-4YOU jack-off lines. We might believe gay love is mostly about incredibly defined abs and extremely hot, but safe, but very very hot sex; that satisfaction is a fantastic spurting come shot and that's as good as it gets.

What of Tom's faint smell of musk? What of this night, this moment, this lover? This is the tender inner world, the real stuff, the hush in his arms. This is nestled like a pair of spoons in the dark, waking and not wanting to part. This is the poetry one man speaks to another with his body, the love songs we have known and remember forever.

Love me tender.

LETDOWN

If you want a place in the sun, you've got to put up with a few blisters.
—Abigail Van Buren

In the beginning, everything is perfect. His quirky way of dressing makes you roll your eyes in mock-embarassed delight. That high tinkling laugh is music to the ear. And who'd think you could tolerate a smoker? But he's amazing! The latest, queerest incarnation of James Dean. You're so into it you start carrying a lighter. Clearly you are about to settle into a life of endless fascination.

But wait, what's this? Months speed by and, on a recent much-anticipated weekend at the beach, something is amiss. It all starts in the car when he tells you the tale of the brief affair with the Australian lifeguard *again*. Later you find yourself clenching and unclenching your fist as you wonder how he manages to so perfectly imitate a hyena in heat when he laughs. Well, the sex is still fantastic, but that fucking smoke afterward! So what if it's raining? He can just put something on, go outside, and give the trees cancer!

Oh-oh. Time for a little Solarcain on the tender spots. In the beginning, love affairs are places in the sun. And if we stay in them long enough, we're gonna get a burn. He's not perfect. Never was. What's called for now is some work, some patience, some setting aside of expectations, some emptiness, some compromise.

It's inevitable, it's okay, it's part of love, and the blisters do heal.

I want my place in the sun.

THE HETEROSEXUAL MODEL

It makes perfect sense to me that people would want to be married. But for me, security is not knowing what's going to happen. Because if I don't know, it could be terrific.

—*Gloria Steinem*

Gloria is still in the minority. Not because she eschews marriage, but on account of her definition of security. Most people prefer the predictable, which is what the "Heterosexual Model" is all about: a set of static choices that are clear, orderly, and advertise happiness ever after.

The basis is an either/or world. Either a boy or a girl. Either single or married. Either in the club or not. Our hots for other guys ruin the whole hetero thing to start with, but once that large thread has been pulled, a lot more starts to unravel.

The alternative to the Het Model is a high option world. Operating in this mode, we realize all the forms, classifications, and predictions are up for grabs. Since we then have no way of knowing what's going to happen, our only real security will stem from getting used to the idea. Which leaves the whole question of what's right and real and authentic entirely in our own hands. Which is pretty terrific.

All the options are open.

HELPLESSNESS

"My darling, you're such a child. You think that by saying, 'I'm sorry,' all the errors and hurts of years past can be remedied, obliterated from the mind, all the poison drawn from old wounds...Take my handkerchief, Scarlett. Never, at any crisis of your life, have I known you to have a handkerchief."
    —*Rhett Butler, from Margaret Mitchell's Gone With the Wind*

There is a limited charm in helplessness. It does arouse the big strong man in us; we imagine ourselves as Rhett Butler, or Muhammad Ali, or Sir Lancelot, or a boy who brings home lost kittens. When it comes to adult men, however, the arousal ebbs away as the warm self-satisfaction we get from performing yet another heroic rescue cools into just not giving a damn.

The degree to which we act out helplessness is the same degree to which remedies will later be required. And those closest to us are likely to suffer the severest wounds. Now we're all entitled to a long spree of youthful foolishness and it's okay to make mistakes. But there comes a point when apologies just don't do it any more. Because what we're doing isn't cute or the least bit charming. It's boring and destructive.

As adults, we have responsibility for creating the circumstances of our own lives. It's a very powerful reality. As for Scarlett, get that girl some help. Just think what shape Tara will be in if she just stops tripping over her own damn skirt.

Frankly, my dear, I'm not the least bit helpless.

HATE

Die faggot die!
—Mail received by a gay public official
after disclosing he had AIDS

Directly or indirectly, to our face or behind our back, each of us has felt the searing lash of hate. Arising from a monstrous pool of fear and centuries-old indoctrination, we are the close range targets of the particular human madness called homophobia.

The face and voice of hate are shocking in their ugliness. The agenda of those who hate is extreme. They want us dead.

To exist openly as gay men and wage our battle against these dark forces requires two contradictory efforts. We must look hate in the eye with impunity, refusing to cower before it. And we must, in the sanctuary of our soul and with people who love us, cry bitterly for the terror and injustice hate inflicts upon us.

If we do not do the first, we grant those who hate a public victory. If we do not do the second, we allow the private murder of our hearts.

Hate has no hold on me.

PASSION

No less an expression of yourself will do: passion incarnate at climax, and proximity to the living, flaming heart of reality. Afterward, walking with him, perhaps, no matter if the view is of buildings and fire escapes or of clouds and wide beaches—you will find your world is charged with grandeur.

—David Loovis, A Guide to Becoming a Sensuous Homosexual

"What do you mean? *Describe* it." He is all ears at the mention of passion, the youngish man in the process of coming out, or rather, in the process of coming into himself, a possibly quite flaming self thus far reserved and protected by a cool, wary and now cracking exterior. Passion can't be described well, if at all, but he notes the concept, seems to awaken a bit more right there, and exchanges a nearly piercing look with his boyfriend, the two of them at the doorstep, unsure, not enough raw lust between them, but the taste of it at their lips.

The dictionary will tell him passion is to suffer, to endure the agony of extreme and compelling emotion. At climax it forces itself upon us—not in circumstances of utilitarian or clinical sex—but when the ability to go over the cliff physically is matched by the same readiness to jump off emotionally. This is not to be taken lightly. What kindles the world with grandeur is tinged by madness.

Afterward? Yes, afterward, once one has endured proximity to the heart of reality, one's sight is affected. This is the story he wanted to hear: In the morning, arising from beneath covers where I had lain the first time molten and breathless with the lover I had cried out to the universe to find, a morning sweet with the smell of spring, we walked the few steps to the next room and as the coffee steamed from its cups, the utensils on the kitchen wall caught the sun and shone silver and gold and deep violet and were, to the eye, the most extraordinary, the most singular and untainted sight.

Passion, and its grandeur, await us.

FIRST KNOWING

I remember I was about three or four years old watching Batman on our very first color TV and I thought, "Yup, the guy in the tights, that's for me."

—*Timothy Rose*

Looking back, we know when we knew. Of course at that time we didn't know what we knew or what it meant or necessarily if it was good or bad although we sensed it probably must be bad or a secret because nobody ever talked about it.

My first experience of attraction to a man happened at Y-Camp when I was 11. There was some totally unmemorable show the counselors put on and in one part the dialogue went something like, "...and we have financial supporters, and we have volunteer supporters, and we have...*athletic supporters!!*" And then the most gorgeous guy—he was slim and dark and hairy, the captain of the high school basketball team—streaked through the dining hall wearing nothing but a jock strap and my body knew something.

We each learn different things at different times. Some of what we first know is new because we are young. Some is new because we have changed as we've grown older. Some memories are suppressed and we can rediscover them to find again the simple, clear, and true things we knew way back when.

I have always known the truth of my experience.

June

FUNDAMENTALISM

Compulsive sexuality—homosexual or heterosexual—is a mental disorder. Gay activists proudly proclaim that the American Psychological Association no longer lists homosexuality as a mental illness. But **Kiddushin,** *the sanctity of marriage and of sexuality in marriage, is fundamentally violated by compulsive sexuality of any type.*
—*Rabbi Barry Freundel, Moment Magazine*

There's no point arguing with fundamentalists. We're damned if we do and damned anyway. They're bound to have the last word, which should be no surprise, since they think they have the answers. Or anyway, GOD has the answers and they're on the hotline with GOD.

This is a fun-house world of definitions and explanations that make all kinds of sense if you happen to be a mental contortionist. It's pretty slick. There's these made-up rules, you just have to buy that they're "Laws of the Universe," and then you know exactly what positions to contort into.

From the good Rabbi's standpoint, homosexuality may not be a mental illness, but it violates a LAW, i.e. the only kosher sex is married sex and anyone who can't live in line with GOD'S LAW is compulsive. Since homosexual sex happens outside of marriage and sexually compulsive people are sick, practicing homosexuals need help. Get it?

Oy! Well, maybe if I keep being a practicing homosexual some day I'll be a perfect one. In the meantime, it keeps me safe from this world of twisted logic that provides fundamentalists their frightful assumptions of authority on matters they, and their imagined Gods, clearly know nothing about.

I fundamentally reject crazy-making outlooks on life.

BELIEF

Believe nothing no matter where you read it or who said it, no matter if I have said it, unless it agrees with your own reason and your own common sense.

—Buddha

One of the wisest things my therapist said to me as I was coming out was not to run headlong from one camp to another. At first I thought he was warning me not to dash straight from the heterosexual world to the homosexual one. Later I realized he had voiced the Buddha's caution: I should never again buy *any* belief system or way of life wholesale.

We all have to rid ourselves of beliefs we take in about gayness. Things we heard and read were simply not true. Somewhere between the pervasive hostility and general hush-up that surrounded our sexuality, we found a separate reason and different sense that eventually guided us to the truth and made us believe it.

Our awakenings as gay men should make us cautious: of leaders, of religion, of anyone—gay or straight—that would have us believe they know better for us than we know for ourselves.

What I believe is up to me.

BLIND DATES

Life is very singularly made to surprise us (where it does not utterly appall us).

—*Rainer Maria Rilke*

Most blind dates are horrifying. This isn't just my opinion, there is general agreement on the subject. Which makes me figure even if we don't find what we're looking for we keep doing this because we love to complain about the appalling experiences that befall us.

If we're single and looking and have about decided to kiss off these blinding opportunities for good, there is, as usual, a catch. We might just miss one of life's singular surprises which, oh ye of little faith, are also a part of a rich blind-date folklore of love at first sight, long-term happiness, and short-term incredible sex. (Okay, so it's not always sex to write home about. Any port in a storm.)

No one really wants to put a stop to this. Maybe it's the gambler in all of us, but most guys are willing to roll the dice just one more time.

Maybe I'll get lucky.

THE MATTACHINE SOCIETY

They were country-bumpkin Monks who had been trained to read and write who would go back into the countryside in masked groups to perform Fertility or Harvest Rituals for a peasantry forbidden by the Church and perhaps also—on pain of death—by their Overlords, to any longer carry out themselves.

> —Harry Hay, describing Le Societè Mattachine,
> 12th and 13th century European cross-dressing troubadours

In Los Angeles in 1950, Harry Hay convened the first Mattachine Society discussion group and set in place a cellular structure that grew and spread into a launching pad for the gay liberation movement that took off like a rocket in 1969.

The Mattachine name evoked its purpose: to come together from respectable cover and create meaning in the face of the forbidden. In an era when homosexuality was "perverse," illegal, and McCarthyist exposures could ruin a man, five original members met in secret and set three questions before themselves: *Who are gay people? Where have we been throughout the ages? What might we be for?*

The inquiry was as gripping as it was daring. They met regularly late into the night and weekend marathons ran 16 to 18 hours. Their first monumental task was transforming the then-pervasively negative self-image of homosexuals into something positive.

From five, the organization grew to thousands, created the first American gay magazine, mined history and literature for the footprints of gays and lesbians, and made the first successful court challenge to police entrapment.

The Mattachine Society was magnetic, attracting gay men from an invisible field and carefully screening us into flesh and blood reality. First one by one, now by the millions, we have emerged to know each other, our history, our rights, and the meaning of our lives.

"No gay person coming into the world will ever again have to feel alone and unwanted and rejected."
—From the Mattachine Society initiation ceremony

LOVING MEN

We must resemble each other a little in order to understand each other, but we must be a little different to love each other.
—Paul Geraldy, L'Homme et l'amour

Men loving men is a difficult proposition. We've been bred otherwise. In nearly all cultures, men learn to compete, not to couple. The clichés are true: we're inclined to hide our weaknesses and cover them if exposed, we're brought up to be out of touch with our emotions, to defend our territory, to think we should fend for ourselves, to always be right.

Given these setups, two guys together do not exactly double our chances for success. We come into our first relationships like emotional ships passing in the night. Usually we're equally scared, don't know how to ask for what we want, don't know how to reach out to each other when the going gets tough.

The patterns are more easily understood than changed. It's well worth keeping at it. Patience, compassion, and daring will win the day. Since it's not so hard to imagine what the other guy is going through, we can start by giving him the kind of rope we'd like for ourselves. We can be bold enough to be a little different. We can uncover more of our ability to love all the time.

Real men love each other.

THE CLOSET

I think Anita Bryant was one of the best things that has happened for the cause of gay liberation. She forced even conservative gays to come out of their closets. But now self-criticism has to be pushed even further. No sentimental shit about gays as poor little victims.

—Rosa Von Praunheim

Out of the darkness and into the light. Even in the third decade of the gay liberation movement, the world's Anita Bryants and Pat Buchanans are still among the best things to force masses of gay men out of the closet. It's one thing to accept a life of dark privacy. It's another to keep the lock on when you smell gas and hear a match striking against the door.

These are the politics of the closet, a pushing and shoving match at the thresholds of comfort. The personal emergence from the closet has its own timing. Political coming out is an immediate necessity—unless we're sentimental about the idea of gays as poor little victims.

The closet is a cramped place to choose and a worse place to be consigned to. Outside there is light. And space. We may have to fight out there, but we get to *be.*

I'm outta there.

ISOLATION

I have come one step away from everything. And here I stay, far from everything, one step away.

—*Antonio Porchia*

Walking through the streets of a foreign city, one can feel completely outside of life. Behind the doors and windows there are people, music, art, business and connections going in all directions...except ours. There are ways to step across the boundary, to learn the language and make inroads, but essentially we remain tourists.

This can mirror our experience where we live. At times, we just don't connect. Which may be deliberate. We take a step back to gain a fresh view, or nurse a broken heart, or really throw ourselves into work for a while. We want to be alone and it's refreshing.

Unwanted isolation is anything but refreshing. It seems like everyone in town is on their way to a great party except us. Being gay can make this a double whammy. We often feel like tourists marooned in Heteroland. If we're reeling from something trashy on the gay side of the tracks, the whole world winds up a pretty unfriendly place.

Fortunately, the roads out of isolation are many and close by. No matter what may have happened yesterday, we needn't be shut-ins today if we don't want to be.

The world is at my doorstep.

COMMITMENT

There are situations in which hope and fear run together, in which they mutually destroy one another, and lose themselves in a dull indifference.
—*Goethe*

Straying from the rote path of dating-engagement-marriage-children, the whole area of commitment is even murkier for us than for our heterosexual pals. Since no one is going to tell us what's "right" we have to know for ourselves what we want, then go after it.

This is where hope and fear collide. Hope that we will be able to depend on someone, trust him, believe him, be our very best with him. Fear he won't want the same things, that he'll bail out—or we will—if the shit hits the fan. Hope that putting ourselves on the line will enable richer things to pass between us. Fear that all we really want is security and are running away from the challenge of making it alone.

Commitment needn't be everything forever all at once. It can be about honesty, small promises, monogamy for now, sharing feelings out loud, about giving something a chance. Knowing how much commitment and what kind means putting both hope and fear on a short rope and trusting our response to the simple questions: What do I want? What am I ready to give?

I'm strong enough to make commitments...and keep them.

ROLE MODELS

Society makes our existence wretchedly difficult at times...I myself am suffering under an absolute lack of models.

—Vincent Van Gogh

While no man can clear our path for us, role models are a vital part of our education. Especially as young men with our sexuality exploding within us, we suffer for lack of models. Many of us were sure we were the only ones who ever felt this way. Or could only connect ourselves with gross stereotypes. No real people. No heroes. No one in our family.

At some point, a light goes on in our heads. We meet someone, find a book, make our first trip to a big city, hear the truth about a person we respect. Then lights start going on all over the place.

They are there for us. Vibrant throughout history and visible now everywhere, in every field, in every stage of life: faerie wizards, faggot kings, queer painters and generals, homosexual uncles and fathers, a gay Mr. Universe, transsexual goddesses. The models are there to light our imagination, telling of possibility without end.

Like others, I am breaking new ground.

BACKS

The aim of life is to live, and to live means to be aware, joyously, drunkenly, serenely, divinely aware.

—*Henry Miller*

The sight of a man's sculpted back is a joyous thing, calling up from our bodies a fullness and a catch of breath. When it is our own lover's back, the joy completes itself in touch.

We give him massages. Sitting astride him, nestled serenely against his ass, our arms move strong and sure in the cooler air away from our bodies. We trace him with our eyes, knead the skin and muscle and draw out his tension. We have healing hands.

We drink in the long beauty of his back another way when we make love. We are flush against each other, kissing deeply, the fingers of one hand leaving marks across his shoulder blades, the palm of the other hand pressing against the base of his spine, fingers falling just below.

The whole of his back against our chest we kneel over him, push into him, his back now carrying us, now reaching, then stretching away, now glistening with sweat, so muscled and beautiful and both of us so aware...

...so divinely aware of being alive.

SELF-ESTEEM

When I'm standing in a restroom sucking a guy off, yes, then I might feel shame because I was brought up to believe sex was a sacred act.
—*Nick R.*

Our self-esteem as gay men is tricky. (No pun intended.) Like other minorities whose appearance, behavior, and customs are ridiculed by the majority, we certainly can't evaluate ourselves by prevailing standards. On the other hand, we have to be careful not to throw the baby out with the bath water.

Standing in a restroom sucking a guy off, the conversation in our mind can't be about what other gay men might think, or what mom might think, or what Jesus might think. The conversation has to be about what *we* think, what we, in our heart of hearts, know to be true.

Any time our essential self is profaned we are weakened, until, sometimes even quite young, the self is depleted, exhausted, unable to exert its protective and life-giving force.

This is a reversible phenomenon. The moment we take a stand on our own behalf, the self begins to be restored. The more we strengthen ourselves, the more we will attract what is essential to our well-being. The more we perform sacred acts, the more sacred our lives become.

I value and honor myself.

JUDGMENT

If you judge people, you have no time to love them.
—*Mother Teresa*

The disease of judgment is among the leading killers of relationships. It goes like this. He acts a certain way. It offends or embarrasses us, we are hurt by it, or angered; in an instant the lines are drawn. We build our case and prepare to throw the book at him. It's about him, him, him. We feverishly amass all related evidence, ready to go on the attack and quash his paltry defense.

The result is mutual withdrawal in the face of overwhelming implications. He thinks, "It's hopeless. If I'm such a brute, what's the point? I might as well leave." We think, "There's no way out for him now. He'll finally have to confess. I'm right. I'm waiting this one out." Enough of this and the trial is over right quick.

The antidote is a different mode of testimony. It is critical to report our reality. "I need you to listen. I need to talk about my experience of something that happened between us and what I feel." We begin curing the disease when we admit our reactions are about me, me, me. This immediately changes the course. We affirm we are two human beings with differing motivations, dissimilar cultural contexts, men who don't necessarily know what we have done has hurt. To simply state—rather than judge—strengthens us, makes room for understanding, charges the atmosphere with love and the potential to heal.

I am not here to judge you.

RITES OF PASSAGE

In the late 1980s the tactics of groups like Act-Up and Queer Nation did not merely shock and anger, but took the logic of shame-abandonment to a thrilling conclusion. To exist within their sudden energy was to be caught in a liberating rite of passage which...exploded many of the cozy assumptions of closeted homosexual and liberal heterosexual alike.

—*Andrew Sullivan, The New Republic*

In a Bar or Bat Mitzvah (meaning literally, Son or Daughter of the Commandments) Jewish thirteen year-olds appear before the congregation, lead services, read in Hebrew from the Torah, and give a speech. This is the official transition to adulthood. The child knows this, feels the difference, says inside, *"I have learned. I have stood on my own in front of everyone. I am deserving."* Then there's a big party and lots of presents.

I don't think Aunt Mitzi and Uncle Seymour are likely to send a savings bond in honor of our participation at the Pentagon "Kiss-in," but then, we probably didn't send them an invitation, either. Gay rites of passage are not so tidily packaged as Bar Mitzvahs, nor so widely and happily celebrated. They are something of a commandment, though, if we are to stand proudly on our own two feet.

The rites of gay men are personally chosen. They are meant to honor no one's assumptions. The sudden energy of abandoning our shame may surge over us standing naked in the waves of the ocean, fucking shamelessly like young stags, crying quietly in our therapist's office, or with arms linked shouting outrage at all the world. In each case there are witnesses. In each case we become free.

I have learned. I have stood on my own in front of everyone. I am deserving.

JEALOUSY

Where jealousy is, love is not.
—J. Krishnamurti

It's quite possible the world of romance hit its absolute low when the early '60s song, "Johnny Get Angry," hit the top of the charts. One can only hope the advent of feminism has had an impact on what young girls consider a thrilling demonstration of interest. But if the stock of brave men and cave men is falling among the het set (debatable), it appears Johnny can still get angry at his boyfriend if he wants to show he really cares.

Chalk this up to theories of delayed social development in gay men or some bizarre side effect of the men's movement, but be clear about one thing: jealousy shows precious little about how our boyfriend feels about *us*. Oh, "Why were you looking at that t-shirt number in the bar?" shows he's observant and values us enough to want to stake his claim. (It means *he* thought t-shirt was worth looking at, too.) But this jealousy thing is about *him*, about his fear of losing us, fear he isn't good enough, fear we'll outgrow him, fear he'll be betrayed, fear he won't be in control.

When he's suspicious and swearing and yelling and throwing a regular cave-man jealous fit, it's tempting to be flattered by all the drama. And it's quite powerful to be able to pull his strings. But this isn't love. It's a '60s song.

There are better ways to show we care.

VALUE

It has taken many accidents, many surprising coincidences (and perhaps many efforts), for me to find the Image which, out of a thousand, suits my desire.

—Roland Barthes, paraphrasing Lacan and Proust,
A Lover's Discourse

Every so often it's a good idea to step back from your lover and just look at him. He may be chubby or svelte, young or old, dark or light. He is, in this moment, the object of your desire.

Such moments should never be taken for granted. It is all too easy to focus on flaws, shortcomings, inevitable small offenses to sensibilities or feelings. It's easy to think your desire so one-dimensional that it excludes challenge and hardship and the sometimes harsh residue of the accidents, coincidences and efforts that cast him into the Image your soul has waited to find.

We do not come together without magic. We do not stay together without pain. Those whose lovers have died know this better than anyone: how extraordinary it is, how precious, that he sits across from you now.

I take not one moment with you for granted.

INDIA

I cut my beard off and wrapped my hair into a bun atop my head. I put on a new white lunghee (a cotton cloth wrapped around the lower body) and draped a towel around my upper chest. The old swamis on the river steps looked on, chanted, and seemed to give me an inner smile. I had taken a step away from the world of males and females into the androgynous world of what in my part of India is whispered to be an "evening person."

—Susil, Tea Seller, *A Lotus of Another Color*

Gayness has many faces and forms in India, which is only fitting given that eighty percent of the nation's one billion people are Hindu and worship many-faceted Gods, including Ardhanarishwara, who is usually depicted as half-male, half-female, and inspires a whole artistry of sexual dualism.

Some Indians will say homosexuality doesn't exist. (They've taken the British colonial influence a bit too seriously.) Others simply shrug it off as a fact of life. The Kama Sutra includes an eight-step lesson in "oral congress," complete with mango metaphors. One of the oldest religious myths represents the "infinite source" as a triangle made up of female twins *(jami)* and the earth, with heterosexuality coming later, at first merely defined as "that which is not *jami.*"

Modern urban gay life has been described, in contrast to the West, as a "virgin continuum," with no liberation movement, no gay press, and with entirely different cultural expectations that would render much of our politics and organized gay life irrelevant. Human loving appears in countless guises, speaks many languages; the unmistakable meaning of men jostling next to one another on the crowded local train, priests and congregations chanting to an ancient likeness of Shiva's penis, gatherings of men who converge on local bars, whispers and smiles of the evening people.

I have taken a step into a different and exciting world.

FEMININITY

Now that traditional notions of femininity have disappeared from the real world, they have disappeared from the gay world as well. So inevitably and possibly against its will, the homosexual community apes its environment. It goes beyond eschewing femininity; it shuns anything that might be called finesse.

—Quentin Crisp

My introduction to the homosexual world came via the theater. As a teenager, I was in an acting company. Partially out of my own attraction, partially due to his magnetism, I found myself among the favorites of the director. This resulted in my attendance at a number of parties in his Victorian home, where I saw and experienced many things new to a boy fresh out of Fargo, North Dakota.

The guests, when it was a theater gathering, were mixed. On other occasions, the place was filled with queens. I remember such a party best. Our host, a man of unabashed sexuality and great finesse, filled bowls with ripe peeled avocados and limes, platters with blueberries and raspberries, glasses with Italian wine. He wore a red sash around his waist and talked of attending parties where the Persian rugs were known to rise off the floor and fly. I looked down at the edges of the carpet under my chair, just to check.

Some 20 years later, I am in a small Manhattan kitchen preparing a cold dinner for my lover on a warm summer night. I am wearing a sleeveless lime green crew-neck shirt, black silk pants, and a touch of lipstick. The table is set simply, but with great attention to detail. My body is fluid, relaxed. I feel feminine and sure of myself. Tonight, more than anything, I am interested in pleasing a man.

The finer things are always in style.

ANTICIPATION

I always read the last page of a book first so that if I die before I finish I'll know how it turned out.

—*Nora Ephron*

We can drive ourselves nuts with anticipation, playing out the various plot lines in advance, preparing for the worst. I had such a terrible crush on one guy I had to write myself messages and tape them on the bathroom mirror to help me remember who I was and how to act. They said great little things like "You're OK" and "Don't panic" and "You can live without him".

The one thing I hadn't anticipated was that we'd wind up back at my apartment that night. The moment we got in, I was in the bathroom grabbing handfuls of notes off the mirror and feeling like a character in a spy novel whose cover was nearly blown. He was none the wiser, since my extensive mental preparations had lent me an air of cool self-confidence. It was a very good night, but the affair didn't last.

There is no way to know the ending beforehand. Unlike literature, in life you actually do have to die to know how it turns out. In the meantime, hoping for the best and preparing for the worst both have their merits, as long as we don't get so caught up with anticipation that we miss what's going on right now.

"You're OK. Don't panic. You can live without him."

OPPRESSION

Nobody really cares who goes to bed with whom finally. I mean, the State doesn't really care, the Church doesn't really care. They care that you should be frightened of what you do. As long as you feel guilty about it, the State can rule you. It's a way of exerting control over the universe, by terrifying people.

—James Baldwin

Power-holding groups—church hierarchies, governments, straight white males—act instinctively and ruthlessly to preserve their hold on privilege and power. There are exceptions, of course. Liberation theologists, Abraham Lincolns, men and women of true and generous character. They often suffer for betraying their class.

Oppressors are in a position to hand out the world's rewards and punishments and would have us believe they guard the gates of heaven. They rule by propaganda which teaches us to oppress ourselves; by exclusion when we fail to be well-behaved; and by force when their terror outweighs ours.

The overturning of oppression starts by expelling these false regimes from our own hearts and minds. This happens well away from barricades, fire hoses, and bullets. It is first of all a private act, a housecleaning that removes the dirt and stain of illegitimate authority from what we do.

Then we are free to make our own choices. Their rewards and punishments lose their hold on us; their ceremonies come up empty. Casting off oppression is an arduous yet exhilarating beginning. We find our power and our true allies and friends as well. Then comes a new test, whether we have learned not to become oppressors ourselves.

I reject all forms of oppression.

COLOGNE

Steeped in flowers, abundant with fruit and heady with spice...a masterpiece of contrasts—it is the mood of the sea, the spirit of the wind, that intoxicating air—captured once and for all.

—Ad copy for a new men's eau de toilette

No, the little blue bottle does not come with an all-expense paid trip to the Greek Isles. But let's give credit where credit is due: things have come a good distance at the men's fragrance bar. (Personal admission: being a brand-loyal consumer of a leading designer name, I still can't resist an after-workout splash of the Old Standard proffered at my health club of choice. Its very rankness makes me feel like a REAL MAN in some inexplicable, reckless way.)

But back to the spirited ode cited above. Popular wisdom has it our sense of smell is the most potent of the five for evoking memories. So naturally, when we've spent the night with a lover, the pungent mix of his scents may stir strong reactions: a desperate dash into a very long shower; refusal to wash our sheets for weeks; or the wish we could wear him every day—and have it all be as heady and available as a bottle of cologne.

Go ahead. Intoxicate me.

ROMANTICS

The dream was always running ahead of one. To catch up, to live for a moment in unison with it, that was the miracle.

—*Anais Nin*

The word *romance* did not use to mean love affair. It referred to a long prose poem, one of those historic *Odyssey* kinds of things recounting the adventures of knights and other heroes. Later, romances became highly fictionalized tales filled with extraordinary events. In its modern use, *romantic* can describe a "fanciful, fictitious, fabulous" dreamer with no real substance, or simply someone suited for romance or lovemaking.

As children, many of us thrilled to stories of adventure; Knights of the Round Table, Swiss Family Robinson, the cliff-hanger journeys of Big Red. But after a time, our romantic imaginations had to proceed in a vacuum. We knew enough, or quickly learned, not to say we wanted to be Guinevere instead of Arthur and actually, it was puzzling why Arthur and Lancelot didn't recognize the obvious solution and banish the girl from the picture.

With no substance to anchor ourselves, our budding romantic natures often drifted into the fanciful, the fabulous, the ultimately unattainable. Upon learning what our dreams really meant, many of us stopped believing in miracles altogether. But we are most certainly suited for romance and lovemaking. And have adventures and tales to rival those of any errant knight. So are we not romantic?

I can catch up with my dreams.

FEELING

If you would have me weep, you must first of all feel grief yourself.
—Horace, Ars Poetica

We walk into the park, the bar, the bedroom hungry to be touched. Not just our bodies, which can be satisfied so impersonally, but more than that. Beneath the skin is the need for richer contact.

We believe the right man understands this. We don't want to have to bring it up. We'll know if he knows because we will *respond*. He will bring feelings out in us, call us sensitive and powerful and rare. We wait.

And wait. And make a terrible mistake. We may die of malnutrition waiting for this. It is up to us to make the first move, to go deeply into ourselves on our own.

We will, at first, sense nothing. There will be emptiness. We may be terrified. Then, little by little, we will fill. We will find deep reserves to nourish us. As feeling men must, we will grieve our emptiness, our losses, the changes in our lives, the movement of time. We learn to stand alone.

The right man understands this. He cannot cause these things in us, but he will welcome them and cry for joy at what he sees.

Feeling deeply is its own reward.

PRIDE

In This Moment
—*Title of a song celebrating the beauty and importance of the moment, by Gary Simmons; theme song for the 1992 GALA festival of national and international gay choruses*

The voices of the combined San Francisco and Seattle Gay Men's Choruses fill the Seattle Opera House. It is the highlight of pride week and pride resounds. Greta Cammemeyer appears on stage and the crowd is on its feet, cheering her courageous leadership in the battle against military madness. A contingent of choristers from England are welcomed. Quilt panels for singers dead of AIDS hang over the stage.

Proud to be gay. Curious concept. Is sexual orientation something to take pride in? Any more than being right-handed? What then? Close to a thousand people are in the hall and as the music pours out, the feeling of pride accompanies it like grace notes.

We are *here,* our openness and freedom won personally and collectively in the face of virulent opposition. We are political, we're funny, we create art that honors its gay roots, we love passionately, we care for our sick and honor our dead, we have created a trans-global network, and we serve as a lightning rod on critical issues of human diversity.

The evening's last encore begins. It's *Over the Rainbow.* Glinda materializes above the heads of the singers and rains showers of glitter over everyone. In that moment it is clear what we should be most proud of: that we dream dreams. And make them come true.

I am *so* proud of who I am and what we've done.

PURSUIT

With the catching end the pleasures of the chase.
—Abraham Lincoln

He was alarmed when I showed up the next day. I thought we had started something the night before. He was already finished. Back home, I called my vastly experienced friend in Chicago. "You were his trick!" he explained. "When he asked for your phone number and mentioned the weekend he was just following trick protocols. Don't think anything of it." Emerging from my embarrassment, I decided I'd been a great trick and hadn't had such a bad time myself. It's just that I was in pursuit of something more.

The catching does end the pleasures of the chase—and if pleasure is all we're out to catch then the whole matter is quite easily put to bed. At times, the chase is everything—we're out for experience, we need to exercise our testosterone, we're into a hunter-gatherer-throwback-phase, we're relationship-aversive, we're just boys who wanna have fun.

At other times, we've had it. No more racing around. We want something, we know what it is, and we wait. When that something comes, catching is no end at all, but the beginning of sweet pleasures we've been pursuing for a long long time.

Let's get caught.

DEBASING OURSELVES

I couldn't decide if I wasn't doing it because I had too much, or too little, self-esteem at the moment. It takes a certain security, I realized suddenly, to debase oneself. To kneel, to worship at the altar of another man's masculinity, or beauty.

—Andrew Holleran, "MMMMPFGH," Flesh and the Word

The electrical charge arcs back and forth as signs of mutual attraction and interest become clear. We know what each other's bodies want instinctively. We feel the same things.

It's easy to turn on, get off, and walk away. To get further, we must face and overcome a host of demons. Common images for gay men's most intimate sexual acts are degrading, used as verbal rape. To fulfill ourselves means debasing ourselves and being secure enough in our sexuality to do it.

This is subtle terrain. Permitting ourselves to *be* debased is an entirely different matter, the province of self-hating homosexuals who use sexual pleasure as a reminder that only a filthy faggot wants to do such things. It takes self-love, enormous self-esteem, to kneel and transform sexual images of debasement into the holy acts we know them to be.

We *are* faggots and faggots want to do such things: to sacrifice at the altar of another man's masculinity, to lie under him and kiss all of his body and touch his soul and make ourselves servants to what we know to be love and a call to worship and a source of life.

With certain security, with joy, I kneel before my lover.

LIVING TOGETHER

[Maurice and his friend Clive] were concerned with a passion that few English minds have admitted, and so created untrammeled. Something of exquisite beauty arose in the mind of each at last, something unforgettable and eternal, but built of the humblest scraps of speech and from the simplest emotions.
"I say, will you kiss me?" asked Maurice, when the sparrows woke in the eaves above them, and far out in the woods the ring-doves began to coo.

—*E.M. Forster, Maurice*

Ah, the joys of our cottage in the woods. "More tea, Morrie?" "Oh, Clively, how perfectly lovely of you to offer, but isn't it my turn to pour?"

Not to be cynical. It's just that cleaning nests out of eaves and gutters is a pain in the ass, living together in real life is about a hundred times more complicated than in romantic stories, and I personally have not heard anyone mention their living arrangements and cooing doves in the same breath since Snow White crashed with the dwarfs.

This is not to deny love's wildly optimistic first blush or the exquisite visions that arise in our minds when we propose to split the rent. It is merely to inject a note of caution in regard to winning strangers with fabulous dicks who reduce us to states of helpless hospitality; a moment of reflection before we conclude any two people who have got on as seamlessly as we have for the past six months will never argue violently about who does the dishes, whether it's right to tell off the landlord, or if the Colt Calendar comes down when mother comes to call.

Oh, it's a grand thing to do, living together, most civilized for those with the desire, intestinal fortitude, and sense of humor to pull it off. We just shouldn't expect to wake up every morning in an English novel...or anything less than the challenge of a lifetime.

It's lovely when the ring-doves coo.

STONEWALL

We are the Stonewall girls
We wear our hair in curls
We wear no underwear
We show our pubic hair...
We wear our dungarees
Above our nelly knees!
  —Song sung by a "chorus line of mocking queens," taunting cops who
  used billy clubs to beat anyone they could get their hands on during the
  Stonewall Riot, as related by Martin Duberman in his book, Stonewall

Beginning late on the night of June 27,1969 and until nearly four in the morning the next day, patrons of The Stonewall Inn joined by people hanging out in New York's Christopher Street neighborhood suddenly exploded in rage during a routine police raid on the bar. The exact moment the riot began is unclear, but more than one account credits a drag queen, who got pissed when a cop grabbed her, with throwing the first punch.

By the time it was over, gay people had been beaten bloody by riot police; a contingent of New York's finest were locked inside The Stonewall Inn, lighter fluid poured in a broken window, and a match thrown in behind (they survived); according to Dick Leitsch in the Village Voice account, a "wild Puerto Rican queen" yelled at a cop about to beat him, "How'd you like a big Spanish dick up your little Irish ass?" (he got away); and it turned out to be as significant to Gay Liberation as the Boston Tea Party was to the American Revolution.

It happened when it did for lots of reasons. It was the late 1960s and the nation's youth were in open rebellion. A bunch of queens in a working bar got drunk and fed up and fought back. Judy Garland's funeral had been that day. All kinds of activists from every walk of gay life had laid decades of groundwork.

Within a year, America's nascent gay liberation movement flared to life in spontaneous combustion all across the land. The day will not be forgotten. The flame will never go out again.

We've made a revolution.

CONTROL

Three words were in the captain's heart. He shaped them soundlessly with his trembling lips, as he had not breath to spare for a whisper: "I am lost." And, having given up life, the captain suddenly began to live.
—*Carson McCullers, Reflections in a Golden Eye*

Many of us struggled for years to suppress the impulses, thoughts, and feelings that ultimately could not be denied. Giving in to them may have been like tumbling overboard into deep and frightening waters.

Three words came from our trembling lips, *"I am gay,"* and instead of drowning, we began to live. Perhaps not the life we had imagined, not the ports of call we had planned to visit, but a different voyage to a hidden and marvelous harbor.

To arrive in this new place—foreign, intriguing, full of heady attractions—we had to give up the illusion of controlling our own destiny. Now we sail on, having begun to live, seeking no control over the tides, or the winds, or the urges of the heart, or any force of nature. Only fixing a course for ourselves guided by the stars.

I have begun to live.

KISSING

Bring your lips to mine
so that out of my mouth
my soul may pass into yours

—*Diderot*

There are kisses and then there are kisses. The peck on the cheek. *Have a nice day.* The lingering brush on the neck. *I'll miss you.* The big moment, hours, maybe weeks in the build-up, in which our whole hard tense bodies say yes to one another and we begin to make love. *Oh God.*

There is the kissing of reaching souls. When the body and mind both recede and we have no awareness of who is kissing whom, but something inside us is reaching, reaching *Oh my love*, and our breathing changes and it isn't just being excited because our full lips and searching tongues and hard-edged teeth are in conversation more clear and memorable than any other language and if we draw back then so we feel breath on our lips and look in each other's eyes, we see briefly what we want to pass into and feel what is dying to pour out of us and it is our soul and his soul and our lips meet again and nothing, nothing is so achingly beautiful as this.

There are moments when the universe pours in.

LIFE

Men must live and create. Live to the point of tears.
—Albert Camus, Notebooks 1935-1942

One morning, a few months after we moved into our new house, my then eight-year-old daughter paused as she was pulling on her clothes, sat down on the couch and said, "Why am I here?"

"Well, honey, " I began, "The other house got too small and I know you miss it, but mommy and I...."

"No," she interrupts, "I mean why am I *here*." My eyes get big as I realize this little slip of a girl, is asking *the* question and asking it with the same curiosity and expectation of an answer as when she wants to know why some clouds make rain and some don't.

I made the mistake of trying to answer, which only frustrated her so she dropped the subject. But she brought it up again about a year later, and cried hard one night a few months after that about how confusing it all is. The next day she was entirely bright-eyed, chattering about school and how many boyfriends she has and what kind of birthday party will be best.

I watch carefully as she grapples with the meaning of life. She has so much to learn. As do I. As do you. So far she's willing to press the hard questions to the point of tears. I hope she never stops.

Why am I here?

July

FAGGOTS

"Faggot," as a sacred male sexual firestick, is a venerable term. The faggot as a wand for divination and sacred firemaking has apparently belonged to the province of Gay male wizards, sorcerers, and priests for thousands of years.

—Judy Grahn, Another Mother Tongue

So much of what is feared in modern cultures held power and sway in ancient tribal times. The unlocking of passions and unleashing of spiritual forces involved phallic-shaped objects and firesticks. These were often wielded by faggots—powerful shamans who stole fire from gods and masqueraded on the line between the sexes—who brought life-giving erotic, spiritual, and utilitarian fire to the people.

The flaming faggot of today pales next to his historic counterpart who would easily outdo him in exaggerated movement, gaudiness of makeup, and ability to stir up a crowd. *(And honey, those ostrich feathers were no run to Woolworth's. I slew that ostrich myself and they are the **real** thing.)* Still, we'd find we have much in common if we got together to dish after things died down around the fire circle.

We are the few who cross over to other realms. We were singled out, initiated, and arouse flaming passions nearly everywhere we go. We're on intimate terms with phallic-shaped objects and get good and hot and wild. We definitely have the best parties, stage the best rituals, and, in crossing all the lines, even suffer the worst indignities.

No matter how we look, dress, or act we are named faggots in this world. We flame. We break the rules. We hold power and sway. We bring life-giving erotic, spiritual, and utilitarian fire to the people.

I am one hot faggot.

IDENTITY

I've always felt so integrated as a gay man, so comfortable with my place in the world. I had other things to write about first. I couldn't force myself to write about sexuality.

—Jon Robin Baitz, The Advocate

Are our eyes gay? Our hands? Our soul? In our younger years, it seems we should be able to account for every part of ourselves. By thirty, we expect to have it down to business card size.

> *Juan Doe*
> *Latino, Lapsed Catholic, Social Worker,*
> *Major Queen, Size 38 Short*

In the long run, none of it really comes in handy except the suit size.

An identity is a lineup of thoughts we collect about ourselves over time. It's useful. We know where to show up for work, which kind of parties we'll enjoy, and can give other people a handle on how to relate to us. But the notion that we *are* things—gay, straight, white, black—accounts for a small portion of our being and only serves to provoke identity crises when we inevitably fail to fit the mold.

Identity is something one grows into; we need it to make meaning of our experience and get a fix on the world. Then it's something to grow out of—so we can see things as they are, touch and be touched in ever-changing ways, and live out the deeper more universal truths of our soul.

My gayness does not define me.

RISK

Spend all you have for loveliness,
Buy it and never count the cost;
For one white singing hour of peace
Count many a year of strife well lost,
And for a breath of ecstasy
Give all you have been, or could be.

—Sara Teasdale, "Barter"

There's no excuse for unsafe sex. This is about another kind of high-risk behavior. It's about men entering relationships *sans* emotional condom, about throwing caution to the wind and seeking multiple, unprotected contacts with loveliness.

Not wanting to get AIDS makes sense. Never exposing ourselves to heartbreak doesn't. It's rare to impossible we won't test positive for emotional strife if we put ourselves on the line, but this is not fatal. If we consistently make ourselves immune to ecstasy, slow death is guaranteed.

We all have a say in this. We can wind up a motley crew of dried-up old men or we can get creative, brace for some pain, and take the risk of opening our hearts to the loveliness and to the tears. For such contact, we *should* give all we have been...and then stay tuned for the singing glory hours of all we might be.

Never mind the cost, sign me up for that lovely stuff.

INDEPENDENCE

I fear nothing, I hope for nothing, I am free.
—Nikos Kazantzakis

Each of us must wage his war of independence from the tyrannies that tax our spirits. An imperial flotilla looms on the horizon: our parents' approval; the emotional aftermath of our childhood; "making it" in the world; a host of heterosexist assumptions; an array of gay categorizations.

It is one thing to gain physical independence—the right job, right home, right lovers—it is another to loosen the tenacious grip on the inner sanctum of our *selves*. Once the battle reaches the heartland, reinforcements are called for. We need skilled strategists, counselors, and healers.

In these battles there are turning points; confrontations with our most dreaded enemy, most crushing memory, most feared reality. The fight for our own ground—even when we are winning it—is enormously taxing. Breaks for rest and relaxation are vital. Little by little, the war winds down; we have vanquished the demons, no longer feel threatened. We know, with humility, that we are free.

I celebrate my hard-won independence.

COMING OUT TO STRAIGHT FRIENDS

The holy passion of Friendship is of so sweet and steady and loyal and enduring a nature that it will last through a whole lifetime, if not asked to lend money.

—*Mark Twain, Pudd'nhead Wilson*

Do we unnecessarily strain our friendships of long standing? Yes—when we *don't* come out to our friends. Keeping this tidbit to ourselves discredits them. We run the risk of offending them by supposing they can't handle the truth.

Now the girl next door we grew up with who has always adored us and inexplicably sends a fruitcake every Christmas and has gone on to be prayer leader for the Mormon Tabernacle Choir may react poorly. We may wish to spare her—and ourselves—the ordeal of upsetting the apple cart.

Aside from exceptional cases, we owe it to friends to come clean. Not that it doesn't cost us. We need to hang in there while they adjust, ask strange questions, and admonish us in concerned, mournful tones to *"Be Careful."* As for friends who flip out, do we really need them if they stop being able to see us and just see a big neon sign flashing QUEER every time we walk in the room?

True friends want to be on the inside of our lives, want to know something so important, will struggle to understand if the revelation is tough for them. Coming out builds trust. And you never know what stunning revelation might be shared with us in return.

Friendship deserves honesty.

COMING OUT TO GAY FRIENDS

We have not even to risk the adventure alone, for the heroes of all time have gone before us, the labyrinth is thoroughly known…and where we had thought to be alone, we shall be with all the world.

—Joseph Campbell

As opposed to the mixed reviews we expect from straight folks, we may fantasize the announcement of our arrival in the gay world prompting exuberant choruses of "Hello Dolly" and a rush of dancing boys eager to show us to the best table in the house.

This is unlikely. It is likely that a number of gay men—guys we've known since high school to the particularly out fellow at work—will be our friends…if we come out to them. (Anonymous sex, tricking, and going alone to bars doesn't qualify. This may be out of the straight closet, but it's into a gay one.) What does qualify is being openly gay among other gay men and open to the companionship, affection, and mentorship of those who are finding their way through this labyrinth just as we are.

In its own way, it's actually *more* nerve-wracking to come out to gays than straights. We fear being judged, misreading signs, making fools of ourselves, or simply not fitting in. We may be used to being alone, but where are we to turn if we feel alienated in this crowd? And coming out to gay friends makes the whole thing more official. It is a strong affirmative statement, a real commitment to say, "Here I am. I'm like you. I want to be a part of this."

Hello, Dolly.

LUNCH

Love is sweet, but tastes best with bread.
—Yiddish Proverb

Noontime is an unusual hour for love. Five days out of seven the world moves at its most frantic pace. There are chores to be done or appointments to be kept and anyway the sun directly overhead is hardly romantic lighting.

Which are all reasons why a lunchtime rendezvous may be a standout. A lazy Saturday where the sole purpose is to be together, no agenda except to share each other's company. Or a weekday exception to the norm—lunch at one of the places rich people go—two hours of a fantasy life. Or forget about food, meet me at my apartment for something more filling than bread.

Whether for a tenderloin or tryst, lunch can be a surprising addition to our menu. Seeing him in the full light, dressed for success, sweaty from a morning in the fields, or in jeans with a weekend growth, we might pause before biting into our burger and remember this moment is exceptional, rare, as is every moment sweetened by love.

Let's do lunch

ACTIVISM

The 15 Church Ladies, who call themselves "performance activists"...introduce themselves, each staying in character: Church Lady Felicity Bundtcake shows off his "earrings that pinch; that's what keeps us angry." Embree O'Conception, in a particularly gaudy knee-length flowered number and sporting major facial hair, strikes up "Amazing Grace" on his bagpipes ("I once was lost, now I'm pro-choice...")

—*The Advocate*

Activism can be fun. We get to express our outrage, make new friends, and those pictures in the paper are great to send home to mom and dad. Showing up in drag at the city council debate on gay rights will be called poor strategy by some, but then what are we to make of the dour pro-lifer who told one of the Church Ladies she liked his dress? One never knows precisely what will bridge the gap.

Activism is important, although not a public sport for the faint of heart. Ask particularly out gay spokesmen how many death threats they've received. Which is precisely why activism on all our parts is needed. The forces of The Dark Side don't take gay clout lying down. As they lose fights here and there, they pop up bolder and more insidious somewhere else.

Not that gay causes are the only things to fight for. Lord knows there's plenty of places to pitch in. Ladies, gentlemen, choose your weapons. Fire off a letter. Send in a check. Take to the streets. Pull on a dress. As the Church Ladies demonstrate so divinely...

It's righteous to take a stand.

OLD TAPES

This whole thing about Mike being a lot more organized and stuff. It's a big issue. I'll feel guilty about not keeping the house as clean as I should and then when he says something about it I feel like this really bad, this really horrible person.

—Johnny S.

Maybe it's time to resurrect "Queen for a Day." In case you're too young to remember, it's the show where the downtrodden housewife with the absolute worst tale of woe—and they were *bad*—got dinner for two at a steak house and gleaming new Maytag appliances. Everything about it was extraordinarily pathetic.

Back in the '90s, how could thoroughly modern Michael and Johnny fall prey to a dynamic we thought went the way of the hula hoop? Not that they're pathetic. Far from it. They're young, hip, good-looking, comfortably out, quite in love, and just bought a house in a retro neighborhood verging on its first espresso bar.

Must be something in their childhoods. Must be something in all our childhoods. Something about needing to please grown-ups who created weird and often impossible standards and then made us feel like really bad, really horrible people when we failed to measure up. It's a big issue and if it doesn't show up over housecleaning, then it'll be the check ledger, or the laundry, or how we behaved at the bar, or any number of a hundred other mundane conflicts that come up between people who love each other and are foils to help each other grow and who sooner or later push every single button we've got.

New tape: I'm great because I care and try.

SECRECY

In 1954, we mimeographed a directory of gay bars on the West Coast, from San Diego to Seattle. There were about thirty-five on the list. We numbered the sheets of paper and we signed out the numbered copies for people to fold up and put in their wallets. They signed for them because we did not want the list to get into the hands of the police. It was that sensitive a matter in those days. We had only about fifty copies. That was all we dared print.

—Hal Call, interviewed by Eric Marcus, Making History

There are people who kind of miss the bad old days. Today's gay world has lost its mystique, the bond that comes from being part of an underground, the rush of being risqué. Flashback: squeaky clean men and women, crew cuts, braids, bobby socks and skirts (on the girls), a smattering of suits (on the boys) (and the girls). A crush of same-sex couples in a dim bar dancing cheek to cheek. A red bulb on the ceiling flashes, the lights come up, and patrons quickly form "straight" couples to charade for the cops who come barging in.

An air of espionage was necessary at a time when being queer itself was illegal if you expressed it in any way. Gay men got hauled in for lewd conduct for a brief good-bye kiss at the train station. You could get arrested in New York City for wearing one too many articles of clothing not expressly assigned to your sex. Just being in a bar might mean getting thrown in a paddy wagon.

These were merely the public outrages. The private outrage of having to hide our fundamental drive for intimacy took its own deadly toll. No, the old days weren't better days, despite the innocence and fun that may be gone. Living deep in the closet was the norm. Self-acceptance was rare. For the vast majority, the idea there could be anything good about being gay was the deepest darkest secret of all.

The real secret is it's great to be gay.

GROWING UP

Most surrender to the vague but murderous pressure of adult confor-mity. It becomes easier to die and avoid conflicts than to maintain a constant battle with the superior forces of maturity.

—*Maya Angelou*

I went to my therapist complaining I had created the struc-ture of a "perfect life," but just didn't feel *alive* in it. "I want a better body, but can't get with the exercise program...I want to get out of debt, but can't stop spending...I want to satisfy my wife emotionally, but can't express my real feelings."

"I'm going to say something now that I believe it's impor-tant for you to hear," he responds. "Gary, *grow up*." "What?" I think, "For this I pay $90.00 an hour?" But we press on and I begin to understand the wisdom in his unequivocal prescription. He knows it's time for me to break through. I must push back against a false state of "happy ever after," resolve my conflicts, and claim who I really am.

It takes a lot—murderous pressures don't yield overnight—but I find out being a grown-up means at least three things: 1) No illusions, promises, or futuristic fantasies about being anything I'm not. 2) The forces of maturity have incredible life-giving energy and though you can't beat them, you can join them. 3) Work hard and be careful what you wish for.

Growing up is good—and hard—to do.

MALE PRIVILEGE

A man will learn more from wearing a dress for a day
than a suit for a lifetime.
—Radical Faerie wisdom as related by Patrick Scully

Men in suits have been in charge of virtually everything throughout our lifetime. Wearing the uniform and acting the part screens us "in." As long as no one asks and we don't flaunt, we're assumed to be in the club and handed the full menu of perks and rigid expectations that come with being male. The membership fee is steep: we get good at playing a man, but we don't get to play with ourselves.

So let's give RuPaul and Billy Beyond a run for their money and wear a dress for a day to see what a little gender anarchy might teach us. Here's some possibilities:

1. What a great feeling it is to have air circulating under and around our crotch while we walk.
2. The degree to which clothes really do make the man.
3. How blindly most of the world accepts dress codes.
4. How blindly most of the world accepts everything.
5. The fact that we are utterly free to define ourselves.
6. What Marlo Thomas must have felt like as *That Girl.*
7. Dress styles that would suit us better.
8. That you have to realize you're in gender prison before you can break out of it.
9. A lighter, looser, and more agreeable way to move our bodies.
10. How sexy we are on our own terms.

I'm privileged to see the world a different way.

AIDS

This is about you. This is about us all. Our planet is sick. Earth has acquired an immune dysfunction. We are all living with AIDS.
—Perry Tilleraas, The Color of Light

AIDS is an inescapable fact. We all know people who have died; some of us have cried for loved ones until we have no tears left. We tend the sick, wage war with government and medical bureaucracies, raise funds, publish black humor journals, and buy passion fruit flavored condoms. We know what it's like to be tested or to decide we don't want to be. Most of us understand terror.

We know this is about us. Each of us has his own AIDS story to tell. Our artists and composers and playwrights and filmmakers are doing the private dark work of creation that gives a public voice and a permanent record and a universal face to our inside view of the workings of this plague. Death and tragedy and injustice beg for meaning to be made. Sometimes there is none. Sometimes human learning is the only possible saving grace.

AIDS has sped the passages of a whole generation of gay men. Some, like time-lapse flowers, withered and died in a breath. Some are braving chronic illness day to day. The rest of us look on with old eyes. We are the victim heralds of something we didn't create. We now have utter responsibility to live more preciously: we and all our fellow inhabitants of earth who teeter together at the perilous brink.

I am living with AIDS.

UNMASKING

Like sheaves of corn he gathers you unto himself.
He threshes you to make you naked.
He sifts you to free you from your husks.
He grinds you to whiteness.
He kneads you until you are pliant;

—*Kahlil Gibran, The Prophet*

The rare spirit enters our lives who loves what is most true within us. He may stay a short while, like the prophet who arrives unheralded, bestirs the people, and moves on. Or he may come to live beside us, bringing comfort and disarming demands.

He is drawn to us out of insight, we to him out of instinct. We are strangely naked in his sight. *"Tell me who you are"*; he is a thresher with his questions. *"Tell me stories of your past, what you saw and felt and dreamt. I want to know everything."* This is not easy love. We become honest by sifting out the truth, removing the husk of pretense that hides the best and worst inside.

There will be times when we are loved so well—and so harshly in the need for truth between us—that we feel pulled between great stones, our falseness turned to powder, our willfulness ground out, until at last something pure is arrived at and we see it as ourselves: fresh, unmasked, strong and pliant in loving hands.

I can remove my mask.

MISTAKES

Every man got a right to his own mistakes. Ain't no man that ain't made any.

—*Joe Louis*

When we are children it is expected we will stumble and fall, scrape our knees, and even knock out a tooth or two in the process of learning how to make it across the playground. When we are teenagers it is expected we will be party to numerous fiascos as we navigate the rapids of adolescence. And as twenty-somethings it is expected we will think no one has ever had their shit together quite so completely as we do.

Mr. Louis helpfully points out we've got a right to our mistakes. This is how we learn. A little overenthusiasm and misplaced trust here. A little arrogance and rushing out on a limb there. Comes a time, though, when many of us think we should be done scraping our knees and just get on with doing everything right.

True enough, we shouldn't make the same mistake twice and caution is a virtue, especially since our errors tend to have greater consequences as we age. Fine. The older but wiser girl for me. Still, when we notice our blunders are down to zero, it's a sure sign we've stopped growing up and are just growing old.

Even the champs blow it from time to time.

CHESTS

It is not sufficient to see and to know the beauty of a work. We must feel and be affected by it.

—*Voltaire*

Worked in symmetry, the chest renders its beauty with great variety; from the fullness and softness of corpulent men to the simple flat grace of the lean. Muscles here bring majesty in bearing; a flush of eagle feathers.

Subtle curves and two dark points suggest themselves beneath starched white fronts, press against tight cotton undershirts, draw our eyes and hands up and inside loose-hanging tanks. Chest hair grows on some in abundance, thick for running fingers through, black in swirling patterns, red and blond catching rays of the sun. Some are hairless; clean and smooth and fine and rich.

Seeing is not sufficient, although we are already affected. Feeling gives our hands their due. Here function matches form: twin sensations of fullness; further provocation. Our fingers press in, trace around the nipples, come together and pinch hard to elicit the gasp of icy pleasure that shoots down his body. Our tongue follows, flat and wet; next teeth, lips. We suck and bite hard, then gently, then hard. Again he gasps.

We know this beauty. We see it and work it. Against the chest we hear the beating of his heart. We return here over and over in our quickening rhythm of heated give and take.

I see and feel and am greatly affected.

REPRESSED ANGER

Anger repressed can poison a relationship as surely as the cruelest words.
—Dr. Joyce Brothers

Signs of repressed anger:
1. They call about the second interview for that job, but you forget to give him the message.
2. You're sure he must have gotten over that food allergy by now, so you just go ahead and put walnuts in his birthday cake.
3. You have frequent fantasies about the touching eulogy you deliver following his tragic accident after which his family and all your friends fawn on you unendingly.
4. You have no qualms at all about inviting your ex-boyfriend(s) to the party.
5. You wear his good suede shoes.

Probable results of repressed anger:
1. Outright prolonged hysteria.
2. The emergency room staff's rendition of *Happy Birthday*.
3. Another frustrated fantasy.
4. Another ex-boyfriend.
5. Nuclear war.

Alternatives to repressed anger:
1. The English Language (or any substitute).
2. Hiring a therapist/bouncer to mediate.
3. Remembering it takes two to tango.
4. The prospect of another ex-boyfriend.
5. Being honest and direct.

I need to get something off my chest...

NORMALITY

"...and who are you?"
"I—I hardly know, sir, just at present—at least I know who I was when I got up this morning, but I think I must have been changed several times since then."

—Lewis Carroll, Through the Looking Glass

Welcome to the Land of Normal where everything is predictable and everyone is the same. (It's a giant hoax, of course, but somehow the general population got duped. Maybe it's something in the water.) Nevertheless, the single most important rule to remember growing up Normal is everyone *but you* is in charge of deciding what goes. Should you forget this, you will quickly be identified as *deviant*, subjected to peer torture and possibly hauled in for formal intervention to get you back on track.

The extraordinary resilience of the deviant population (controversy rages over its size) can be traced to the unexplained conviction in the minds of the deviants—which many report was present from an early age—that *they* were normal and at pains to exist in a parallel reality with the hostile forces surrounding them.

Life in Normal is rocky these days. It turns out car mechanics, Olympic athletes, rodeo cowboys, and macho movie stars are all having tea with Mad Hatters and shaking everybody up. The giant hoax is crumbling. Because when you get up close to the looking glass, little is predictable and no one is the same.

I am who I woke up to be.

DISSATISFACTION

It's terrible to pretend that the second-rate is first-rate. To pretend that you don't need love when you do or you like your work when you know quite well you're capable of better.

—Doris Lessing

How often we choose to fool ourselves. We get restless and come up with a distraction. We make a few adjustments around the edges of our lives, but hang back from dramatic improvements.

Adapting to the second-rate does terrible things to us. We develop a cynical edge that puts a face of worldly wisdom on our own disappointments. We bury the desire for what we really need under addiction to alcohol, work, or sex. Or we quietly fade out as human beings without ever seriously going after what we want.

When we step off the merry-go-round long enough for our heads to stop spinning, we see the level facts of what's wrong with our lives. It's right to feel dissatisfied about the second-rate. It's good to want love. It's important to do our best work.

I want a first-rate life.

STYLE

Geraldo Rivera: *Please answer me. What* are *you? Are you a woman trapped in a man's body? Are you a heterosexual? Are you a homosexual? A transvestite? A transsexual? What is the answer to the question?*

Holly Woodlawn: *But, darling, what difference does it* make *as long as you look fabulous?*

—*Dialogue from 1976 ABC TelevisionTalk Show*

Gay men are peacocks in the menagerie. Not that straight birds don't show their feathers—they do—although a bit more modestly in order not to upstage the female of the species. Us, we just egg each other on.

The more attention of the right kind the better. Hoots, cat-calls, tipped hats, and come-hither-looks are all welcome. While some of us take preening a lot more seriously than others, it's always a pleasure to take in the scene and, on our better days, it ain't bad to consider ourselves one of the attractions.

Some say gay men are into style because of all the extra time on our hands—no kids to raise, etc. etc. Some say we're constantly coming on to each other and want to look good to improve our chances. If you accept the "everyone gets 15 minutes of fame" theory, then some of us stake our stardom on killer muscles, others on rhinestone-studded boots, others on giving Diana Ross a run for her hair.

Me, I'm into the show. Watching it, being part of the cast. Forget all the definitions. I mean darling, what difference does it *make* when it's all so fabulous?

Style is part of the fun.

LEGITIMACY

The one disgraceful, unpardonable, and to all time contemptible action of my life was my allowing myself to be forced into appealing to Society for help and protection...

—*Oscar Wilde*

We must never view our crusade for equal access to opportunity, full inclusion, and protection under law as an appeal for legitimacy. This is ours to grant to ourselves.

Every segment of our community has its place in the pursuit of social justice: the men and women with the patience to work within political process and deal with "you scratch my back, I'll scratch yours" realities; the men and women who battle in court to strike down laws and bans that provide cover for discrimination; the outright nonconformists who shout and shock and pay penalties for their passion; the quiet daily openness of thousands who win the slow change of individual hearts and minds.

From these many interlocking actions, society as a whole grows more tolerant; justice is slowly achieved. Indignity has been suffered, careers ruined, lifeblood drained in bringing us to this point. Traditional society rarely provides the affirmation and strength necessary to carry on; this must originate from a fierce inner knowledge of our own legitimacy.

I have no need for society's sanction.

ANONYMOUS SEX

Sex is. There is nothing more to be done about it. Sex builds no roads, writes no novels and sex certainly gives no meaning to anything in life but itself.

—*Gore Vidal*

The protocols are well understood. Signals of mutual intention followed by satisfaction of mutual drive. Speech is rare. No relationship assumed. Simply sex. No strings, no questions, and no meaning attached.

We find this in riverside clearings, hidden by bramble and sumac, secluded pleasure spots where lush afternoons and moonswept nights witness the nude and partly clad couplings of men and groups of men seeking sex with the wind at their backs, seeking burning sun on their bellies and cocks, seeking shadow and dark anonymous hands and the scent of danger.

We find this in bookstores and back rooms and baths and cellars. We find this in San Francisco and Selma and Tokyo and Rome. We find this because we like it or need it or want to see it or don't know how else to have it. We find men of all descriptions, men of specific tastes, men who bore us, men we come back and search for again. We find sex. Glory hole grass stained grab ass dirty kneed sun drenched Mr. America come fast come slow come all over me sex.

It builds nothing. It has no meaning. It simply is.

We find each other but don't touch each other.

LOSS

What is this darkness? What is its name? Call it: an aptitude for sensitivity. Call it: a rich sensitivity which will make you whole. Call it: your potential for vulnerability.

—*Meister Eckhart*

Loss is a severe teacher. We do not suffer her lessons gladly. Loss brings pain, pain brings darkness, and darkness opens our eyes. We see that we are fragile, that everything we want or love is tenuous. We learn we own nothing.

We know much about loss. We are not afforded a comfortable view of the world. We have lost jobs, families, former identities. We have lost trust, innocence, and dreams. If this were not enough, we have also lost leaders, lovers, and many friends. Such darkness might embitter us, the line between our sensitivities and our agonies too thin to tread.

Here is one of life's supreme ironies: it is only loss that teaches us the sensitivity that makes us whole. Vulnerability is forced upon us. We learn life offers only its moments. We can shut down this sensitivity or we can use it, turning our eyes to the expanding glow of a sunset's brightening then dimming color, knowing full well that what follows is darkness.

From the darkness of loss comes light.

RUSSIA

I am aware that my inclinations are the greatest and most unconquerable obstacle to happiness; I must fight my nature with all my strength.
—*Peter Ilyich Tchaikovsky*

Mixed news out of Russia these days. The iron curtain lifts slowly and what was crushed beneath it comes only wrenchingly back to life. Things are better than they used to be when being gay was a big nyet-nyet and getting caught meant postcards from the Gulag. It's still not exactly Castro on the Volga, but at least now the guys have got a chance.

Twasn't always so in Mother Russia. Homosexuality and bisexuality had their day. In the 11th Century "Legend of Boris and Gleb" (okay, to the modern ear the names leave something to be desired), Boris had this magnificent golden necklace made for Gleb "who loved Boris beyond reckoning" which, after they were both brutally massacred, could not be undone from around Gleb's neck which necessitated severing his head. The two are annually commemorated together as Saints of the Russian Orthodox Church.

Russia's history is nothing if not turbulent and the place of homosexuality in society had numerous ups and downs. Up during the 16th Century rule of Grand Prince Vasily III when gayness was prevalent and open among all classes; up again due to Peter the Great; down as 18th and 19th century homophobia crept in from the West (no help to poor Tchaikovsky); a regular rollercoaster in the revolutionary period, and then down for the count as a symptom of "bourgeois degeneracy" under the Soviets.

A succession of turn-of-the-century poets reflect the stream of male love that ran so often below ground. Vyacheslav Ivanov, Mikhail Kuzmin, Nikolai Kluyev, Sergei Esenin. Their very names evoke the sense of this complex and tortured land, a giant in all ways, a place where spring does not come easy or soon.

We have grown in even the harshest soil.

HIGH SCHOOL REUNIONS

How many cares one loses when one decides not to be something but to be someone.

—*Gabrielle (Coco) Chanel*

A strange ritual for taking stock, those brief biographies we write for the reunion program. Take just a moment to fill in the blanks, then send the form back to the Reunion Committee (the pep squad rises again) along with a recent photo.

1. What is your strongest memory from high school?
2. What has been your most important learning experience since high school?
3. What accomplishment are you most proud of?
4. Who was the secret crush of your senior year?

It is with extravagantly mixed emotions that many of us greet these every-half-decade flashes from the past. Decisions, decisions! Whether to go. Whether to go alone. Whether to fill out the form. Whether to fill out the form honestly. Whether to go if we *don't* lose those 20 pounds. We get an unexpectedly powerful reading of how we feel about ourselves, how we relate to our past, what cares we still have, what cares we have finally lost.

Conventional wisdom is as follows: 5 years, everyone is out to impress; 10 years, everyone is out to show off their husband or wife, or make it with the person they really wanted back then, or both; 20 years, it's amazing how much better the women look than the men (with a few notable exceptions); 25 years and beyond, except for the unredeemable assholes, everyone has been tenderized by life and anyone who shows up just to be who they are has a good time.

It's powerful to be someone in a place I was something else.

PROGRESS

If I went to a gay gathering of some kind, I was sure to have at least one person come up to me and say, "I wanted to meet you because I wanted to tell you what you saved me from." I'm thinking of a young woman who came up to me and said that when her parents discovered she was a lesbian, they put her in a psychiatric hospital. The standard procedure for treating homosexuals in that hospital was electroshock therapy. Her psychiatrist was familiar with my work, and he was able to keep them from giving it to her.

—Dr. Evelyn Hooker, interviewed by Eric Marcus, Making History

In 1974, the American Psychological Association officially removed homosexuality from its list of mental illnesses. In so doing, the mental health profession was standing squarely in line with groundbreaking research done by Dr. Evelyn Hooker and first presented to her professional peers in 1956.

Dr. Hooker did what had never been done before. She took on the prevailing belief that homosexuality was a form of mental illness. She did so with evidence gained from impeccable scientific methodology and rebuked experts of the day who were convinced a set of standard personality tests would select the queer boys out as misfits.

So congratulations, we're not crazy! Which isn't news to most of us. But it was major progress at the time. And each bit of progress, each newly enlightened heart or mind, is worthwhile because someone, somewhere—in ways we can never know—is saved from senseless suffering.

People I have never known helped clear my path.

SEXUAL FREEDOM

To love without role, without power plays, is revolution.
—Rita Mae Brown

In the beginning we are relative strangers, drawn together by an attraction that proves to grow. Ignited inside, we do as lovers do and use our power with each other. We have to test, want to know how far we can go. There are limits: fire out of control destroys. As does freedom without constraint.

We play out the roles. Provocateur. Master. Tease. Seductress. Conquered slave. We go the long route of mock resistance, showing our ability to withhold. We beg we can wait no longer, concede complete power to arouse. We become more bold, allow shy powers within to show their face. We whisper fantasies into each other's ear, invoke the power of spoken truths.

We become different men, each freer than the last, many lovers in one night. I have the hungry body of a nineteen-year-old boy; the full lips of a woman promising much when you kiss me; the powerful loins of an animal that runs, fights, and kills. We share our power now. What is mine is yours, what is yours, mine. This is sexual freedom. All of who we are, beyond role, beyond any need for control.

The revolution is trust and love.

LOYALTY

It is not enough to say that one was a brilliant poet, scientist, educator or rebel. Who did he love? It makes a difference. I cannot become a whole man simply on what you feed me: watered-down versions of black life in America. I need the ass-splitting truth to be told so I will have something pure to emulate, a reason to remain loyal.

—Essex Hemphill, Loyalty, Men & Intimacy

In the beginning it was essential, and later loomed large, our wired-in need to be wanted, to meet the measures of belonging, to be a pride to our family, our community, our race.

We pursue multiple paths as we grow into ourselves, setting out and fulfilling expectations. "Look, mother, my poem won a contest at school." "Look, brother, I am paid for the sweat of my brow." "Look, man, I am here for my slice of the pie." "Look, father, I have sinned."

It's not good enough. Maybe for them, but not for us. They stop asking who we love—it's enough if we show up ghostly, much paler than we really are, much less black, less Jewish, less hometown, less pure if we fail to stand up to the tribe and say, "Include me, *goddamn it. Now!* Let's have the truth, let's have it out, let's peel back this rotting look-alike veneer. There is no reason you can give me to betray myself and remain a broken part of you."

Faced with no real choice, no real history, no real love, we will leave all the familiar places and go out into a new place where there is a chance for something pure, *I need the ass-splitting truth,* a chance to be born. I am loyal to nature, my mother; to the earth, my sister; to the sky, my father; to the other men assembling here, my brothers.

I will be a whole man.

MAKING A DIFFERENCE

Whoever sustains one life...it is as if he sustained an entire world.
—*Talmud*

The work we do to turn back the tide of prejudice can be thankless and overwhelming. The ignorance is so vast, hatred so deep, discrimination so entrenched, that our efforts can feel insignificant as grains of sand on the beach. Unless we're up against a crisis in our own lives, we may fail to see the point. Day to day, things aren't so bad and after all, how much of this stuff is really life or death?

Unfortunately, a lot of it. Gay men are beaten to death. Gay men die prematurely for lack of access to adequate health care. One-third of all teen suicides are committed by gay youth.

Every effort we make is of enormous value. This is not just about battles for civil rights and decent public health policy. It's about how we live our lives. Every bit of personal healing sends a ripple. Every open statement that affirms gayness makes a wave. Every act that claims our rightful place makes the world safer for us all.

Because we do these things, somewhere out there a young man we will never see will somehow feel the strength to get through his pain. And it will be us—from another place and time—who sustained his life.

What I do makes a difference.

BITTERNESS

It's a kind of test, Mary, and it's the only kind that amounts to anything. When something rotten like this happens, then you have your choice. You start to really be alive, or you start to die. That's all.
—James Agee, A Death in the Family

Every gay man comes in contact with the world's rottenness. As the victim of bullies, in a crude and unloving church, at workplaces that demand we lie about who we are, at the hands of selfish and insensitive lovers, in the form of a random mindless disease that savagely cuts men down before their time.

No matter what happens to us, we all have our choice. Really being alive is no day at the beach. We must accept all of life, from extreme suffering to intense joy. When we act from bitterness, we feel we are throwing our pain back at the world, "Here, I've had *enough*." But we throw away more.

Bitterness repels life like pitch spread over cracks in the heart. Salty tears sting, but run off. Laughter's deep release doesn't penetrate. Beneath the protective surface, rottenness has taken root. It festers there.

Still there is a choice. Always. To the last breath. The way back may be long—the toughest journey on God's earth—but a sweet wind rises at our back the instant we choose to live.

I will not be bitter.

SWIMMING SUITS

A thousand fantasies
Begin to throng into my memory,
Of calling shapes, and beck'ning shadows dire,
And airy tongues that syllable men's names
On sands and shores and desert wildernesses.

—*Milton*

Artistic excellence in the swimsuit competition is truly a marriage of content and form. If you're ever in Florence, Italy, stop by the Chapel DiMedici and Uffizi and then head for the municipal swimming pool if you really want something to write home about. Modern male poolwear in the Renaissance capital is a classic statement of less equals more. These Italian guys strut their stuff.

There's also plenty on view right here. Let's talk Speedos. It's in the design: downward and upward lines of the body converge and are caught in a thin, calling shape that both beckons and throngs. As the swimmer races, so does the mind. How can so little hold so much? Is it better if he leaves it on or takes it off? Doctor, doctor, what does it mean that I'm jealous of a small piece of black and lavender nylon?

And what of the airy knee-length styles? Much better on some models. Not to mention the Chariots of Fire fashion with t-shirt thrown in. Oh, a thousand fantasies may be too few! Sun, water, sand, cocoa butter. Let me at that tan line!

Life's a beach.

August

ADDICTION

People who drink to drown their sorrow should be told that sorrow knows how to swim.

—*Ann Landers*

Addiction is a like a broken record. The needle gets stuck and our lives don't go anywhere. There are a million excuses (it's part of the disease) and one of them is just not "getting it." So a few key points to clarify the picture.

Number one: The difference between something that feels good and an addiction is just that. Sex, food, alcohol, drugs, high-demand work—they all start out feeling good. When they're feeling bad and we still do them, we've crossed the line.

Number two: Addictions cover up underlying sorrows—and a gay man without sorrow is about as likely as a virgin street queen. Unless the causes are dealt with, chances are good we'll conquer one type of self-defeating behavior just to fall into another.

Number three: No reason to get all hung up on the question if everybody's addicted to addictions. If something is beginning to feel unmanageable, don't be shy, check it out. And no scoffing at the meetings and programs and counseling that plenty of people who've been through hell and gone will tell you saved their lives.

Final point: Addictions provide instant gratification. Facing sorrow isn't like that. It's more like sink or swim and the water starts out damn cold. The payoff is a subtler, better, and much longer-lasting high.

I am a very strong swimmer.

RECOVERY

"Come here," I say to him, blinking away the moisture in my eyes and holding my arms out.
He walks slowly into my arms, his body slumps against mine. How fragile he feels, how thin and vulnerable. I wrap my arms around him, as I wish someone had done for me years ago. As I tighten my embrace, his body begins to fade, then disappears altogether. I am left alone, my arms encircling my own body.

—Rakesh Ratti,
Visit from an Old Friend, A Lotus of Another Color

There is no precise moment we walked away from ourselves. We were pried apart little by little almost from the time we were born. We learned to live separated. One half went into hiding. The other turned to the outside world and attempted to manage the unmanageable.

A void grew between us. Which at times went unnoticed as we pursued our interests and intrigues. At other times, the void was overwhelming and we desperately filled it any way we knew how. Along the line we pronounced ourselves gay and reached out to each other with doubt and fear and anger and hope all flashing back and forth in an instant. Some of us emerged from hiding then. Some ran further away.

When we're ready, we can stage a full-fledged reunion. It's a matter of recovering all parts of ourselves, the ingathering of exiles, letting ourselves collapse into our own arms. Then, with help, with perseverance, we can knit the fragile pieces into a whole.

Come here.

SENSUALITY

To be sensual is to respect and rejoice in the force of life itself, and to be present in all that one does, from the effort of loving to the breaking of bread.

—*Phyl Garland, Sound of Soul*

When my parents sold our house, friends thought I should give out souvenir remnants of the multicolored wall-to-wall shag carpeting that covered the basement walkout family room which played host to high school hippy scenes of scented candle-making (jasmine and spice), fireplace-lit sessions of orange peeling and massage as directed by our sensuality do-it-yourself-book, *Sense Relaxation Below the Mind* (there were naked art photos), forays into transcendence via the expanding harmonies of The Moody Blues' *OM*, dinner parties providing an early outlet for my talents as Maitre d', a guys-only night that turned into crawling-in-the-dark-tag that turned into the first time I was groped (and hungrily groped my soon-to-be first lover in return), the place of *many* love scenes, the place where we did what our parents were worried we might be doing.

We all have places and periods that remain rich in our memories because of their impact on our senses. Dewed hay at sunrise. Skinny-dipping. Rockefeller Center lit up for Christmas. Barbecue from the corner shack. We can relegate sensuality to nostalgia. A part of sex. Or we can claim sensuality as central and vital to our everyday efforts to love and to live.

I make the most of every sense I've got.

AKHENATEN

How manifold it is, what thou hast made!
They are hidden from the face of man.
O sole god, like whom there is no other!
Thou didst create the world according to thy desire...
                    —*Hymn to the Aton, Akhenaten, 14th Century B.C.*

This was one busy Pharaoh. In his 17-year reign, he revolutionized Egyptian religion with the concept of one supreme God (lesser Gods made a comeback after his death), changed art from strictly formal portrayals to a more naturalistic style, built a new capital city, wrote poetry, and after his chief wife Nefertiti's death, installed a 17 year-old prince, Smenkhkare, as his co-ruler (who, lest there be any confusion regarding this boy's rank, changed his name to Nefertiti) and, thanks to the staying power of stone, left the first example in recorded history of a homosexual relationship.

The carving in question is quite simple. The two men sit side by side, Smenkhkare's arm around Akhenaten's shoulder, the Pharaoh's hand—a key gesture—tenderly posed under his young consort's chin. Open homosexuality was uncommon at the time, but Akhenaten's public display is consistent with his religious and artistic bent: he attached his name to the phrase, "Living in Truth," which indicates respect for natural creation.

Many Pharaohs have fallen into obscurity from the progression of leadership that spanned 27 centuries and 30 dynasties. We can never know how Akhenaten came to be so creative and bold or what combination of qualities allows him to arrest our attention in the long shadow of time. We do know the fact of Akhenaten's immortality distinguishes him greatly on his civilization's own terms.

Living in truth is powerful.

THE PETER PAN SYNDROME

"It was because I heard father and mother," he explained in a low voice, "talking about what I was to be when I became a man." He was extraordinarily agitated now. "I don't want ever to be a man," he said with passion. "I want always to be a little boy and to have fun. So I ran away to Kensington Gardens and lived a long time among the fairies."

—J. M. Barrie, Peter Pan

Oh, it's tempting to refuse to grow up. We can work off an image of ourselves as *Golden Boy* or the *Great Black Hope* forever. We can keep our stomachs flat, teeth gleaming, and hairlines intact. We can devote ourselves to always having fun, play with gangs of boys, avoid responsibilities that tie us down, and make absolutely sure not to fall into the grown-ups' trap.

It sounds swell—and who doesn't have days when they'd just as soon skip their exit off the freeway and drive and drive until reaching Neverland? But drive or run or fly as we might, we're not Peter Pan (or Wendy) and there is no Neverland. Our available world is full of nasty pitfalls for those who shun responsibility and the deepest satisfactions are missed if we refuse to become a man.

Peter Pan has his charms and adventures—as should every boy. Men need more: work done well, real relationships that stand the test of time, the sense we have grabbed hold of life at its core. Peter had a bittersweet knowledge of what running away to Neverland meant, "He had ecstasies innumerable that other children can never know; but he was looking through the window at the one joy from which he must be forever barred."

I want the deepest joy life offers.

BODY HAIR

We find great things are made of little things,
And little things go lessening till at last
Comes God behind them.

—*Robert Browning, Dramatis Personae*

The aesthetics are as varied as God's handiwork. We can take groups as a whole; the tendency of Asians toward smoothness with deep black below the waistband; the tight curls and rich dark patches close to the skin of men who are black everywhere; the wonder of redheads, striking in their variations of natural colors that don't always seem possible.

We can take each part of the body one at a time, finding great things. A happy promise is made to bear-lovers by the volumes of hair that spill over t-shirts and out the collars of men who have to contain this upward surge with a razor. A delight of contrasts is found on lumberjack arms graced by a sweep of softness. A lessening pattern on the legs leaves a patch of bare skin inside the thighs that causes our mouth to water.

With seductive trails in so many places, we can choose which one to take. The movement across and down the chest that swirls around nipples. The tiniest blond line below the belly button of an otherwise hairless body that falls into pants like a sigh. A full, hairy ass, powerfully inviting at the center.

We go with our eyes, our hands, and more. We go with our own nature and come close to such tiny wonders that gather around and into great ones.

The right amount of hair is *so* sexy.

RADICAL FAERIES

We're transforming society by being ourselves.
—Kelly K.

He sits across from me, just returned from a week-long Faerie gathering in the Kawashaway* Sanctuary and his sky-blue eyes definitely have a new twinkle in them.

It wasn't what he expected, he says. He thought he'd be on the outside looking in. But something happened. He describes an event that sounds half high school prom, half midsummer night's dream, half terrific encounter group with the no-sex rules suspended. (And never mind that there's three halves.)

He didn't expect the Big Man, kissed good-bye by his husband and told to have a good time, who took him into his tent the first night and every night thereafter. He only brought one dress, but everyone shared, and an airy, rescued from thrift shop, anarchistic, alter-ego, madcap reality set in. Talismans, firelight, and each faerie around the circle speaking her truth had an effect. A delegation was sent when his love cries from a remote tent with Big Man worried the other faeries that he had been mauled by a bear.

He didn't expect this wild-eyed troupe that disperses under urban toadstool roofs and gathers in tree-shaded gossamer tents would become his tribe. Nor did he expect to proudly wear a bracelet roughly woven of old skirts and ceremoniously bestowed on him to prove it.

Allowing the unexpected transforms everything.

* A Native American name meaning, "no place between, a spirit land."

RUSHING

The trouble with some women is that they get all excited about nothing—and then marry him.

—*Cher*

Okay we get a little overexcited sometimes. "So what if he came and ran? He was clean. And he does have a *job*. Which is more than I can say for the last one. There's *two* good reasons to marry him: he washes and he works. I think he wants to move in...it's so romantic, only three days...I'd better grab him."

We don't need to marry guys to keep them around. And we don't need to sell ourselves short. It's charming when visions of china and crystal flash though our eyes just following the first orgasm, but there's every reason to slow down. If it's real love it won't go away. And if we think quickie domestic bliss will keep him from straying, then we are *definitely* deluding ourselves.

When it comes to really knowing someone, time is on our side. There is the phenomenon of love at first sight—and the story of the guy who went to dinner and never left—but even true love has its variance and rhythm and generally is not to be rushed. If we're the marrying kind, we need to make a pithy list of what we're after in a husband and then be patient until we find him. Besides, if we're all tied up getting prematurely tied down, we don't make ourselves available for that Mr. Right who's out there shopping for us.

What's the rush?

HESITATION

One must act in painting as in life, directly.
—Pablo Picasso

Unlike the artist's brush stroke, once we act in our lives we can't paint over, erase mistakes, or simply keep the canvas from public view. There are times when he who hesitates is smart: we know how much easier it is to get ourselves into a scene than out of one. But he who hesitates all the time loses out: when we can't make up our minds, they get made up for us.

The tendency is to keep our options open. "Don't push me," we say, "I'm not ready." Not ready for what? Not ready to be challenged, held accountable, depended on? Not ready to show our true colors? Not ready to be cared for and loved?

We can produce sketch after sketch, always backing off when the time comes to act directly and create something meant to last. This will never produce a masterwork. The only chance any of us has to fulfill his potential is, at some point, to banish hesitation, defy doubt, and step across the brink.

I can create great things.

WOMEN

She is a friend to my mind. She gathers me. The pieces I am, she gathers them and gives them back to me in all the right order. It's good when you got a woman who is a friend of your mind.

—Toni Morrison, Beloved

Gay men have a curious relationship with women. We imitate them, parody them, make a fuss over them, complain about men with them, dress them, do their hair, decorate their homes, ridicule them, call each other Mary or June when we trip over things, have them as best friends, have them as ex-wives, wish we were them, become them, loathe them, and love them.

Many of us enjoy a special ease with women. The absence of sexual tension allows an intimacy and playfulness between us— we can both let our hair down without fear anyone will get the wrong idea. We can also be the nastiest and most dismissive sexists. Not only do we carry the same cultural baggage that straight men do, we don't see where women are good for *anything*.

When I was a teenager, I talked with my mother about my bisexuality. The greatest fear for me that she could express was that I would miss out on knowing what it was like to be loved by a woman. I have been lucky. I have been loved—and loved well— by more than one.

Sexual orientation need never be a barrier to a meeting of the minds. Nor a meeting of the souls. We miss out a lot if we're missing out on women.

It's *very* good when you got a woman who is a friend.

COMPROMISE

Try to calmly accept the fact that Baryshnikov is straight. Don't take an overdose every time you see him photographed with a woman.
—*Tony Lang*

It is apparent to most people who have relationships that we can't always get what we want. The question is, do we get what we need?

Compromise on practical matters is relatively easy to manage. Tantrums will be thrown, but after a while—assuming we aren't on Mission Impossible—we can come to terms on the electric blanket question, the smoking or non-smoking table question, and even the who-does-or-doesn't-go-with-who-to-what question.

The more difficult compromises are those we confront after he has made it clear he's gone as far as his ego, his ability, or *his* needs will allow. At that point, the process no longer directly involves him. It's up to us to decide whether we can face life without Baryshnikov—or without other ideals, values, and fantasies we might prize. Close attention and creativity are called for. When there's no way to get what we want, we have to look hard for solutions that still give us what we need.

On complex compromises it's crucial we know the difference between giving in and giving ourselves away. Too much giving away and there's nothing left for either of us. Too little giving in and we're off in La-La Land all by ourselves.

I can compromise with him as long as I don't compromise myself.

THE HOMOPHILE MOVEMENT

*Foster had drawn up a proposed set of "aims and purposes" for the orga-
nization that did include "the firm establishment in society of the homosexual as a first class citizen," but went considerably beyond civil rights
in asserting that "the unqualified acceptance by society of homosexuality as a wholly natural personal trait, and a highly valued expression of
human love" was "the chief over-all long-range aim of the movement."*
                    *—Martin Duberman, Stonewall, quoting the
          "Proposed Set of Constitutional Aims and Purposes for NACHO"
                (North American Conference of Homophile Organizations),
          first drafted by Foster Gunnison, Jr. in 1966, finalized in 1969*

Homophile: from the Greek, meaning love of same. Has a pleasant "secret society" ring to it not unlike those wine clubs where the
guys wear gold tasting cups on velvet ribbons around their necks.
The term had some popularity during the '50s and '60s. Early
activists thought it better than homosexual (too clinical for some,
too sexual for others), but it fell out of favor as the more straightfor-
ward *gay* proved a worthy—and radically positive—alternative.

Our homophile predecessors were busy boys back in that
strange American interlude when most everyone apparently was
asleep until Kennedy got shot. The country was in a paroxysm of
denial following the big war. People wanted everything to be normal. No problems. No shortages. No commies. No fairies.

In 1966, the first national conference of homophile organiza-
tions was convened. It included, among other groups, the
Daughters of Bilitis, San Francisco's SIR (Society for Individual
Rights), ONE, Inc. of Los Angeles and San Francisco's Council on
Religion and the Homosexual. Chicago's Mattachine Society
attended, but New York's wouldn't have anything to do with it.

By 1971 the organization had served its purpose and disband-
ed. History had been made. Amidst the arguments and divisiveness
and disapproval over tactics and boring speeches and brilliant
speeches and hotel room affairs, a movement's words were written
and spoken and acted upon in a way that has served to change all
our lives.

Affirmation: Many labored for our movement to be born.

DIFFERENCE

This...possibility says that there is a reality to being gay that is radically different from being straight (note: different, not better or worse). This gay reality is inside of us, and it is substantial and meaningful. It is real. We can feel it in our hearts and in our guts. And it has nothing to do with hetero mythologies, either negative or positive, about what it means to be gay.
       —Don Kilhefner, Assimilation or Affirmation? Gay Spirit

There is significant disagreement over just how different we are. Some contend being gay is a special gift that goes well beyond our particular sexual bent. Others insist sexuality is the only factor distinguishing us from straights.

Until any one of us truly learns about himself—through experience, introspection, the mirror of relationships—our sense of who we are isn't genuine. We reflect our upbringing, our culture, the intentions of those who educated and shaped us. This is particularly true of the element in our nature that is gay. None of us encounters this cleanly. Of all things about us, it is perhaps most overgrown with distortion, myth, and others' realities.

Deeply experiencing our nature requires finding out what the feeling in our hearts and guts is all about. Hetero mythologies can't guide us. And those of gay culture only lead us so far. Crossing the border into our own territory, we encounter substance and meaning. The question of difference ceases to matter when we radically become ourselves.

I am what I am.

INTERNALIZED OPPRESSION

The most dangerous myth facing African-Americans today is that middle class life is counterfeit and that only poverty and suffering, and the rage that attends them, are real.

—Brent Staples, The New York Times

Rage is a natural consequence of oppression and a necessary stage in overturning it. Its character is passionate, hard, and deeply distrustful. Its essence is destruction. Rage is powerful and blinding. It attacks anything in its path.

A people's movement out of oppression is messy and painful. As the pressure from without shifts and cracks, deep damage within must still be healed. An example of such damage is the myth that poverty, suffering, blackness—and therefore loyalty, authenticity, and passion—are inextricably tied together. A comparable myth is that proper queer identity requires alienation, counting all things heterosexual counterfeit, and jumping into the backlash against safe sex.

These myths are mistakes. They cause needless division and tragic deaths. The answer isn't a move to the suburbs. It's what it has always been—self-determination—which means fighting for blacks and gays and everyone else to make choices free of oppression from without and free of oppression from within.

I shall determine what's real for myself.

THE ARTS

Like a gaudy East Indian purse; outrageous in color, embroidered in cliché design, the worth of these plays lies ultimately in the tiny mirrors woven into the fabric wherein we catch our reflections.
                    —Harvey Fierstein speaking of Torch Song Trilogy

In two renowned galleries in Florence stand sculptures of David. The more famous of the two, Michelangelo's David, is a towering statement of physical perfection, a demigod. One is awed. Donatello's David stands in the Ufizzi. He is slight. A graceful boy. I walk slowly around and around him, myself a slight 20 year-old boy, entranced by a sculpted image in which I find my own reflection.

When I finally leave the gallery I am changed. I have seen a new vision of heroic masculinity that includes a vulnerability and soft beauty I didn't know belonged in the picture. I too can slay Goliath.

Works of art take us places and give us things. We have our imaginations stirred and souls filled. We feel connected to history, other people, other worlds, to ourselves.

Gay people have always made art. And while often hidden or disguised, we have always been reflected in it. Of late, openly gay themes and artists weave new and brilliant strands into the embroidery. Some are gaudy, some subtle. Some illuminate gayness, some shed light on much more. Each is another mirror for us. And for all humanity.

Art has the power to change lives.

FATHERS

My father's gifts...are daily surprises: my love of naturalness, the tone of my voice, my very face, eyes, and hair.
—Alice Walker, In Search of Our Mothers' Gardens

This father/son business is a complex testing ground. How well he does is his business. *Our* grades are what matters to us. Chances are the courses include Standing Up for Ourselves; Intro to Forgiveness; and Surprise Gifts. Let's see how we do.

1. **Since dad can't relate to you as an updated model of him, he can't seem to relate to you at all. Do you:**
   A) Educate him about homophobia?
   B) Suggest playing cribbage like you did when you were a kid?
   C) Make sure you're not a disappointment to yourself?
   D) Tell him to quit pouting and act like a man?

2. **Dad's basically an asshole. As long as you can remember he's been drunk, distant, disapproving, and, on occasion, abusive. Do you:**
   A) Refuse to take any crap whatsoever even if that means refusing to see him?
   B) Confront him and give him a chance to apologize?
   C) Try to understand what made him that way?
   D) Get therapy before you turn out like him?

3. **By a strange coincidence, you meet an old friend of your father's who goes on and on about what a great guy he was and how much like him you seem. Do you:**
   A) Agree and enjoy the chance to reminisce?
   B) Tell him you're sure he's got the wrong guy?
   C) Go home and look in the mirror a long time?
   D) Understand more about the gifts you got from your father?

Surprise! No wrong answers. Passing the test is a matter of unwrapping the gifts, then making the most of what we got.

It's up to me to put value on what he gave me.

QUEERS

Homosexual persons should make no effort to try and join society. They should stay right where they are and give their name and serial number and wait for society to form itself around them. Because it certainly will.

—Quentin Crisp

Funny how things come full circle. A queer was not what you wanted to be. The name snarled off the tongue of playground kingpins, high school quarterbacks, and vicious attackers. It had to do with girlish mannerisms, or not wanting to fight, or wanting to rub your stiff cock up against your best friend's when he slept over, or not knowing how to be one of the guys and treat girls like sex objects, or wanting to be treated like a sex object by the guys and somehow they figured it out before you did.

It's a powerful word. You're dirty, an outcast, strange, threatening, disgusting, unusual, and shocking all in one fell swoop. It puts everything right out front. No secrets. Which accounts for its skyrocketing popularity as the name of choice for many gay men and women.

As queers, we stand our ground completely. It's a whole truth. They know we know they think we're disgusting and it's quite clear we don't intend to buy in. Threatened? Go deal with it. We like being queer. Rubbing our cocks together is nice and dirty and queer and we like it. Anyway it's a big lie that people are not strange, unusual, and shocking. Everybody is. Queers are just among the first to stop apologizing for it.

I'll just relax right here while everybody catches up.

SENSITIVITY

Men of sensitivity are like good, much-played violins which vibrate at each touch of the bow.

—*Wassily Kandinsky*

The "sensitive homosexual" is a stereotype which, like all stereotypes, has some basis in fact. It's a chicken and egg question: which came first, our sensitivity or our gayness?

The gayness school of thought has it that our composition is inherently sensitive beyond the norm. It's our extra dash of *yin* (the receptive female element) added to the *yang* (the assertive masculine element) that does it. It is that—nothing to do with sexuality, really—that tends to stand out early. And it is that—still nothing to do with sexuality—that accounts for our over-representation in both the fine and decorative arts as well as in other fields that require emotional finesse.

The alternative school says our experience of being gay in the world is what sensitizes us. Because we are almost never encouraged to be who we truly are, each of us has to discern a truth and find a path by his own wits. Between this challenge and the experience of homophobia, it's no wonder we've got a reputation for being high-strung.

It doesn't matter which, if either, school we think we've gone to. Sensitivity is a gift. Whether it's ingrown, inflicted, or cultivated, the sensitive man plays with fullness, resonance, and range.

I'm a Stradivarius.

SPEAKING UP (PART I)

I made speech my birthright...talking back became for me a rite of initiation.
—Bell Hooks

It's incredible how much energy can go into deciding whether to speak up. Not to mention the Monday morning quarterbacking wherein we second-guess our calls.

There are at least four types of situations that put us on the line.

- Presumption of heterosexuality *(Are you married?)*
- Subtle homophobia *(She's a lesbian, but you really wouldn't know when you meet her.)*
- Obvious homophobia *(We don't rent to your kind.)*
- Political incorrectness *(I don't see why gay people should have special privileges.)*

The dilemma in every case is the same: what does it cost if I speak up vs. what does it cost if I don't?

This mental rite provides initiation for the birthright of speech. We're likely to zigzag through phases—avoidance, self-righteousness, loyalty to the cause, fatigue—finally getting to a place where we consciously choose our battles. Our voice may or may not change the world, but every time we speak we gain more of the dignity and power that comes with holding our own ground and refusing to be intimidated or silenced by anyone else.

I have the right to speak.

SPEAKING UP (PART II)

Speech is civilization itself. The word, even the most contradictious word, preserves contact—it is silence which isolates.
                                        —Thomas Mann, *The Magic Mountain*

Well, yes and no. The conversation with the woman next to me on the plane took a decidedly chilly turn when I explained I was "going to see my lover." Not that I cared about preserving contact. I said it as an experiment to see how she—and I—would react.

All words have power, but it seems words having to do with being gay take special vitamins. I like being deliberate (when I've got the energy). So far, I've got seven different words for *boyfriend* depending on who I'm talking to and what kind of reaction I'm up for:

- Lover: conveys romance, shakes up a conversation, or, if I'm feeling a little belligerent on the subject, makes it clear I *sleep* with him.
- Friend: a sort of halfway measure around certain aunts and uncles, the word I suggest my mother use, and my choice with people I'm not quite ready to come out to but whose suspicions I want to either reinforce or arouse.
- Love Interest: has a nice classical ring to it and makes it clear I've got a great life when I have no desire to bring gayness into the picture, e.g. in response to a question from the dentist while I'm lying there waiting for the Novocain to take.
- Thank-You-But-I've-Got-A-Place-To-Stay: for travel agents, clients' secretaries and when my personal life—or if I even have one—has no place in the conversation.
- Partner: ideal for making an impression of stability—on others or myself—like in discussing Bat Mitzvah arrangements with the Rabbi.
- Husband (or wife): when I'm feeling especially appreciative, outrageous, or bitchy.
- Boyfriend: the most casual and lighthearted. My favorite.

We've got tons of choices here. And while silence is isolating, sometimes engagement is worse. If we keep quiet altogether, civilization certainly won't get anywhere. But we needn't have Christ complexes, either.

I'm entitled to protect myself when I choose to.

BELLIES

And his hands closed on the naked body of the other man...They seemed to drive their white flesh deeper and deeper against each other, as if they would break into a oneness...So they wrestled swiftly, rapturously, intent and mindless at last...

—D. H. Lawrence, Women in Love

Laying naked against each other, our cocks press into one another's bellies, creating double sensation for us both. Arms and hands closed around the body of the other man, faces buried in necks, we push forward deeper and deeper with all our might, feeling softness and hardness in front of us and hardness next to us and hardness within us like we might burst against him.

We slide down, our hands loosened from behind him and pull his body toward us from the flanks. We move with our mouths, feel the change in texture of his skin. Our lips reach his belly, unique in its softness, with our fingers trailing across his nipples, or locked together behind the small of his back, or holding the cheeks of his ass, or one hand behind him and one flat against the juncture of belly and thigh as we bury our whole face next to and around and over his hard cock lying up against him.

We return again to press our whole bodies into each other, now wet and slick below, more intent, rapturously, and it is almost as if his pushing is matched by your opening until he feels like he has come inside of you and you inside of him and you push and push against him, more swiftly against the grip of his belly, and want to finish this way, mindless, in a hot rush against him.

...as if we would break into a oneness.

LOVE

When you love someone all your saved-up wishes start coming out.
—Elizabeth Bowen, The Death of the Heart

Love is complex. And yet the most clear and uncomplicated of feelings. It's full of paradoxes. You know—complex yet simple, easy yet hard, painful yet soothing. Because when love is present, *everything* starts coming out.

Love is devious. When first it rears its gorgeous head we see nothing but beauty. We may not have known we wished to meet a man whose feet we were compelled to kiss, but there he is, the very first morning after the very first night and what we want to do is worship at this shining altar. Already more wishes than we knew: to be inspired, captivated, humbled.

Love demands. In the eyes of love we eventually become more naked than we have ever been. Love reveals our deepest needs, our greatest fears, our hidden talents, our delicate aspirations. We wish to be protected, nurtured, to be assured a security that doesn't exist, to become more completely ourselves.

Love is enduring. Whether our time together is brief, our ending traumatic, or our lives permanently intertwined, that which is called out of us and illuminated by love is touched and changed forever.

I wish to know love.

REALITY

If you're never sad or angry, you don't understand what's happening.
—*Sam Keen, Inward Bound*

The provocations are many. The media carries the latest attack on fragile civil rights laws by the Radical Right, a lesbian mother is declared "unfit" and restricted to weekly visitation with her child, the Rainbow Curriculum's minor mention of gays and lesbians sparks a vitriolic school board battle which we lose.

Close to home is the latest assault on a gay man in a local park, a couple at the synagogue gay rights forum outraged at the prospect of being blessed on their 25th anniversary at the same Friday evening service a gay couple will be honored for their commitment, the tears in the eyes of a neighbor's eleven year-old son asking, "What can I do? They tease me and call me a girl!"

If we are never sad or angry we're simply out of touch. If we keep attuned, we could go nuts. The temptation is to just shut down.

We mustn't. Shut it off from time to time, yes, allow our anger and sadness to just be. We have to talk or write or sing or cry or walk or just sit and stare. The critical thing is to stay connected to reality. Because if we don't understand what's happening with this part of our lives, we're unlikely to know what's happening at all.

My reality includes sadness and anger.

TWO SPIRITS

To us a man is what nature, or his dreams, makes him. We accept him for what he wants to be....If nature puts a burden on a man by making him different, it also gives him a power.
> —Anonymous winkte, Sioux for male homosexual,
> Tinselled Bucks, Living the Spirit

The Gay American Indians History Project has compiled a list of 133 tribes known to have acknowledged gay, lesbian, or alternative gender members. In many tribes, such "two spirits" people were honored with special roles, however the great majority of these tribal traditions were lost or drowned by the tidal wave of genocide and forced assimilation brought about by European invaders.

It is incorrect to believe all tribes esteemed their two spirits, or *berdache* members, as they were called by French explorers. However, in many cases, the Native American respect for the whole of what nature presented was extended to the individuals who received in their puberty visions the gift of an exceptional nature.

M. Owlfeather writes, "They had a special and sacred place. They were the people who gave sacred names, cut down the Sun Dance pole, and foretold future events. It was considered good luck to have a berdache on a war party." What was different was assumed to be useful and often was venerated. It has also been reported the gay boys' teepees were "the best made and decorated in camp."

There is sorrow and rage when one studies what was lost in the decimation of native cultures. A growing number of contemporary gay Indians are retrieving their inheritance and reviving its traditional power.

Our difference is a gift to be honored.

GENDER

As far as I'm concerned, being any gender is a drag.
—Patti Smith

So much for the Total Woman. The pendulum is in major swing from a history of gender-based roles dating back to the 1950s (or the Stone Age—whichever came first). Granted there have always been those who crossed the great divide, but owing much to modern feminism, the potential for living beyond rigid expectations for both men and women is greater now than ever before.

For some, being the *wrong* gender is a drag. Solutions range from weekend changes of clothes to hormone treatments to full-time cross-dressing to surgically correcting nature's mix-up. The options are manifold: more than one man I know self-defines as a lesbian.

The best thing about how out-of-the-box all this has gotten is the great freedom it allows. I wouldn't quite put it like Patti does, as far as I'm concerned...

Being any gender is a joy.

LIES

Anthropologists from the early 20th century reported that homosexuality in Bali was confined to prostitutes but never explained who used the prostitutes.

—*International Gay and Lesbian Archives*

There are two ways to lie. One is to tell a falsehood. The other is to withhold the truth. Although the "out and out lie" is generally classified a more grievous ethical violation, either type pulls the rug out from anyone trying to get a serious grip on themselves, on a relationship, or on life in general.

Gay men know a lot about lies. Others' and our own. Some of us sensed early on that the picture was heavily retouched and we have all been shaken by the magnitude of what was brushed out. Unfortunately it isn't just a matter of neglecting to note who used the Balinese prostitutes. It is also the depiction of homosexuality as child abuse, mental illness, and the work of the devil himself.

Being intelligent boys, we learned to lie in order to protect ourselves. As grown men, deception is self-defeating. We do confront situations in which we painfully find our best choice is to doctor the facts. But to ourselves, certainly—and to anyone we care for or respect—we owe the truth, the whole truth, and nothing but the truth.

I want the real deal.

MONOGAMY

To know what you prefer, instead of humbly saying Amen to what the world tells you you ought to prefer, is to have kept your soul alive.
—*Robert Louis Stevenson*

There was a time in the gay world when monogamy was laughable. Someone had to be kidding. Even though we knew of couples who were exclusively devoted to one another, most gay men had internalized an image of ourselves as permanently excluded from the joys of marriage, or, conversely, lucky enough to forever enjoy the life of colts let out of a barn.

Since AIDS made coupling more socially acceptable—and our notions of what's available to us in general underwent drastic improvement—the thorny issue of monogamy is front and center for many.

The conventional world says we ought to prefer it. Maybe, but what exactly is it? Some say it's primary commitment with plenty of room to play around. Some pluralize it—primary commit*ments*—and maintain the integrity of more than one at a time. Some allow outside flirting, an occasional kiss, and even more. Some practice it serially. Some reject it absolutely. Some find restricted but perfect happiness only to be anguished when a perfect stranger appears and sets their soul to aching in a way that should not be denied.

We are people who have learned to honor their preferences. There is nothing honorable in saying Amen to a monogamous bind. There is everything honorable in making commitments based on our own truth.

I commit to keeping my soul alive.

DANCING

If I can't dance, I don't want your revolution.
—Attributed to Emma Goldman

We squeeze out to the middle of the crowded floor under black lights and the latest laser effects. The Relentless Beat makes more sense now that the Absolut & Tonic has taken effect. My friend and I dance. He incorporates some new moves into his own style. Looser than a year ago. Nice. I dance *with* him a bit, making air contact next to his body. He smiles, likes the interaction. I'm in the mood, so I unbutton my shirt, let The Beat drop lower into my body, and look around.

Black drag queen with outrageous tits, bare midriff, and leather mini-skirt dancing very nasty with white construction worker type. Shirt and sweater guys with little sense of rhythm working at it seriously. More straight couples on the floor, clearly here to enjoy our revolution. A clutch of young pretty boys, blasé with beer bottle in hand. I'm bumped into and caressed on the shoulder by way of apology.

Better music now and the pace picks up. I return my attention to Karl. He's sprung a sweat. The Beat has moved into my whole body. Head flung back, arms open, men flashing hot white all around, for at least one freeing instant, all I do is dance.

We've got the hottest scene going.

DETERMINATION

There is in this world no such force as the force of a man determined to rise. The human soul cannot be permanently chained.

—W.E.B. Du Bois

Bursting out with pent-up rage on New York's Christopher Street, the gay liberation movement has come further since the Stonewall Riots of 1969 than almost anyone could have imagined.

Indeed what broke out of its chains was the human soul. "No more," cried the soul, "No more will I endure these humiliations in silence. Today I am free. Today I begin to tell a new story." It has proven an inspiring one. From a violent flashpoint to a radical national movement to the best party in town to a cultural explosion to a network of caring and advocacy for the sick to a political force that helps elect presidents.

It is done moment by moment, man by man. In our own determination, each of us commands the power of entire movements yet unborn. When it is the force of the soul that breaks free, watch out.

I can move mountains.

INTEGRITY

Who told you that you were permitted to settle in? Who told you that this or that would last forever? Did no one ever tell you that you will never feel at home in the world?

—*Stanislaw Baranczak*

Among the highest compliments one can earn is to be known as a man of integrity. It implies many things: the public and private selves are consistent; one cannot be bought at any price; principles are balanced with concern for people; suffering, loss, misunderstanding, and isolation are all prices one will pay to stand by a conviction.

Decisions made with integrity demand the sacrifice of comfort. Settling in becomes rather silly—it gets just that much harder to move to the next place. Integrity searches for grounding in the present and a positive vision of the future. What is true now? What will be best tomorrow? Integrity knows that movement and change mean giving up attachments, that improbable things last, that we are guests of life, not the host.

Yet integrity gives us a home. It is not a home in the world, but a home inside ourselves where the breadth of who we are— and the depth of what we can understand—is continuously sought. It is our base camp from where we move, and observe, and attempt to act wisely in the world.

Doing what's right isn't easy.

LOVE AND RACE

Trust me, I'm here to love you,
not to hurt you.
to relieve your fears,
not to put chains on you.
Make love to me, as you once did,
a long time ago, by the oasis,
as the sun set
our black bodies glistened in the moonlight.

—*Sugar Bear, Oasis, Men of Color*

"Momma, I've got something to tell you."

"Yes, honey?"

"I want to bring someone home for the holidays, someone very special to me."

"Well, that's wonderful, baby! There's always room and you know I've hoped for a long time you'd find someone."

"There's something more. I've kept this from you a long time. I just didn't know how to tell you. Momma...*damn* this is hard to say...Momma...he's white..."

Love and race is a heavily loaded subject. At some time, at some oasis, men within every racial and ethnic group have loved each other. But at few points anywhere have elders of different races approved of mating outside the tribe.

For most of us, color counts a lot. Some actively seek the other: the added allure of difference, the high contrast of our bodies against each other, something in us that wants to fly in the face of the norm. Some, on the other hand, are separatist; some racist. Still others mix easily but prefer the ease of our own kind and there's an eclectic lot who simply can't predict where they'll end up next.

It doesn't take a man of a different race to put chains on us. Anyone can do that. And it's not just men of our own race who are trustworthy. No matter what color he is, if he's decent and good it'll go a long way toward easing momma's fears.

I'm here to love you, not to hurt

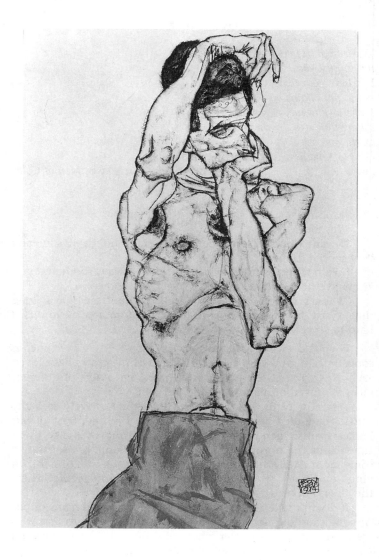

September

THE BOYS IN THE BAND

It's like watching an accident on the highway. You can't look at it and you can't look away.

—Matt Crowley, The Boys in the Band

Should the day come when you're in a serious self-hating mood and just can't seem to come up with enough bad thoughts about being gay or how gay men treat each other or enough negativity about life in general, then make a beeline for your local video store, check out "The Boys in the Band," and settle in for a look at the wreckage up close.

I saw this movie in 1971. I just saw it again...at least as much of it as I could stand to watch. It's well-written, well-acted, has some wickedly funny lines, and even a brief rear end nude shot of one of the better bods. This I could look at.

I had to shut it off, though. I got too sick to my stomach witnessing the sweeping damage the world had done to these characters, the birthday party turned hate fest, the consistent equation of gayness with shallowness, sadism, and masochism. I can't remember my exact reaction at age 18, but I have to believe some part of me went running hysterical into the night screaming for an ambulance.

This was a breakthrough film. It had a lot to do with making homosexuality a legitimate topic of conversation. At this point in time, it's an invaluable reminder of what we've survived, a harsh spotlight on the carnage, an experience comparable to the driver's training films of broken and burning bodies that were meant to horrify us into steering clear of such danger every single day of our lives.

It's amazing what we've had to overcome.

GAYDAR

The pilot emerged from the cockpit. As Michael disembarked, the ancient, unwritten but unmistakable eye signal passed between the two men.
"Welcome home," said the pilot.
"Really!" said Michael.

—Armistead Maupin, More Tales of the City

It rhymes with radar and we've got it for each other. Sometimes it's obvious from a mile away. Sometimes that extra millisecond of eye contact capped by a barely observable flex of the eyebrow gives us a surprise right up close.

Its benefit is directly opposite to its electronic namesake. We don't use it to search and destroy. Nor do we track each other to make sure we don't collide. It's an invitation to pursue things further: a conversation with verbal cues leading to an exchange of phone numbers; a preview in the shower at the gym becomes prelude to an X-rated afternoon.

It's also more than a constant state of automated cruise control. Unless we live in a gay ghetto, we spend most of our time outnumbered at least ten to one. Even in affirming environments, we are likely to feel isolated. The "sign" provides connection and, even if momentarily, gives us a sense of safety and being at home that other kinds of friendliness simply do not.

There are confusions, of course. Misreadings, undercover cops, UFOs, sorting out the friendship frequency from salutations signaling sex. We always have the option of shutting the system down. After all, being an air traffic controller is an extremely stressful job.

I'm on the right wavelength.

EFFORT

Conquest is not heroic. What's heroic is to make love last.
—Gérard Dépardieu on being married for 23 years

There is absolutely more drama, more suspense, more "...then *he* said...so I said...and then I just reached down and started unbuckling his belt and the *look* in his eyes, but he didn't do a *thing* to stop me and *then...*" in last night's conquest than in last week's brief debate on whether or not a Black & Decker Heavy Duty Dustbuster is really an appropriate Christmas gift between boyfriends.

It takes boldness, self-confidence, and a certain amount of cunning to win a lover. It takes a great deal more to keep one.

We have to learn him...no easy task. How does this man want to be loved? Birthdays and anniversaries have never been our forte, but they mean the world to him. We wanted to move in two years ago. He still thinks distance is a good idea. I want diamonds. He wants a Dustbuster.

Then there's the really tricky stuff: how to be with him when he's depressed; how to always encourage each other to grow; how not to panic if things get painful, or confusing, or dull.

The efforts of 23 years aren't necessarily spellbinding, though a long and successful love affair requires many heroic qualities: generosity of spirit, going beyond limits, coming through with the grit and commitment to make things last.

If it's love, it's worth the effort.

COMING OUT TO OUR CHILDREN

Mommy says Daddy and Frank are gay. At first I didn't know what that meant. So she explained it. Being gay is just one more kind of love.
—*Michael Willhoite, Daddy's Roommate*

If, when, and how we come out to our children provides a crystal-clear reflection of our own understanding and issues as a gay man.

Whether they are five or fifty our presence in our children's lives is like bedrock. If they reject us, it would be devastating for us both. But how much power to give the gay issue? If our bond is solid, then it's just one more kind of love. If we are sure of ourselves as gay men, then we will show them a good and right thing.

It's simple when they are very young. Gay, shmay, it couldn't matter less: *Daddy, can we play catch now?* More complex as they grow older and homophobia enters the picture, but *our* degree of comfort is still the major cue. Teenage years are likely to bring embarrassment and anger no matter how wonderful we've been. And the older they get the more honest we'd better be prepared to be.

Once we come out they'll need time, perhaps a lot, to fully understand and accept, but unless we've raised religious fanatics or deeply insecure kids, they're more likely to be incensed by deception than truth: didn't we trust them (do we trust ourselves?) to love us as we are?

My children deserve the very best: my honesty.

INHIBITIONS

One more drink and I'll be under the host.
—*Dorothy Parker*

God, it's nice to let go! Everyday life is just Inhibition City. We have to keep ourselves from punching jerks on the job, staring at hunks on the subway, and from sliding under the host— all quite practical constraints lest we wind up fired, slashed, or the talk of the town.

Prior to AIDS, many of us prided ourselves on a complete overturning of the puritanical outlook and claimed promiscuity as a political statement. *Down with the repressive, heterosexist patriarchy!* Today we have to be a lot more careful about mixing politics with poppers.

It does take some trial and error to learn the difference between which passions to inhibit and which inhibitions to get past. There's no need to give in to the forces of "if it feels good, *don't* do it." Within safe boundaries, we can reach for a truly uninhibited place, a place where our bodies speak to us their instincts and passions, where our pleasures run deep and wild with love, where we know one another with abandon.

I go all the way.

SAFE SEX

For me the act is beautiful. But afterward, I will replay it and replay it and I'll wonder, "Was I safe? Do I have a disease? Do I have AIDS?"
—Afzal S.

They're fairly anti-erotic, those little safe sex thoughts that creep in while we're busy tasting his sweat. "Shit, I wonder if that shaving cut is completely closed...He said he was tested last April, let's see, that's four months, so if he's had other lovers since May...Now what did that article say again about pre-seminal fluid?"

Okay, so it's basically a drag and last week there was this weird condom that was supposed to be lubricated, but somehow when it rolled on there was this horrible suction feeling and by the time we got it off with a scissors his penis felt like it had been run over by a vacuum cleaner and it really ruined a hot scene.

And yes, our bodies (which are sometimes loosely connected to our minds) have different ideas and something just takes over and we're in the back room, or in a dark car, or pressed against the mattress by his hot hard weight and this is so close to what we've fantasized and our blood is pounding and the sense is just go ahead and do it, it couldn't be that dangerous, I want it so much, Oh, he's doing it, *he's doing it...*

The acts are beautiful. The terror is not. It takes a cool head and a firm resolve (firmer than anything else) to figure out the boundaries and stick to them. The safe stuff leaves us feeling a little unsatisfied, a little cheated, but when we replay it and replay it, *Was I safe?* what answer do we really want?

I coldly calculate the cost.

FORGIVENESS

My very earliest memories are of being tortured and tormented about feeling acutely different and knowing that something was really out of whack, that I wasn't seeing anyone in my world that looked like me or thought like me. Waves of emotion pass over me whenever I come back to the Midwest. For a long long time I didn't come home because it was too painful.

—Michael Callen

Each and every insult stands out in perfect detail: where we were, who said and did what, vivid hateful words. There may be a blur: shadow figures spit in our face, chase us with stickbats, choruses chant *faggot, faggot,* laughter trails around a dark corner and leaves us alone, discarded, hurting. Something is horribly out of whack and there is *nowhere* to turn.

Coming home to these places takes a long long time. We need to go back, but let us be very careful about who we need to forgive. There are some who apologize. Parents, teachers, brothers, friends who say, "I didn't realize, I didn't understand, I am horrified now, I was cruel or allowed others to be. I hope you can forgive me, I am sorry." These people we must forgive or we end up men with blocks of ice where our hearts are supposed to be.

The rest is not about forgiveness. It's about history; stark, impersonal, meaningful. It comes back to us in the terror dream state where we hold the key to unlock the door and run from the intruder with the knife, but are paralyzed and awake screaming. How not to have terror in our lives? How to bleed out the bitterness it leaves inside us?

Lacking apologies, knowing it's wrong to forget, still we must heal. Forgiveness then can be for ourselves. I can say to the me of yesterdays, the child, the younger man: *What happened was painful and unjust and terribly wrong. There was nothing I could do. I am so sorry for what you suffered. It's over. I am here to protect you now.*

I forgive myself. I forgive those I can.
I give no power to the rest.

SUFFERING

To become a deeper man is the privilege of those who have suffered.
—*Oscar Wilde*

It would be nice if there was a way around it. There isn't. Which is not to diminish the pain of suffering or pass it off as something we should be glad to have. Suffering is a part of life. And while it is appalling to witness on the evening news and wretched in whatever form it enters our own lives, we will always learn, always become deeper if we let it sink in and have its way with us.

No martyrs or masochists, please. If you choose it or like it you're missing the point. Physical suffering is in a category of its own. It's a real stretch to accept this as any sort of good thing, except it makes you real grateful when it's gone. Emotional suffering is different. There is something gripping in it, a voice that begs us sit up and take note.

If we pay close attention, the voice teaches us, sometimes multiplies into a choir chanting to us, falls silent and bids us contend with emptiness. We understand that suffering is universal, all human beings hurt the same. We learn compassion. We remember stories—Jacob wrestling with the angel of God, Jesus alone in the desert, the coyote testing the strength and powers of a brave—and we are there.

Our hearts grow when we inch past anger, blame, and fear and hold close to the flame, to the strange and beautiful and awful teacher that suffering is.

It is a privilege to grow deeper.

COMPASSION

Please call me by my true names so I can wake up; so the door of my heart can be left open: the door of compassion.

—*Thitch Naht Hanh*

My name is fear. I don't sleep. My instincts to defend are sharp and built in. I will take as much power as I am given. I can be taught to see danger where none exists and react as if my very life is threatened. I am ruthlessly misused by tribes and nations and all others who wish to protect their desperate squatter rights to wealth, conformity, family, and God. I stand squarely in front of the heart's door and know its opening is my destruction.

My name is care. I seek to alleviate pain. I am naturally awake in some, aroused by duty in others. I am sometimes confused with selfishness, even arrogance, when I care for myself. My natural companion is courage. I must be stopped by force, but I fight with persistence, not violence. I sit with the dying. I soothe the skin of those in misery. I rest in the doorway of the heart. My tears well up as a mighty stream, cleanse as the waters recede.

My name is love. I bundle suffering in my arms. I understand what others feel. I am often recognized by the name compassion. I reach out in the dark, stand steadfast though afraid, and know the true meaning of names for me the world scorns. I live deep inside the heart. Men suffer much and find boundless comfort who find their way to me.

Please call me by my true names.

JOY

...this insistent reality which comes back at me, wells up from inside, frightens me by its nearness, shocks me by its inclusiveness because it's in the things I love, the lustiness and vigor and lavish things, and abandon—which before I had put aside as outside, not God.

—Joanna Field, A Life of One's Own

There is a bar in Minneapolis called the Gay 90's (makes things easy for out-of-towners). It's actually eight bars in one and makes for a nice little romp through gay nightlife. You enter into a giant Wild West Saloon—mirrors, red velvet, lottsa wood—which is dominated by two go-go boys with marginal talent and maximum pecs who dance on the bar and work the room in a sort of disinterested way and occasionally sit on the faces of men in booths who then put folded up bills into the dancers' Caribbean Surf briefs that you're sure you saw marked down in International Male.

From there is the small Black dance floor, the pick-up bar, the leather bar, the disco (black lights, laser, video, multiracial), a passage through pinball alley then upstairs to the billiards bar, the piano bar (very Rainbow Room, local stars sit in after hours), the country western bar, and the Casablanca Show Lounge open Friday through Sunday and featuring Miss City of the Lakes as Minnehaha costumed by Liberace along with a parade of some greater and lesser drag queens lip-synching their hearts out to everything from Ethel Merman to Madonna.

The place is filled to overflowing with lust, vigor, and lavish things: all things I love. Real life happens there. Heartbreak, hope, desperation. Stars are born, flame, and fade. I am shocked by its inclusiveness and something does well up inside, a strange joy, unsanitized and real, where nothing is put aside.

God goes to the bars.

SOCIAL CHANGE

Change does not roll in on the wheels of inevitability, but comes through continuous struggle. And so we must straighten our backs and work for freedom. A man can't ride you unless your back is bent.
—*Martin Luther King, Jr.*

The changes wrought in the last decades by gay and lesbian activists may appear to have been inevitable. They were not. Nothing would have happened without the great struggle and intense energies brought to bear against a formidable status quo. The battle is far from over.

Our agenda is ambitious: full equality everywhere, a radical social transformation that eradicates homophobia and replaces it with a truly welcoming spirit toward all. There are countless ways to join in this work, every one of them important, every one requiring a straightening of the spine in the face of difficulty.

We confront ignorance. Apathy. The wistful desire for things to just stay as they are. When we engage in the work of change, we encounter odious laws, actions, and attitudes. We must be armored against ruthless enemies—and sometimes against people we thought our allies. We must be living in the new world inside, have rejected the power of any outside authority to determine the rightness of our souls.

This is the struggle less spoken of. What it takes to enter the belly of the beast—wherever hatred or brutishness reside—and stare it down. To keep it outside, not me, not a burden I will carry.

I stand upright, straight, and strong.

COCKS

There's a strange frenzy in my head, of birds flying, each particle circulating on its own. Is the one I love everywhere?

—*Rumi*

It is completely, profoundly, magnetically mysterious and I have no desire whatever of a solution, only more of it. More of the sight of it, more of the heat of it, more of its absolutely right weight in my hand, on my lips, pushing its way into me from behind.

There is a strange frenzy in my head as a short question and answer session plays out each time you are naked, your cock ready for me, and I ask, "May I? Is this true?" and you say, or your hand on my head and pulling me by the hair down on you says, "Yes. Right now. Have what you want," and my mouth closes over you, your so beautiful, so right tasting smelling feeling dick being where I want it, closer to the mystery, deeper inside me; I am so hard and beginning to drip myself, I need this, worship this, am hungry and want everything.

I do this with my eyes open, my whole body shuddering for pleasure, then up for air. Please, more clues, hover above me, drag the weight of your balls and cock across my neck, my face, my chest. Turn me over. I want your power surrounding and inside of me in the way that makes my sight dissolve into shiny particles and I am all feeling, flying, understanding birds, and animals, and water.

Oh, baby, why is this so right? Why is my dick pressed to yours so wet and hot? Why when you come is it like warm spring rain?

I want you everywhere.

THERAPY

When the mind is ready, a teacher appears.
—Zen saying

I am a little suspicious of anyone who has never been in therapy. A few prove to be rare healthy specimens who managed to grow up intact, others are true self-healers, and there is the occasional Mad Hatter who would prove a loss to us all should he change one bit. These are the exceptions. The question for the rest of us is, what are we doing with our pain?

"Wait a minute," you may protest, "Who said anything about *pain*?" And that's exactly the problem. No one did. *Expectation:* everyone is fine. *Reality:* hardly anyone is. *Expectation:* normal, competent people figure it out for themselves. *Reality:* real men get help. *Expectation:* confusion, anxiety, cold sweats, and boyfriends who fuck with our minds are just normal parts of life. *Reality:* things that don't get better get worse.

What we're likely to do with most of our pain most of the time is suppress it, deny it, or figure we deserve it. Learning a different way—at any point in time—starts with the desire for things to change. Our palms may sweat during that call to make an appointment. *(Get a referral from someone you trust.)* It's scary stuff. In the course of good therapy, we may learn truths that shake our foundation, that cause a house of cards inside us to collapse. It's also very good stuff. We can get a real shot at the better life we're ready to have.

The right teacher helps me learn from myself.

SIMPLICITY

We never reflect how pleasant it is to ask for nothing.
—Seneca

This sounds suspiciously like something someone would say who already has everything. We can just picture him. He looks great in muscle shirts, expensive suits, or sequins, has just the relationship(s) he wants, lives in a perfect rent-controlled loft, has a summer place overlooking the ocean, earns tons of money in a great job even through he ran away to Belize instead of finishing college, has all his hair, and he's really close with his brother who works for the airlines.

Oh, we could go on and on, painting the composite picture of the perfect life, but I'm afraid it just gets depressing. Which is precisely the point.

Here's a little exercise. (If you like it, you can do it every day.) Exempt yourself if you lack basics—decent food, clothing, and shelter. Exempt yourself if you are struggling with illness. Now, exemptions aside, try this: you are where you are right now. Take a deep breath. Take in your surroundings. Close your eyes and ask for nothing.

There is so much in each moment.

QUEENS

Sensual, barbed, informative, revolting, political—Fairy speech is a living art. They called each other the names of particular movie stars—Miss Garbo, Miss Horne, Miss Taylor, Miss Davis, or sometimes just: Miss Thing. Their usual character of speech is a spewing of a running stream of advice, predictions, protection, commentary, gossip, "truth saying." Queens can be found holding court wherever court may be…
—Judy Grahn, Another Mother Tongue

At face value, it's all great fun: the repartee, highbrow put-downs, mock shock at an unending string of double meanings…"Oh come, *come*…" "Why, *Priscilla*, aren't we in a *hurry*…" and dish from here to eternity. It's a tight insider thing. (Umm, sounds good.) Sharpen your wits, stick out your tits, and honey, you is the biggest queen outside Buckingham Palace.

Cut deeper and you have to wonder. Hilarity as a steady diet ceases to be filling. Where's the beef? Miss Thing acts out a heightened sense of self-importance: are high voltage verbal trip wires really in her best interest? This is about distancing, keeping each other at bay. When court adjourns and we've applied our Noxema, do we actually fall asleep at night dreaming of better hair days?

Not enough of us are genuinely secure in our royalty and too many of us pretend to the throne. We build fabulous castle walls and are frightened to invite people inside. It's a shame. Our exuberance is a joy to behold. Kitchen Queens, Opera Queens, Dairy Queens…the underlying insecurity runs deep, but so does the creativity and strength. Precious few of us knew how to believe in the majesty of our being, but all of us turned out to be Queens.

Just call me Your Grace.

FANTASY

Imagination is the mad boarder.
—*Nicolas Malebranche, Recherche de la vérité*

Who knows where they come from, these transient residents of the garrets and cellars of the mind. Each must be welcomed, made to feel at home. Each barters his rent, pays by disturbing or exciting us, adds a fragment to the life we dream.

Some we assign a permanent space, our private erotic library. How many times have we jacked off to the Dance Floor Fantasy, coming simultaneously with the hot slim blond in our face and the hairy muscleman behind, dark bodies in mist all around, they got us so drunk, we wanted to be stripped while the music turned slow, to be forced and watched. A sweeter mood, The Beach Fantasy, he comes walking at the edge of the water at sunset, the sand still radiates warmth, everyone else has packed and left...

Many more rooms in the library, scenes from past lives, an array of visitors at the door. The open mind invites its future. The maddest boarder may yet appear, one who has collected fragments over time, connected them, and made them flesh and blood. We will know him, recognize him with all of ourselves, helpless in pleasure, heart soaring, tears streaming down our face.

I dream my life.

DOUBLE LIVES

The important thing is not to believe your own propaganda.
—Adlai Stevenson

<u>Ministry of Propaganda</u>. File: *What they don't know can't hurt them.* Forty-one-year-old male is happily married, has two sons, both athletically inclined. Subject is successful in business which necessitates frequent overnight trips. Intensity of work and need for "client socializing" demands late hours. Telephones wife and sons daily, dutiful in all ways, brings gifts. Although exhausted and distracted much of time, has sex with spouse every second week, keeps in shape at gym, and often cheers boys at weekend games. Wife is busy with child-rearing, managing home, volunteer work. Leads balanced and rewarding life. Wife's recurring and increasingly violent migraine headaches are a mystery to everyone.

* * *

Some of the glossed truths are obvious. Some not so. His story is quite believable. We've probably met him. It's an illusion that he—or we—really get away with this sort of thing. The pressure always builds. There is always a cost. Someone is always suffering.

Most aspects of our own double lives don't qualify as made-for-TV-movies. A little failure to come out here. A little withholding of truth there. The biggest farce is the underlying one: that there is such a thing as a double life. It's a lose-lose scenario. We lose, the people we cheat on—in big or small ways—lose, too. The way out isn't easy. Ditching the propaganda is a decent place to start.

I deserve a single, rich, honest life.

POSSESSION

We made a vow to each other that he could own me, my mind and everything I knew, and my body, and I could own him and all he knew and all his body, and that we would give each other ourselves, so that we possessed each other as property, to do everything we wanted to, sexually or intellectually, and in a sense explore each other until we reached the mystical "X" together, emerging two merged souls.

—Allen Ginsberg, Gay Sunshine Journal

Not the stuff of first dates. And an extremely unpopular concept—for good reason—in feminist circles. The idea of possessing another person conjures repugnant caveman images of female bounty dragged off to dark places where ownership is brutal and absolute. More contemporary renditions hold no more appeal.

Here, as in so many things, historic notions need not apply. Between equals—whether men or women—the power dynamics can be another story altogether. Domination and control are clearly destructive, but what we're talking here is free exchange. Two *self-possessed* individuals, deeply rooted in who they are, offering themselves to one another lock, stock, and barrel.

The trust factor is enormous. I'll show you mine if you show me yours. Open exchange. Complete revelation. Participation in an ownership agreement that assumes one bottom-line agreement: we emerge enriched souls.

**At the right time, with the right man,
I can give myself completely.**

AGING

Youth, large, lusty, loving—Youth, full of grace, force, fascination. Do you know that Old Age may come after you, with equal grace, force, fascination?
        —*Walt Whitman, Youth, Day, Old Age, and Night*

Wet behind the ears, we strike out into the world. As young men, we lack sophistication and our force generally outweighs our grace (Oh, oh...how'm I going to get out of *this* one??). We *are* fascinated—with new sights, with sex, with ourselves, with treasure troves of music and art, with a gaudy array of *experience*.

Youth, it is said, is wasted on the young. How much more we would savor that winter in the Ventura beach house with our quieter set of tastes. What scenes we would recast knowing all we know now; with what grace reenact them.

The life truly lived ferments one's passions. Naive force grows to wisdom. Our fascinations run deeper and yield more. Aging is ripening: the full-bodied payoff beyond the random samplings of youth.

I welcome the gifts of my age.

COMPARISONS

Be gentle with yourself...and patient. I've learned to look more at my progress over time rather than measuring myself against some ideal standard. How many times did Rosa Parks give up her seat on the bus before finally saying no and setting ablaze the civil rights struggle?
—*Richard McLellan, B & G Magazine*

It's easy to feel like we've failed if we can't count ourselves the best little gay boy in the world. Comparisons to an ideal produce a long list of shortcomings: a non-rippling abdomen, not out enough, a few sexual inhibitions; inability to attract and retain perfect boyfriend(s), inability to get rid of extremely imperfect boyfriend(s); lack of interest in memorizing lines from *Whatever Happened to Baby Jane*; nagging sense of superiority toward at least one segment of the gay "subculture"; nagging sense of inferiority in regard to (choose one) a) Denzel Washington, b) Rod and Bob Jackson-Paris, c) Jeff Stryker; failure to chain oneself to the doors of judges' chambers who refuse custody of children to entirely fit lesbian mothers.

It's enough to keep the covers over our heads for weeks! And clearly a mistake to go down this path. Comparisons dead-end quickly. Each of us has our own hard-won victories. Not that it's wrong to have ideals, goals, and heroes: we need them to stretch beyond our comfort zone. But progress is ultimately made by patience, persistence, and taking the necessary next step. As Rosa Parks tells it, she wasn't thinking about a civil rights movement, she'd just had a really hard day and needed to sit down.

Gently, patiently, I take my own next step.

WORKING OUT

My dear, you used to be quite a dish; now you're quite a tureen.
—Somerset Maugham to his lover, Alan Searle

Given the range of appetites, this could be a case of more being merrier. So let's get past the boy beautiful syndrome right off and muscle in on the real fun. Bodily perfection is unquestionably a joy, but if all we're focused on is the product, we miss out on the pleasure of the process.

And a pleasure it is, whether class at the barre, weights at the gym, wheelchair basketball, or a brisk walk around the block. It always takes a little time to get in the groove, for the blood to really start moving, and then in almost every session there is at least one perfect moment, a blend of pain and effort, breathing and concentration, a moment we experience our bodies as complex and perfect.

The Surgeon General recommends this, of course. It is so extremely good for us, so healthy, so wholesome. Personally, I'm in it for the endorphin rush and yes, even though I am, shall we say, beyond my salad days, I'm far from ready to give up being saucy. And one more thing. All the other dishes on the table. Some days at the gym are a regular feast.

Please pass the soup.

PSYCHOLOGICAL WARFARE

Those whom we love we can hate; to others we are indifferent.
—Henry David Thoreau

I remember a particularly no-holds-barred battle with my wife about three years into our marriage. I don't recall what point she was trying to make, but I remember the extent of my resistance and the ruthless tactics I employed.

I was determined to outflank her, disarm her, destroy the morale of her troops. Whatever she said, I mocked: the reasoning, the motives, the style of delivery. I thought she would surrender, admit that my stunning maneuvers had shown her the folly of trying to hold even an inch of ground. I wanted her begging for mercy.

She didn't. She got very quiet and said, *"What is wrong?* Why are you trying to hurt me?" I couldn't tell her the real answer. Which was in that moment I hated her. I hated her for having insights I didn't. I hated her for calling into question my ability to be intimate. I hated her for exposing my defenses. I hated her for having a better idea of what she wanted in a relationship than I did. All reasons I loved her.

It isn't kind, what we sometimes do to our lovers. It's messy and awful and part of most intense relationships. Outright abuse is never acceptable, but some amount of warfare is to be expected. To get anywhere, we also have to make peace offerings, own up to our issues, say we're sorry, and tend the wounds. Indifference, ultimately, is the certain crushing blow.

As often as we can, let's call a truce.

MASCULINITY

As soon as you trust yourself you will know how to live.
—*Goethe*

About a year after I came out, a straight friend and I were dressing in the locker room at the club and he said, "There's something different about you...something more male...more masculine." Now granted, we were heavy into this testosterone number and I tend to reserve my queenier behavior for gayer company, but even so, he was right, and it's ironic because this change in me is a direct result of coming to know myself as a gay man.

Masculinity is about power, turf, and potency—things the world has always said it's about—but it doesn't come from the symbols and places the world advertises. It comes from inside, from trusting ourselves.

Power is the ability to make things happen, but so what if they're not the things we really love. Right up close—in the tender spots macho guys pretend they don't have—I love a man. And the more I open myself to him—my mouth, my heart, my ass—the more powerful I become.

Turf is our territory, where we live. It's not houses or land, it's our selves. Coming through what coming out demands—and healing ourselves—makes us lord of our castle. Neither society, religion, family, nor our lovers can cast their shadow inside unless we let them. A little butch? You bet.

Potency. What else if not knowing how to live? This is the ultimate measure of men—that we seed our own lives, that we find our destiny and live it, full force, drawing from the enormous range and depth that nature planted within us.

I am learning to trust myself.

FLANNEL SHIRTS

I will thank you because I am marvelously made; your works are wonderful and I know it well.

—Psalms 139:14

In the storehouse of memory, sense memory from the time we were boys, are imprints of tackle football, our hands slipping down sapling bodies; tropical pools where we dove for fast fish; harsh city hours where pleasures were only imagined; butter popcorn and horror movies on a mattress in the basement with Kevin, Brad, Stephen, all boys with tough demeanors and soft flannel shirts.

We experienced ourselves and our days as sensuous and pleasing or difficult and confused or unbelievably hellish. We wanted simple things we understood and complex things we had no way of understanding.

Today, on late afternoons of days growing shorter in the same cycles as they did then, we are older boys remembering the smell of burning leaves or first snow or salt spray or diesel exhaust and we lay next to another now older boy who wears wool or silk or flannel and we reach across his chest and unbutton a single button and slip a hand inside and know well the wonder of him and what we will do with our bodies and how marvelously we were always made.

I feel peaceful and complete.

VULNERABILITY

To be vulnerable is to be alive.
—Alexis de Veaux

We must have the trembling moments when we risk emotional bruises. Otherwise, there is only safety and then only something less than being alive. Vulnerability doesn't mean being wide open all the time to everything—only madmen live that way. It means being able to be deeply touched, by beauty as well as by pain.

The learning curve is long and demanding. Many of us have formidable walls inside. We built them to fend off insult and injury, to protect delicate hopes, to store our love and overwhelming grief for lost lovers and friends. Reclaiming life in the shadows of these walls can mean getting a whole lot more vulnerable—at least for a while—than is anywhere close to being comfortable. But it's worth it to push ourselves, perhaps worth more than anything else.

We emerge tentatively, not sure what all the choices mean, not sure how to be open and safe at the same time. We are alive to greater range, moved by our own experience and that of others, become vulnerable to bitter hurt and disappointment, learn how to protect ourselves at the core, become vulnerable to ecstasy and love.

I can live beyond the walls.

PARTIES

Society is no comfort
To one not sociable.
—Shakespeare, Cymbeline

It *is* a matter of how we feel about ourselves, isn't it? Making an appearance can be grand—when the weight is where it belongs, self-esteem high, a particularly good catch on our arm or awareness of what a particularly good catch we *ourselves* happen to be. It's terribly nerve-wracking. All that getting ready. Wondering if there'll be anything to talk about, anyone especially pleasant to talk *to,* if we'll have something worthwhile to offer, if we'll have to fend anyone off, if there'll be anyone we don't *want* to fend off. A last dash of *Eternity* or Patouli behind the ear, a final once-over in the mirror, and we're off.

It's hard to say which are the best parties, they fall in categories. Gatherings of old friends win for warmth, leaving with a live favor to unwrap extends the celebratory mood, and there is the rare evening of delicious food, delicious conversation, and at least a few delicious men that produces in us a euphoric sociability in which we ourselves and the entire supporting cast bask in the glow of humanity.

At least it seemed that way at the time. Or was it the champagne? We're not 100 percent sure, but didn't the gossip at one point get a little, shall we say, indiscreet? And speaking of indiscreet, maybe we shouldn't have spent quite so long in the bathroom with that foreign physics student. At least it wasn't dull. But then, dull would have been a little less challenging in the morning. Oh well, so it goes with parties. You never know quite what to expect.

When I feel lovely, I have a lovely time.

LATIN AMERICA

Outside, someone says, "That was a shot," but only when it is not repeated does he go to the spot where the noise came from. He enters the washroom on the run, fearing that what he suspects may prove true. And he calls to his fellow-soldiers to come and share his horror: "It's Evaristo!" he cries out, shouting like a madman. "He's shot himself in the bathroom."
—Luis Zapata, My Deep Dark Pain is Love, translated by E. A. Lacey

I don't think I want to move there. Latin America, that is. There are pockets of tolerance in Argentina, Chile, Mexico, Cuba in its better days, Brazil (Ah, Rio, gay Rio...), and elsewhere, but by and large the combination of a dominating Roman Catholic Church, a string of repressive governments, and a severely ingrained macho ethic proves lethal.

The plot of the short story cited above goes like this: boy meets boy, boy begins to understand his "deep dark pain is love," boy's soldier/soccer team pals start to suspect, boy is exposed, boy decks would-be lover in barroom brawl, boy shoots himself in the bathroom. There were other choices. He could have moved away, found gay friends, boasted of his conquests, and thereby kept his sense of manhood intact. Even if he did, though, the deep dark difficulty would always be there with drunken stupors and cocked pistols standard painkillers of choice.

An interesting flip side is the fate of drag queens. Unlike bound-up macho tops, the girls have a respected place alongside other "fallen women" who work red-light *zonas de toleráncia* and find acceptance, even respect, there. A final redeeming factor seems to be the land itself. Writers of the region express deep longing to recapture the lost magic of youth, a time when the wild nature of jungles, animals, and cliffs was intertwined with their own. And certainly, in barracks, in barrios, and in high pastures, they break through harsh training and rigid roles, and two by two, they succeed.

Love is not the source of the pain.

SERVING

Govinda bowed low. Incontrollable tears trickled down his old face. He was overwhelmed by a feeling of great love, of the most humble veneration. He bowed low, right down to the ground , in front of the man sitting there motionless, whose smile reminded him of everything that he had ever loved in his life, of everything that had ever been of value and holy in his life.

—Hermann Hesse, Siddhartha

The two old men meet again after many years' separation, Siddhartha an unassuming ferryman whose life is movement back and forth across a river in service to travelers. As boys, they set out together, sharing a quest for life's meaning. Siddhartha threw himself into the world, played many roles, and eventually found peace. Govinda held himself apart, believed the world an entrapment, and faces his old friend blighted in spirit.

Like these men, we go out into the world seekers. Many of us long for and find a man to travel with us. Often, we hold ourselves apart from him. We await assurances, must be convinced in a thousand ways over time that we are valued. We add them up, notches on the ego. We give back in kind, not wanting to be taken advantage of. This is how we have been taught. We measure our worth by what we get.

Yet there are moments his smile tells us of everything we have ever loved and in these moments we must know that he comes to us to teach. We learn, unlock something humble and real, when we are able to serve him. He is not easy—this is not meant to be easy—at times carrying him, catering to him, confronting him, playing many roles, washing his feet, licking his wounds. In our veneration we may be judged the fool, but our hearts will know what it is to serve what one loves and that, invisible and holy, will be enough.

Princes, servants, we bow to one another.

TERMINOLOGY

Fag, faggot, dyke, queer, lezzie, homo, fairy, mary, pansy, sissy, etc., are terms of abuse. If you don't want to insult, the words are gay, lesbian and homosexual.
—*Gay Activist Alliance and National Task Force, 1973*

How times have changed! Here it is 1994 and the local gay book store advertises its phone number as 379-MARY. What's going on?

For one thing, the melting pot idea is dying its well-deserved death and the former ingredients are renaming themselves more to our taste. Orientals have become Asian-Americans, most Hispanics have become Latinos, Blacks (who hold the record for most changes in the shortest time) have become African-Americans, and so on. Given our history of invisibility and the fact that all terms for us were used abusively (remember "admitted homosexual?"), us homophiles writing our own book of social etiquette was a landmark event.

That was then. This is now. We're here, we're queer, we're dykes on bikes. We wear t-shirts that say, "I can't even *think* straight." We do what our lover likes best and he marvels out loud, saying, "You are *such* a faggot." We are entering mainstream "Miss Sugar Beet" pageants as acknowledged cross-dressers and *winning* them. We are walking up to creeps who yell at us, grabbing them by the collar, and telling them if they don't like queers they should find another part of town.

If you don't want to insult us, you should probably still call us gay ("bachelor uncles" is kind of nice). But since our self-respect is now beyond question, we can enjoy every bit of being a fairy, sissy, homo, or queer...and all that that implies.

Term me unabashed.

UNFINISHED BUSINESS

While dressing today, I went to Barry's closet and, with a certain amount of relish, took a tie of his...Tying the knot, I knew how handsome he thought me in it—perhaps how handsome I looked to him now, from some cloud—and I wept.

—Stephen Greco

With death's finality framing the picture, it is clear what is finished and what is not. The fact that we never dealt with our father's abuse makes our tears bitter. Or leaves us with dry eyes altogether, unable to cry for him or ourselves. Worse are apologies we intended to make, but never did. Poignant and wrenching are the compliments unpaid, the "I love yous" not said, the worry if he knew, *really* knew, just how handsome we thought him in that tie.

Unfinished business falls into two categories: wrongs never righted, and worthy deeds left undone. Which may sound like the credo of King Arthur's Court, but chivalry isn't the point. Tying up loose ends is something we do for ourselves, for the freedom it affords, for our own peace of mind.

There's no reason to wait for death's knock at the door. We can open the cedar chest of yesterday's intentions right now. We can reach in and pull out what we have not yet fully worn: our bravery, remorse, passion, our wild-eyed notions. We can decide not to hesitate, not risk being too late. With a certain relish, perhaps with faces streaked by tears, we can decide now is the time to take greater hold of our own lives.

I've got important business to attend to.

—— October ——

LOVERS

...his heart was so full that his ribs heaved and ached on the left side and he couldn't speak at all but he was thinking this is love, this is love, this is love, this is my lover;
—Neil Bartlett, Three Wedding Ceremonies, Gay Short Fiction

A lover might stay just a night, be ours only stolen hours each year, or arrive for an expanse of time. There is a fierceness to it. It seems the world is opening up, we are traveling to another, far deeper place, our bodies go to instinct and our spirits rush to welcome this man, this wonder, this rarity.

A range of factors will dictate how long we can tolerate being pulled open, how much we will respond to this nearness that takes our breath. We have found one another over God knows what distance. Here, together, much is desired; everything is possible.

Pull closer, closer. Let my heart beat in this painful singing way. Let me remember and come back to this time and place with you, I am awash with your body, Oh, I dreamt true things, this is love, this is love, this is my lover.

This is exactly where I belong.

EMOTIONAL TERRORISM

When Nazism split husbands from wives, children from parents, when apartheid or slavery broke up familial bonds, it was clear that a particularly noxious form of repression was taking place. But the stigma attached to homosexuality begins with such a repression. It forbids, at a child's earliest stage of development, the possibility of the highest form of human happiness. It starts with emotional terror…
—Andrew Sullivan, The New Republic

The mind recoils. Was it really that severe? Nazis have names, faces, uniforms. Apartheid was an official policy of separation, brutal exploitation, minority control. White slavers are money-crazed creatures of centuries past.

Who do we cast in their roles in our own lives? Our parents? The nuns at school? The kids down the block? If such a monstrous crime was committed against us, where are the perpetrators? Where is the evidence?

Below the surface of the gay world are the clues. Call them alcoholism, drug addiction, sex addiction. Read about the grisly murders of men who invite death picking up damaged merchandise at after-hours sidewalk sales. Notice the man who likes to be fucked but who flinches when touched. Visit the S & M parlors where we act out our darkest needs. Observe a certain obsession with the superficial, a hypercritical eye for dress, body type, haircut. Note how viciously we attack each other's politics. Watch the male-male couple discreetly close the shades each and every night long before they go to bed.

Early in life we were marked, demeaned, cruelly pulled apart from each other. Getting close to the truth is nearly too much to bear. It's real. It happened. It's terrifying.

They have disappeared, vanished like masked terrorists into the backwaters and alleyways of our lives. We were their victims then. If we allow the past to terrorize us still, we are our own victims now.

The greatest human happiness is my birthright.

THE PINK TRIANGLE

And as You've given me an all-seeing eye, and an all-hearing ear, give me, as well, the strength to scourge, to caress, to uplift. And grant that these words be not empty phrases, but a credo for my life. Towards what am I aiming? Towards all that which is best in the world, and of which there is a spark within me.

—*Hannah Senesh*

The Pink Triangle was invented by the Nazis to mark homosexuals with an insignia that specifically identified our crime and positioned us near the bottom of the subhuman strata that determined who would live by torture and who would die by torture in Hitler's hell on earth.

This symbol attests to our presence, along with Jews, political dissidents, the handicapped, Jehovah's Witnesses, communists, and others—9 million in all—as victims of the Holocaust. There is no honor in having been victims. But there are many lessons. And there are obligations.

We aim for a world in which it is safe simply to *be.* All around us we see and hear those who would deprive us, us and other undesirables, of this basic right. Caring for our lives, for life, means confronting every force that diminishes even a shred of our humanity. The place to make a stand is not starved and broken at the gas chamber door. The place to honor the legacy of The Pink Triangle is wherever and whenever the faintest spark is under threat.

I am a protector of humanity.

FIGHTS

I don't go looking for trouble, but I've gotten in fights. I've used my fists to defend myself. You can't let some things go by. You have to stand up for yourself.

—*Craig W.*

I have to admit I was a little surprised to hear this from my hairdresser. He's a slight, pretty man—some Italians and Mandarin Chinese must have cross-fertilized somewhere on the family tree. There is a hint of urban tough that lurks beneath the Vogue Homme haircut, half-dozen earrings, and tales of perilous twenty-something romance. There's backbone, too. A girl who gets butch when it counts.

Craig says he doesn't go looking for trouble. I hope that also means he knows how to scram when trouble comes looking for him. Getting in the face of gutter-tongued punks makes sense and a swift knee to the crotch may be just the "it was him or me" tactic to disable a would-be basher. Let's be perfectly clear, though: there is murderous danger out there and if we sense even its slightest possibility, then walking with eyes straight ahead, crossing the street, or just screaming and running like hell are among the intelligent and self-protective choices at hand.

There's no earthly reason to take any shit. But neither does stepping into the line of fire earn medals for meritorious self-defense.

Don't fuck with me.

THE HEART

Gracious kindly soul,
who so sympathetically
stretched welcoming hands to love,
though my crude style
(and I recall it with sorrow)
may not succeed in honoring you
as my heart would wish,
which constantly forces me
to tell of your charming ways
and of what humility dwells in
your adorable and girlish body,
Still will I recount with that zeal
which love will inspire in me from the
*   third heaven.*

—Renaissance Italian Madrigal, Anonymous,
translated by H. Colin Slim

Sweet, excitable soul,
who so grandly
opened doors and windows to love,
your deep concern
(and I receive it with gladness)
is misplaced given striking success
as my heart bursts to tell,
which sings out so loud a song
and softly attunes me
to the wary shyness within
your spiced and sculpted body,
Only attend to my soft cries
which unguarded passion rains over a
    greening earth.

I listen to the language of your heart.

THE MAHU

A belief of the…young Tahitians is that being sucked is like feeding the mahu *[traditional term for gay cross-dressing figure] with the penis. "He 'ate' my penis," one man said. He said that the* mahu *believe that semen is "first class food for them." Because of that* mahu *are strong and powerful.*

—*Judy Grahn in Another Mother Tongue, paraphrasing the observations of a member of the London Missionary Society, 1801*

Welcome to this week's 60 Centuries, where courtesy of our sponsor (Have you ever wanted to time travel? You will.) we are pleased to bring you, in simultaneous translation and sensurround, an interview from the unexplored South Sea paradise, Tahiti.

60 Centuries: Thank you for taking time away from that lovely cloth you're working at to talk with us.

Raere: It stays where it is. Thank you for visiting.

60 Centuries: Tell me, how do you spend your days?

Raere: I live among the women. I have worn the dress of women since I was small. This is the role I was born to. I make things, useful things such as mats and painted cloth. I am told in some places the Mahu organizes many activities of the people.

60 Centuries: But you are not a woman.

Raere: (Laughing) A strange question. What does it matter? I do as I do.

60 Centuries: Forgive my boldness, but what gives you pleasure, sexually?

Raere: Asking about pleasure requires boldness? You are from a strange place. I take the man in my mouth. This gives me great pleasure. And him.

60 Centuries: Where I come from this is not common. And now is considered dangerous. A man can become sick and die in this way.

Raere: I am sad for you! How do the Mahu get their strength? You must miss this salty sweet taste, it is the taste of life flowing.

60 Centuries: Thank you, but our "time" is nearly gone. Any last thoughts?

Raere: Please, if you return, bring the Mahu of your village with you. I would like to see how beautiful he is.

We share our beauty and strength in many ways.

LEARNING

The important thing
is to pull yourself up by your own hair
to turn yourself inside out
and see the whole world with fresh eyes.

—*Peter Weiss, Marat/Sade*

No one can do this for us. No therapist, no teacher, no friend. Learning is a commitment we make to ourselves. Luckily, there's plenty of fun mixed in with the hair-pulling along the way.

Seeing the world anew is the important thing because the vision we've had pounded into our heads isn't just cloudy, it's crap. The heterosexist details are so deeply imbedded we have to shake ourselves but good to be rid of them and even then we find corners and crevices of our minds that haven't been turned inside out quite enough.

It isn't just the notion of being sexually straight that has to go. With that part of the lesson so badly bungled, why feel assured anything we were taught was right? Thus the agony: giving up so many illusions and old ideas. New learning is constantly challenging. If we believe we have it all figured out—and start living that way—we've begun to die.

Our gayness offers entrance to a fresh world. Thus the fun: finding our way somewhere open and big, a fascinating place rich with possibility and an infinite number of things to learn.

I'm learning all the time.

RAPTURE

A thousand little Persian horses were sleeping in the moonlit square of your forehead...

—*Federico Garcia Lorca, Divan del Tamarit*

Within each of us is the capacity for rapture. We can be temporarily transported by the majesty of mountains, music that touches other worlds, by the wash of moonlight on our lover's face.

Movement of this kind requires that we let down our guard. Disarming ourselves can be simple enough camped out under the stars or secure in our seat at the symphony. But allowing such vulnerability with another man, even as he sleeps under our gaze, exposes us to anything from heartbreak to humiliation.

Rapture is rare and unpredictable between two people. Its presence is announced by our racing pulse, tiny hoofbeats overtaking us both. We might whisper, *"I love you,"* and find not a small moonlit square, but a night-swept meadow in which—at least for a moment—heaven and earth are one and we find ourselves among the thousand horses dancing.

I am willing to be enraptured.

COMMUNION

They ate nothing but what was offered them in the villages and every day at dawn they were on the road once more at the same hour the migratory birds are on the wing. They ate from the same bowl and slept under the same cover.

—Alain Danielou, *Fools of God*

The life of a sect of Hindu monks who travel the countryside on foot exchanging wisdom and songs for the basics of life is so austere and devoid of material trappings as to be nearly inconceivable to a Western mind.

There is no room in this life for the responsibilities of marriage and child-rearing, but there is room for love. As described, it is a complete and unquestioned love, a love between men, a love of simplicity, devotion, and communion. *"Moni felt that he and Suresh became like a single being and that in this physical communion something passed from one to the other and each had become the other somehow and he was no longer completely himself."*

Few of us are likely to travel America like Indian *sadhus*, bedroll and small copper bowl our sole possessions, enduring hunger and hardship, devoted only to one another and the legends and songs of our gods. Not a very practical possibility in our world.

In our hearts we can wander thus. Linked. Unworldly monks. Sharing life's necessities, warming each other in the night.

I offer my tender devotion.

SAN FRANCISCO

The light of the day disappears on the great bay; from the ocean arrives an immense, intruding feeling of loneliness. Now the night is above us, and we leave, as if to run away towards the north, past the Bridge, speeding along the curved freeway cut into the hills of Marin...
—*Giovanni De Simone*

Of course it would become the gay Mecca, the recipe is perfect: take one part fairyland architecture, one part golden bridge, two parts adventuresome history, a pinch of Haight Ashbury, a dash of seaport, and roll over all of it with a heavy fog.

At its height, the Castro District was extraordinary. Imagine Disneyland's Main Street of America done over as an all-gay attraction. Even the picture frames in the corner drug store follow the theme with Kodak-moment display photos of happily embracing men. The comfort zone extends beyond Castro Street as well. BART stations all over town carry advertisements for gay cruises, male couples are in restaurants everywhere, and the City Council has about lost count of its gay and lesbian alumni.

San Francisco extended the summer of love an extra decade for gay men. The Cockettes performed their camp send-ups of everything and Halloween was the most important holiday of the year. Gay boys from across the world came with flowers in their hair and Armistead Maupin chronicled it all in *Tales of the City.*

Today, San Francisco has a hole in its heart. You can feel it. Gay life goes on to be sure, in some ways much as before, in some ways richer. But the epidemic has been horribly cruel and The Castro is full of ghosts. It's good to be there—everyone should go. It's the gay city, a city that now also bears a great intrusion of loneliness.

I left my heart...

WORLD PEACE

I still believe in world peace. I still believe in those values from the '60s. And if we were all holding hands, no one could push the button. And if we all had a great big dick in our mouths, no one could speak ill of another. Let's start by holding hands.

—*Roseanne Arnold, Christopher Street Magazine*

Seriously, true confessions, I do think highly of sucking dick, but I never *realized,* I mean I never actually took *in* what a sig*nif-*icant contribution it was to world peace. It makes me feel a little, well, *guilty* that I haven't done enough for such a noble cause.

But then, maybe I'm *still* not looking at it right. Depends on how you think world peace might happen. There is the United Nations approach, that sort of top down idea that if all the governments got it together, peaceful coexistence would seep into the consciousness of the masses, but so far it doesn't look like the old U.N. is quite the right ticket.

That argues for the bottom up approach: peace starts at home. And come to think of it, that is just how I *do* feel, I mean, strange as it may sound, when I've got my lover's dick in my mouth, what I feel (among other things) is absolutely *peaceful.* And the last thing on my mind is speaking ill of anything at all.

Hey, this could really work! There'll have to be an exemption for lesbians, but that's okay, they can come up with something else. So what do you think..."I suck dick for world peace" bumper stickers?

Let's start by holding hands.

THE GENERATION GAP

Not long ago, I gave a reading at the Lesbian and Gay (or should it be retitled "Queer"?) Community Services Center. I read an essay about the changes I had seen during my quarter-century in Greenwich Village. When the applause was over, a gentleman who looked about 70 years old came up to me and said, "You should have been there in the '40s. That's when we really had fun!"

—*Arnie Kantrowitz, NYQ Magazine*

Suppose we had these giant intergenerational symposiums to keep each other informed on all the best ways to have fun. There'd be workshops on everything from how to pick the right sized cock ring to shaping your eyebrows to look like Joan Crawford's. The older guys could take their uniforms out of mothballs and do skits about sex on World War II troop trains while the younger ones dazzle us in tuxes and demonstrate taking your boyfriend to prom. Queer Nation could caucus with veterans of the Gay Liberation Front and figure out some way to outrage us all. Oh, it'd be rich!

But improbable. We're too mad at each other. Queers think gays are hopeless assimilationists, gays think aging queens are simply hopeless, and aging queens think we should all be sent to finishing school. Young people are pissed the older generation didn't give us a more perfect world and those who've already put in their time think the younger crowd ought to stop whining, show some respect, and get to work.

Ladies and gentlemen, life's too short. Each generation defines its time and in turn is defined by it. We all pick up a few tricks along the way, so let's get past this silly arrogance and learn to share. Everyone's got something to teach.

Pooling our talents, we stand to have the most fun yet.

SEPARATION

The truth will set you free. But before it does, it will make you angry.
—Jerry Joiner

We swore it would never end. Unbeknownst to us, the seeds of our separation were there all the time, germinating underground, roots spreading, finally cracking up through the surface and announcing the truth loudly, painfully to our face.

Just as growing together is a process, so is growing apart. "Two years to get over each one I really loved," reflects a friend. "One year of getting over it for each year it lasted," is another rule of thumb. "It takes a long *long* time," says a woman who prefers not to count out months or years.

Anger is a big part of it. That he wasn't, after all, who we thought he was. That we somehow failed. That he betrayed us—or that he *didn't* and it would just be nice to have a clear reason why it had to end. That he's got a new lover. That the person we used to talk to about hard things like this is exactly the person we can't talk to now.

Separation doesn't happen all at once. The truth at each stage, each revelation, each passage makes us angry. Past the anger there is always sadness, then emptiness, then freedom.

Good-bye. Again and again, good-bye.

VIDEOS

Let's see, that comes out to just under 20¢ per penis. Not bad! However, the key word here may be *revenge*. This one has all the makings of a sinister plot: gay aversion-therapy deceptively packaged as an underwear tour of New Orleans.

I shouldn't prejudge, I haven't seen an inch of this one. I do know the genre, however: bad lighting, odd music, plot lines that just never seem to get up and go anywhere, and these huge cocks banging away hour after hour until it looks less like sex and more like some bizarre rig on Mars pumping for oil.

This is to eroticism what Gatorade is to Chateau Lafite. Gorgeous video does exist. And it's worth seeing. The cool glass of our TV screen is no substitute for warm flesh, but hey, why not ride bareback with Cowboy Bob at Homo on the Range Ranch, join the revelers at Carnival in Venice, or admire Le Beau Mec under the Eiffel Tower? Travel enlarges the mind.

At its best, gay video is an image world of beautiful men loving each other. It backfills our heads with what we never saw, were told never to see, never to want.

At its worst, it's revenge of the penises.

If it's not a turn-on, I'll turn it off.

COMING OUT TO STRANGERS

To be overtly homosexual, in a culture that denigrates and hates homosexuality, is to be political.

—Michael Bronski, Reform or Revolution?
The Challenge of Creating a Gay Sensibility, Gay Spirit

Timothy sits down for dinner next to an internationally known politician at a table for eight. The other six people appear to be straight couples. The luminary, being an expansive host, announces, "Well, you'll be my date!" and suggests everyone go around, introduce themselves, and tell what they do. When it's his turn, Timothy says he is communications director for the Gay and Lesbian Community Action Council, then turns to his dining partner and quips, "I've always wanted to meet you. And I promise to tell your wife you were a *perfect* gentleman."

Timothy, of course, has a lot of balls, a lot of practice, and is quite at home in the rough and tumble world of politics. He knows what it is to be overt in the protective company of liberal statesmen and in the menacing sights of small-town bar patrons demanding to know if he's the "faggot on the news." As long as he held down the Action Council job, at least he didn't have to be bothered with decisions about when to come out.

Others of us don't have to be bothered either. We gave up trying to hide it because it was useless in the first place or we made an unequivocal decision to reject the hypocrisies that come with even marginal covering up. Some see it differently. A private matter. Nobody's business. Still others have no stomach for it, or come out defensively, or never come out at all, fearing for our jobs, our homes, our families.

Paradox: The world isn't safe to come out in. Coming out is what makes the world safe.

If we're frightened, we're not free.

FOREPLAY

And some people don't even like to kiss, which I cannot comprehend. All sex is a pretext for a chance to kiss. And, of course, to come. And of course to work out and work through or perhaps merely to practice issues of submission and dominance, or whatever.
—Tony Kushner, Esquire Magazine

This term primarily refers to the activity leading up to the male's penetration of the female, which, for those who haven't been there, is not necessarily a pleasurable business (for her) if there has not been sufficient foreplay, or to put it less clinically, if there has not been sufficient kissing, fondling, sucking, pinching, panting, stroking, talking dirty, practice of submission and dominance, or whatever turns her on.

Back to the homo world, let's see how things translate. Where to begin? Which, of course, is always the very first question. Dropping to our knees the minute he gets in the door is certainly an option, but in less steamy periods or just in case he needs a little longer to unwind after a hard day on the road crew, a more subtle, time-release strategy may be in order.

They say the male of the species needs no foreplay. What the hell do they know? Do they ever slow dance? Do they ever kiss? Do they ever strip by candlelight to sexy music? Do they ever lie naked on their back, hands knotted in a silk tie, with a slow tongue working its way up from their toes to between their thighs? Granted a hard-on speaks for itself, but what does it say? Does it say, "Put your heavy lips to mine and kiss me and wake up every sense in my body until I'm wet and open and my cock is so hard it's a torture and I'm begging you please, oh please I want to come, I'm gonna come, *let me come...*

I'm just getting warmed up.

HANGOVERS

I lay in bed till noon listening to the bloodcurdling screams of the pigeons on my fire escape, the relentless timpani of my pulse and a somewhat softer popping sound. Probably my cells dividing.

—Joe Keenan, Blue Heaven

Oh honey, what a *night*. When we're in the mood, getting just slightly plastered is a great low-cost vacation. Now I don't know about you, but the days when I could throw down seven Stingers without ending up praying on the bathroom floor have gone the way of the Brontosaurus Rex.

The body is a fickle fellow. On the one hand, we get these delighted neuro-messages saying, "Yes yes yes. Relax me. Soothe me. Make me dance!" And the next morning, we're sternly told, "What the hell do you think I'm made of, bulletproof glass?" We flop into bed humming *Cabaret* and wake up an extra in *Lost Weekend*.

You know the moral of the story:

Vice has its price.

ASSES

It passes from the eyes into the heart
In a split second. Thus all beauties may
Find by this means a wide and generous way;
And so, for countless men, desires start.

—*Michelangelo*

It was not the sort of invitation one passes up, being asked to join my strawberry blond photographer friend to meet his new lover and two other boys for a late rendezvous at the new queer bowling alley. It doesn't turn out to be an exclusively queer bowling alley. Better than that, it is a step into the new reality. Good cookies and muffins, good wine, good coffee, very loud Janis Joplin sounding better than before she merged permanently with the kozmos. At least half the boys there are queer, the other half seem to be having almost as much fun.

The boyfriend is a shaved-head, silver-earringed Adonis in blue jeans and thick belt all fitting tight and loose in a strangely timeless way. Much ado about how to keep bowling scores. Finally, balls having been weighed, examined, chosen, and heavy boots exchanged for soft shoes, we begin.

They hold hands, they bowl, strikes and spares earn wet kisses. The new lovers are in molecular connection, have recombined in a liquid state. Little patches of dew glisten from the bench. Beauty stands to address a set of pins, pulls himself up straight and strong. His frame is perfect, classically proportioned. In a split second, it passes from the eyes into the heart. He is completely naked, visible, the muscled whiteness of his ass graced with soft black hair. Slowly, then swiftly, he moves down the alley, delivers the ball, his right hand rising open and sure into the vibrating air.

And so, for countless men, desires start.

HEARTBREAK

ADVANTAGES OF HEARTBREAK:
1. More room in bed.
2. Time slows to a crawl.
3. Opportunity to get in touch with our weeping.
                                    —*Matt Groening, Love is Hell*

1. At first, it's possible to become quite superstitious. *Maybe if I leave plenty of room on his side, he'll just come back. I'll wake up in the middle of the night and it'll be like other middle of the nights and he'll crawl in smelling great like soap and toothpaste and bothering me in a way I like.* Later on, wishful thinking having gotten us nowhere, we take over the entire expanse of bed. In the middle of the night it's just plain empty and in the morning there's plenty of space to throw our arm out where his chest is supposed to be and feel nothing but room and room and more goddamn room.

2. Was there ever anything good on Saturday night television? Early, that is. Prime time. (Okay, maybe Golden Girls.) Being back in circulation was a little exciting there for a while. The flight attendant from Georgia was a nice surprise. And not bad company in the morning. But he flew off and the scene feels really tired. Time to just stay home. All evening. Alone.

3. *Fucking son-of-a-bitch bastard!* That's the last of his crap out of the closet. I want to put my fist through a wall, through his face, through my own face in this goddamn mirror. My eyes are burning, I'm burning, my face is stretching open. I am wet and pounding my fists and choking and screaming. *He broke it! It's broken! He fucking broke my heart!*

Some people pretend it doesn't hurt.

HEALING

And this will go on for us, as if we were being slowly lifted and filled and washed by a soft singing wind that clears our sad muddled minds and holds us safe and heals us and feeds us with lessons we never imagined.
—*Doris Lessing, Shikasta*

We each have the task of our own healing. And it is our pain that takes us to it. For many, "hitting bottom" must happen before work can really begin. Or we may catch ourselves sooner, take our aches and muddles to heart, know that we deserve to feel better and more whole.

Healing is a forward and backward journey. We're finally in so deep we want out. Or we grasp a momentary vision: it comes at a concert or standing before rocks and waves; we feel it in our lover's arms and are drawn forward, we want to move. So we go backward, open wounds, pull out the shards of insult, cruelty, and neglect. And we go forward, into caring hands, caring circles. And back to deeper pools of anguish and despair. Then forward again.

So we lift and wash and fill. The safety healing brings is lasting, untouchable. The lessons are there for us: we can feed and nourish ourselves; we can learn things we never imagined.

I will heal.

MATURITY

One of the many things nobody ever tells you about middle age is that it's such a nice change from being young.

—Dorothy Canfield Fisher

In one's teens and twenties, middle age looms as a vast wasteland of early bedtimes, tired music, and absolutely no adventure. It is true the young possess the ability to chronically stay up into the wee hours and still navigate a straight line in the morning, always find their generation's music superior, and are likely to try anything at least once.

It is also true the young wonder if certain things were worth staying up *for*, if their music—or anything else—will answer nagging questions about who they are, where they're going, and what it all means, and are lucky to have *certain* adventures while fortunate to survive others.

The nicest thing about middle age is knowing ourselves better. It's fairly clear what sort of deck we've been dealt and we learn to play from strong suits and compensate for weak ones. We don't have magic answers to all our questions, but we've got a few things figured out and trust more will come in time.

As for staying up late, in the right circumstances we'll pay the price. Music? Ours is better, of course. And when things get dull, we just build a fire in the fireplace and reminisce about the adventures of our youth.

I enjoy the merits of my age.

STRAIGHT GUYS

I hate the term "straight." What does that make everyone else, twisted?
—Audrey Anderson

If these are the only two choices, I prefer the latter. How dull, how narrow to be "straight." It seems the tables have turned. Uptight, insecure, straight men still run much of the world, but, in an ironic twist, are far from being envied. To the contrary, as The Flirtations put it, they suffer being "homosexually impaired" and are, in their frailty and utter lack of fashion sense, to be pitied.

Now don't get me wrong, some of my best friends are heterosexual. And to prove the extent of my acceptance and freedom from prejudice, I would be perfectly happy to have my daughter marry one. I was brought up to be broad-minded and can see no reason whatever to write off an entire class of people just because they fail to exhibit the desire to have sex with me. Not that that stopped a number of them.

Given fag-bashing and the like, I blame no gay man for being suspicious. Or for avoiding the cruel pitfalls of unrequited love. But I have known far too much nobility of spirit in the company of straight men, had my mind opened to the beautiful and strange, and shared too much pain and sweat in the struggle for justice to ever stereotypically do unto them what so many have done unto us.

It's twisted to classify anyone.

ADVENTURERS

There are encounters, there are feelings, when everything is given at once and a continuation is not necessary. To continue is, after all, to put to the test.

—*Marina Tsvetaeva*

Among us are adventurers. They do not seek and are not cut out for hearth-and-home relationships. Such attachments get in the way, create unbearable ballast. This is a chosen life, a matter of respect for one's internal makeup.

The object, then, is to travel light. Comfort is as easily taken on woven sleeping mats as in perfumed featherbeds. Such a person may appear enviable, the quintessential male: assured, self-contained, a man in every port, nothing owed to anyone. But meeting his match, does he miss out on sustained passion, perhaps the greatest adventure of all?

Maybe so, maybe not. What's important is to be alive, prepared to give everything at once. Commitment is to the present. What security there is with no need for continuation! Anything might happen and anything does. Sex at a price in the markets of Thailand. A searing encounter that lasts 36 straight hours in a plush Los Angeles hotel. Love in installments that flare to life after months or years of absence.

We err by putting such men to the test—if we expect they will stay, if we attempt to alter what drives and compels them, if we misread depth and intensity for a promise on tomorrow.

To each his own adventure.

ANCESTORS

Some people are your relatives but others are your ancestors, and you choose the ones you want to have as ancestors. You create yourself out of those values.

—Ralph Ellison

All cultures honor their ancestors. Holidays commemorate victories and miracles, mythic dramas engage modern audiences with the struggle of gods and men, sepia-toned pictures of great-great-grandparents hang on our walls. Histories and epics abound, but most of us have never heard or seen one that includes the likes of us.

Chances are slim we'll go home for a visit to the farm and sit down to hear granny tell the real story of grandpa and that special pal he went hunting with. Nor are high school classes in Greek mythology likely to linger too long on the relationship between Patroclus and Achilles. Popular culture is coming around, but gay and lesbian ancestors are quite deeply entombed. We feel their absence as a gap; hunger to find a basis for self-creation rooted more deeply than the brief history of our own lives.

They do exist. As surely as the great uncle we never met who sang opera and escaped the Bolsheviks by walking all the way from St. Petersburg to Palestine. God only knows what we'd hear if all the real stories came to light: how our uncles and grandfathers managed to love in worlds that refused their existence, what exploits and miracles they made, what glories they recounted and performed lit by dancing flames of bonfires in the night.

I claim the deep-rooted wisdom of my ancestors as my own.

INFILTRATION

People don't expect me to be Larry Kramer but I am. I'm just as pissed off as Larry is about most things. It's just that it doesn't show up in my work as clearly because I think I can be more subversive.

—Armistead Maupin, OUT Magazine

The young man on the synagogue "inclusion" task force hardly considers himself a radical. He has chosen to be closeted in his corporate job, his taste in clothing and conversation runs conservative, he may admire the no-holds-barred accomplishments of Larry Kramer and his ACT-UP cohorts, but thus far has chosen a within-the-system approach.

Strange, then, to find himself odd man out, the impatient change agent, the confrontative hard-edged voice saying, "We've waited long enough. I grew up here. I'm sick to death of being a second-class citizen. Enough *process*. What about change? What about calling it discrimination? What about *right now?*"

Five years of diligent attendance at committee meetings and he's got a right to be pissed off. He's become subversive. He's acting up. He's drawing fire. He's making everybody uncomfortable. He wants justice.

The older man joining the inclusion task force already knows himself to be a radical. He chooses a different route. He infiltrates. He is quiet, makes a few jokes. He has lunch with the older straight folks, fits in at their parties, seizes his moments, sets off little bombs that explode their myths, holds them accountable to high standards in invisible ways.

To the untrained eye, all the action is where the commotion is. But acting up is not the only way to skin a cat.

Never judge a book by its cover.

LIFELONG COMING OUT

If a bullet should enter my brain, let that bullet destroy every closet door.
—Harvey Milk

If Harvey were still alive what would he be doing? Perhaps he would be Mayor of San Francisco. Or Secretary of Health, Education and Welfare. Maybe he would have returned to Castro Street and run a hospice for people with AIDS.

Harvey Milk was the first openly gay man elected to the Board of Supervisors in San Francisco. In 1978, he and then-Mayor George Moscone were shot and killed by fellow Supervisor Dan White.

Harvey was a passionate opponent of the closet. He understood it as a conspiracy of silence, as a solitary prison, as a tool of the bigot, as a refuge for the frightened. He knew there was more work to dismantle it than could ever be accomplished in one lifetime. He sought to recruit all of us in this work.

We initially come out for our own sake. Harvey wanted us to help ease the way for each other, for the next generation, to keep coming out for everyone's sake, to "once and for all, break down the myths, destroy the lies and distortions." He knew that he was at risk for his life. He asks that we remember and keep hammering at every closet door.

Today I will come out again.

THE FUTURE

Someday the gross repair work will be done. The oceans will be balanced, the rivers flow clean, the wetlands and the forest flourish. There'll be no more enemies. No Them and Us. We can quarrel joyously with each other about important matters of idea and art. The vestiges of old ways will fade. I can't know that time—any more than you can ultimately know us. We can only know what we can truly imagine. Finally what we see comes from ourselves.

—Marge Piercy, Woman on the Edge of Time

The manifesto of a turn-of-the-century German homosexual group offered deep gratitude for the rare "rays of sunshine in the night of our existence." The publishers of One Magazine in the 1950s begged understanding and acceptance of society's "deviants." Conservative critics at the dawn of the new millennium complain "the love that dare not speak its name" has become the love that won't shut up. Our most modest plea has met with undreamt success. Our most entrenched enemies organize vast resources against the looming reality of our power.

The gross repair work is begun, but it is far from finished. We yet suffer from centuries of dumping of raw lies, our own minds do not flow clean, we are asked to plant ourselves elsewhere. Still, our world is all but unrecognizable from a century ago—our freedoms, our celebrations, our outlook.

We see a future growing relentlessly bright. Children with picture books of daddy and daddy at work on sand castles at the beach. Sweet boys, smooth and ruddy with youth, exchanging name bracelets with their first crush. Men of passion and devotion arguing, fighting arm in arm against intrusions of darkness, making love and theater and outrageous art. We see an end to AIDS. We see understanding and acceptance sweeping the globe. We imagine this world, this fine and fragile world, as home and sanctuary to us all.

What we imagine can truly come to be.

LUST

An erection has no conscience.
—Old army saying, per Gore Vidal

And not too much in the way of restraint, either. Get hard (or hard up) enough and things quickly get out of hand (hands are good, but some things are better). The circumstances may be right, or not so. With things bursting at the waistband, it's quite inconvenient when cops come busting out of the bushes. Lust fails to be a convincing defense in court. We may think twice next time, but hey, there's a physiological problem here. With so much blood rushing to the lower extremities, the brain is at a disadvantage.

The good news (once we've paid our debt to society or done our best to explain to an indignant boyfriend or pulled the covers over our heads against the harsh light of day wishing three aspirins could cause selective amnesia), oh yes, the *good* news is that lust, when conscience rears its head (yes, I said *head*) and a quick but thorough inventory reveals nothing and no one to send us skidding into pools of regret, the good news (we're getting there, keep it up) is when he wants us as much as we want him (and no one is looking, at least no one we don't want to be) and we proceed, erect and shameless, to rip off each other's clothes and rip into each other with raw animal lust, raking each other everywhere with not a shadow of a thought of anything except what our raging body wants and now, *right now,* will have.

My conscience is clear.

PURITANISM

That writer, like many others, took the position that sexual promiscuity was the one freedom we had and that we had to fight to maintain it—even if it killed us. And it did kill us, a lot of us.
—Larry Kramer, interviewed by Eric Marcus, Making History

Sexual freedom does little for the dead. Surrendering to the gloating forces of puritanism does nothing for the living. Our brief revolution more than made up for lost time. We unlocked every repressed instinct there is, from the darkest to the most exalted. We gloried in anarchy and ecstasy and were headstrong and drugged with it.

We are not to be blamed. Our sexual outburst is part of a vital corrective course, a rising tide exposing puritanism as anti-human and a morally bankrupt front man for straight white privilege's lock on power. We rode a deep swell of anger and defiance, held our bodies in vast anonymous partnership as wave after wave of pleasure rushed over us. We had no idea the fluids held seeds of death.

To fear sex is to fear being human. To be degraded by sex is to betray being human. The answer is not a retreat into strict puritanical codes; we have to keep having sex and keep insisting on our right to have it. At the same time, we must confront the notion of promiscuity devoid of care, because we are older and wiser and sadder now and must be willing to love ourselves and love each other and love the world enough to make it safe.

I stand for life.

GAY COMMUNITY

And if there were only some way of contriving that a state or an army should be made up of lovers and their loves, they would be the very best governors of their own city, abstaining from all dishonor, and emulating one another in honor; and when fighting at each other's side, although a mere handful, they would overcome the world.

—Plato, Symposium

Like such an army of lovers and their loves, so have we held the dying in our arms. Embattled all around, men of valor have risen—imperfect, unprepared—and applied cool washcloths to each other's feverish foreheads, flown to the ends of the earth for cures, banged with outraged fists on the doors of uncaring powers, appealed for safety, stitched our tributes into a monument of honor and tears.

Put to the most severe imaginable test, we have responded with activism and deepest compassion: proof enough of our mettle, but there is more. Crisis lines, volleyball leagues, churches, scholarship funds, beauty pageants, schools, theaters, lobbyists, newspapers, Tupperware parties—we've got it all. We look out for each other. We plant trees for the next generation.

All this is true. True as well is the petty backbiting, second-guessing, bitter editorializing, and simple viciousness that is part of our community. As collective victims of oppression, we are to be forgiven. As individuals, we're not to be let off so easy. This is not a call for group hugs every time someone behaves boorishly. It is a call to be the very best possible governors of our own city, to allow our leaders their flawed humanity in the seldom gratifying effort to move the community forward, to think how we wish to be cared for in our greatest hours of need.

Let us emulate one another in honor.

HALLOWEEN

Round about what is, lies a whole mysterious world of might be, a psychological romance of possibilities and things that do not happen.
—Longfellow, "Table-Talk," Driftwood

Happy Celtic New Year! A holy day celebrated by tribal Fairy people and later by the Celts as the time when the ground we walk on and the underworld collide, the spirit population emerges, and we humans are in danger of being swallowed into the realm below if we are not well disguised.

Halloween provides the perfect opportunity for us modern fairies to act out what might be. Otherwise wouldn't-be-caught-dead-in-a-dress Brooks Brothers types emerge as drop dead drag queens, having spent enough time getting ready to put the Gabor sisters to shame. I personally once appeared at a college party as a Kabuki Goddess, sat on a couch for two straight hours passing joints, and then spent who knows how long staring in the bathroom mirror intoning, "I am your dream....I am your dream....I am your dream." I think I got laid by Rapunzel.

So there's more to this whole deal than meets the eye. A chance to delve into mysterious realms, a hallowed eve when anything might happen, a direct tie to a common pagan past that hadn't yet written off wild tricks and handsome baskets full of treats for those who acknowledge *all* the possibilities.

What do you think, the chiffon wrap or the snake wig?

November

DINNER

They asked me the other day my definition of the perfect lover. And I had it for them, too. A man who can make love to you until four o'clock in the morning—and then turn into a pizza.

—Charles Pierce

The way to a man's heart is through his stomach. Then again, some people start a little lower. Guess it depends on your aim. Either way, dinner figures prominently in many a romance.

God, it can be fun! Preparing the hors d'oeuvres aware that we ourselves are one of them. Loving his face in the soft evening light. This meal is often a prelude to things to come, but in itself is a mainstay of relationship. The dinner hour serves as a time to sit down together, to share details of the day. It puts us in touch with the simple tasks of living. Picking up, preparing, or dialing out for food. Setting the table. Doing the dishes. Taking out the trash. We extend our circles at this time, too, plan who to invite and consult our Julia Child, or light the grill, grab a cold beer, and toss footballs in the backyard with the guys.

And restaurants. Our rituals may include serious perusal of the wine list, feeding each other from a steaming pot of mussels, or knowing the small size basket of fries is plenty to share. Whether or not he transforms to a pizza later on, it's perfect enough when four a.m. rolls around and he hasn't turned into a pumpkin.

Let's discuss it over dinner.

BISEXUALITY

Many people seem to think that bisexuals are just interested in fucking around and will grab anything that moves...When people take roles too seriously, they oppress themselves and the person they are with...It's not about being lesbian, straight, or bisexual, it's not about being politically correct or incorrect; it is about being human.

—Kamini Chaudhary (A pen name),
Some thoughts on bisexuality, A Lotus of Another Color

The earnest participant in the homophobia workshop raises his hand and asks, "Now who do these gay guys date? Lesbians?" Hmmm. Let's do the math. Wouldn't that be bisexuality to the second power? The possibilities multiply geometrically. The formula actually runs like this: primary orientation + individual attraction over time = reality. Yes, it's subject to change.

One would expect this to be a non-issue in the gay community and for the most part it is, although a much hotter topic in lesbian circles where the issue of selling out to the patriarchy brings added controversy. Selling out is what raises eyebrows. It's like they're just not facing the truth and the rest of us who've done the whole piece on coming out shake our heads with a mixture of pity and disdain. Or is it envy? According to Woody Allen, bisexuality doubles your chance of getting a date on Saturday night. But then he's thrown out the rule book altogether.

That's at the bottom of it. Rules. Roles. Assumptions about lifelong orientation and the odd willingness of gay men and lesbians to promote the same sort of restrictions that victimized us in the first place. Let's get in the habit of claiming the truth for now: an apolitical anti-oppression stand respecting anything that moves.

I'm about being human.

LEGS

When you love a man, he becomes more than a body. His physical limbs expand, and his outline recedes, vanishes. He is rich and sweet and right. He is part of the world, the atmosphere, the blue sky and the blue water.

—Duke Ellington, Music is My Mistress

I come in late, weary, cold. You are asleep with the light on, stir, murmur. I darken the room and slip naked beside you, shivering. You reach for me and envelop me with your legs, pull me all at once between them. My arm goes around and under your thigh and the fullness and strength flows into me. You send heat so quickly from your center that I cease shaking almost instantly and the lines between us are already disappearing as I grow hard against you and the light changes from emptiness to a rich midnight blue.

My arm is the first to move, sliding out and reaching down the silken contour of your leg. My hand comes to rest on your calf which tightens against it, then releases. I feel you expanding from deep inside your limbs. A new shiver moves through me. You are sweet and right, waking up with tired kisses. Everything is receding into a rocking softness, I go deeper and downward, my hands under your thighs, the rest of me pinned tight below.

I am licking you, we are under the sky, you are moaning and writhing as I move wet and warm, my nose and forehead against your strongest and tenderest parts. I kiss all up and down your legs, covers thrown back, your fingers reaching through my hair. I come to curl around you, my legs pulled up as a child dreaming, and I bring us to the rich right place where we both see distant stars and then we stretch and kiss and vanish, long and blue next to one another, into sleep.

Put them around me dark and strong.

BAD BOYS

You're a bad boy, go to my room.
—Saying on a t-shirt

Oh, we are bad bad boys. We watch our living color video fantasy lean taut against the bar, turn and catch our eye, smile wickedly, then push the butt of his cigarette against the neck of the beer bottle as he tips it to his rose-red lips and with a slow relish, pours it into his throat. We mentally order him to our room. He flicks his ash.

Never mind. We're probably much badder than he is. We deserve a spanking. Later we get one. It hurts just right, sends a fast burn wake-up call right through our body, elicits a gasp, puts us at full attention as a wave of pleasure rolls in behind it. Our mouth and ass and hands and everything wants to dive all over him. He does it again. We dive.

Yes, we must be quite bad to have this sort of thing happen to us. We are *really* bad boys if we like it. And we are *very* bad, *very* dirty boys if we *love* it. Which we do. Licking and sucking him as he lords it over our face and sweat runs down our spine, as we make him gasp out to stop, as he puts cold metal and hot leather to us and we reach for it, and he rolls us over rough and we submit to him, buck under him, beg him to be as bad as he can be with us.

I'll be in your room.

OUTING

"Philip—the man's pushing seventy. He grew up in a completely different world! Anyway, what are you mad about? That he hangs out with famous actresses? So would you if you knew any. Besides, it's not as if everyone doesn't know, anyway."
"Then why doesn't he just acknowledge it?" I asked. "The man's a fucking billionaire—he doesn't have to live by anyone's *rules."*
"Except yours, *apparently."*

—*Joe Keenan, Putting on the Ritz*

To out or not to out, that is the question. Who gets to be in charge of the truth? Is this about truth? Or do we just want to throw a few tantrums?

So there's all these closet types who can now spend their weekends with anonymity in great bars from New Orleans to Seattle because a lot of out types fought long and hard to end police harassment and make the world safer for queers. So what? Who's having more fun? And should we ruin the delicate balance some men have struck with their families, their cultural communities, their careers as teachers, nurses, or cops?

But what about preachers who say one thing and do another? What about the guy who does risky shit and goes home and sleeps with his wife without telling her? What about the politician fucking us over in public who can't wait to be fucked by us in private?

It's scummy and repulsive to watch people play both ends against the middle. It's not okay to let anyone hurt us and it's sickening to think how someone's irresponsibility might ruin other people's lives. So how to answer the question?

Let's think long and hard before deciding to play God.

BASHING

It didn't take much to knock me to the ground. He was bigger than me and muscular...He had on boots, and when I fell down he kicked me in the shoulder, and it snapped off the end of my collarbone. They just kind of laughed and kicked me once more. "You faggot! Stay off the streets!" Then they left.

—Greg Brock, interviewed by Eric Marcus, Making History

It's happened to us or a man we know. Some survivors have permanent damage or chronic pain as lifelong mementos. All of us have psychic scars. We learn to look over our shoulder, we put an extra lock on the door, we learn to hate, we struggle mightily to forgive, we enroll in self-defense classes, face him in our nightmares.

What can be going on in their minds? It's a place we'd rather not have to go, a place of terrified manhood, hell and brimstone sermons, cruel expectations. We witness a mother sobbing, her lip split open, a boy throwing himself at his father, *"I'll kill you! I'll kill you!"* He is knocked to the ground, kicked by someone bigger, muscular. The child barricades himself. He has no options and no outlets. He is a cult of violence. He plays it like a sport that demands a drunken pact signed in blood to make the team.

We are faggots on the streets of his town. We don't deserve to live. Not if he can't. We are men who prove men can love. He is desperate to prove he is a man. We do the unspeakable, kiss, are tender. He hates us. He hates men. We have to look over our shoulder. And further. It matters what created him. It matters that there be laws against his crimes. It matters that the cycle be broken.

We are all potential victims.

DISCRIMINATION IN THE MILITARY

I got a medal for killing three men and discharged for loving one.
—Inscribed on the gravestone of Sgt. Leonard Matlovich

The whole thing is really too ridiculous. Of course we have to continue fighting the ban and any compromise with it. Us gay boys have given up just taking things lying down. Minneapolis columnist Lori Dokken sums the whole "new" policy up nicely, *"What a bunch of bullshit!"* The Joint Chiefs can shoot their mouths off all they want. In this war of words we've got the advantage of being right.

But what strange bedfellows it makes! We've got Our Hero *Barry Goldwater*, showing up from Republican retirement to lecture everybody that "We've wasted enough precious time, money and talent trying to persecute and pretend." And any number of us are surprised as hell to be carrying on about our fitness to serve when being queer was the saving grace that made sure we wouldn't *have* to.

You could chalk the whole thing up to entertainment if the stakes weren't so high. Not only for the gay men and lesbians who desire military careers, but because discrimination is disgusting and threatens us when given quarter anywhere. So everybody's getting quite an education. If the enemies of the USA are anywhere near as homophobic as our troops are, we should dismantle the nuclear arsenal, have an all-gay military, and simply scare the other side away.

I just die for men in uniform.

OTHERNESS

We view the world from an inside out upside down perspective.
Being an outlaw lets you do that.

—*Phil Oxman*

He looks anything but the outlaw. He and his partner are courted as prize members by synagogues eager to demonstrate their inclusiveness, their home reflects a tasteful upper middle-class range of choice, his Italian-style loafers and alligator shirt complement black jeans betraying a slight middle-age bulge. He serves on a number of gay and greater community boards, walks every spring with his partner through a park where they helped finance and plant a daffodil garden commemorating friends dead of AIDS.

When asked to reflect on how he experiences his gayness at this stage of the game, his thoughts go to otherness, the inescapable awareness of being marked by the world. He feels other eyes note an embrace of his lover in the synagogue sanctuary, breaking his comfort in a place it should not be. He talks of low expectations; the world-weariness of the Jew acutely aware of what majority cultures are capable of steals over him. He speaks of being doubly other. Today, always, he sees from the outside.

This is the fact and the curse and the blessing of our existence. We may be at home in our hearts, in the sanctuaries where gay men gather, but we walk outside at an angle. Not straight. So we have more vantage points. We are perfectly positioned to turn things inside out, to break many laws, to turn the world upside down.

I see through the eyes of the other.

NOURISHMENT

If a man finds himself with bread in both hands, he should exchange one loaf for some flowers of the narcissus, because the loaf feeds the body, but the flowers feed the soul.

—Muhammad

We are fortunate if we find ourselves with bread in both hands. People everywhere go hungry, die huddled and skeletal from starvation. The truly religious remember God when taking nourishment, praise the intelligence and bounty that brings forth bread from the earth, work daily to extend the blessing to others.

What we hold today has not come easily. Long secret and hidden, we now recognize our gayness as the very staff of life. We sit openly at our own table. It is laid sumptuous and large with our history, our savory tastes, our bodies, our sacred moments. We enjoy at last the privilege of nourishment, the possibility of fulfillment. We are to go on then, give of what we have to others still hungry. We engage with the world at large and follow the scent of the narcissus to where our soul is fed.

Let a thousand flowers bloom.

DISCRETION

The secret of being tiresome is to tell everything.
—Voltaire

There are precious few people who love us enough and have been our friends long enough to really mean it when they say, "Darling! Tell *all!*" In these rare relationships we actually are allowed periods of tiresomeness. We can go on too long, we can bare the breadth of our pettiness in reaction to some creep, we can even whine. True friends are tolerant. And will stop us if we cross the line.

Now holding forth publicly is another story altogether. A great deal more judgment is called for. Here are four tips from Connie Conversationalist:

1. Very little of our business is anyone else's.
2. Most humans have a relatively short attention span. If popularity is our goal, we shouldn't stretch their limits.
3. Never break a confidence.
4. Refrain from saying things about people we won't say to their face. Not that anyone will stop us. Our audience will just assume we also do it to them.

Being discreet is, for many, an acquired skill. Here's a final guideline: when in doubt, shut up. If this is a struggle, first visualize yourself as Garbo. Then shut up.

The secret of being interesting is to tell just enough.

PENETRATION

The penetration of the self—not merely the body, but the gestalt of body, mind, spirit, and memory—is, by almost any definition, an entry into the most private and sacred zones of individual identity.
—Frank Browning, The Culture of Desire

I: I want to enter you

A sensation begins in the heart. There is instinctual rightness to it; a standing cautionary note from the mind. There is unquestionable expanding in the region of the heart. I stare and listen, am ready to make hesitating contact. I ask permission, "May I?" before my hand, not trembling, goes first to an exposed place just above your wrist, so beautiful, black hair in a graceful curve. The sensation spreads throughout the body, becomes fascination with your eyes, brown cisterns of memory and spirit. Soon for both of us I am above you, inflamed, I want to plunge into you, have you receive me, give way around me. I know that everything, the deserts and rain forests of your life are inside. I will be there with you. I want to be inside of you.

II: I want you to enter me

Extraordinary allure battles mistrust. How safe can this be, asking another presence inside? We are on the beach, no moonlight. Eerie fires dance in the distance. You pull me to you and we are breathing as if one windswept body. You feel other, stronger, will I enslave myself by giving you entry? You bring life, growth, are astonishingly fertile. I decide. You prepare me, rub me with oils of ancient scent. You are rough, animal. I become quiet, everywhere open, stretch to meet you. I want you, my lover, I want to be under you, I want you inside of me.

We enter private, sacred realms.

SIZE

Lately, though, I've had to ask myself some pretty tough questions like, What am I doing wrong? And why do I keep picking the wrong men to fall in love with? I don't know what I'm doing wrong, to tell the truth, but I do know that one of my major weaknesses has always been pretty men with big dicks.

—Terry McMillan, Waiting to Exhale

Size counts. Not a pretty fact, but it's true. I've heard the issue cast as a prejudice, "sizeism," but I don't foresee it joining the list of "isms" to be addressed in the next diversity workshop. No straw poll needed: there's a major weakness for big dicks out there and no prediction they're going out of style.

They say it's not what you've got, but what you do with it, and if we stop *picking* men to fall in love with in the first place and properly leave Cupid to his own devices there are surely many instances when the issue is easy enough to overcome. But it *is* an issue. Both for those less endowed and the lovers who cope with feeling deprived.

Penile implants are one recourse. Just getting over the disappointment is another. There are plenty of artful possibilities and, presuming no one present is an insensitive cad, I haven't heard reports of smaller men enjoying sex any less than guys with dicks comparing favorably to those of vertebrates that stopped short of us on the evolutionary climb.

So are we doing something wrong? Well, we've all got our shortcomings, but in the greater scheme of things it's absurd to give something like dick size a major say in our lives.

I'm just right.

BOOKS

These books made the fantasies of happiness I'd imagined when looking at the photo magazines even more complete. In a real sense, their stories laid the groundwork for my eventual coming out as an activist. They were helping me and others perceive of a happiness that we had been told homosexual men couldn't achieve.

—John Preston, Flesh and the Word

Chances are a few more years will slip by before "Sweet Valley High" and "Saved by the Bell" (two pre-teen love/adventure/perils of school series that are current favorites of my daughter and son) will include story lines with budding gay and lesbian youth in leading roles. They'll make great titles someday: *"John and Eddy, Prom Kings!"..."Jasmine's Secret"..."Theodore Comes Out."* Won't it be fabulous?

In the meantime, another queer generation will do as we did and discover, little by little, a part of the adult reading world that speaks in a gripping language we find we understand. There was a time when most of us wished we didn't understand. Our first encounters with hot novels, whether highbrow or low, caused our throats to get dry and our undies to get wet. We knew—we'd been told or we *just knew*—that what we were seeing and feeling was somewhere between impossible and illegal.

Now we know differently. Impossible? Not in the slightest. Illegal? Gay tales grace better bookstores everywhere. Important? There's a long road for every homosexual man from the world of nonexistence to the achievement of a complex and full happiness. Many books point the way, with eroticism, with humor, with portraits of lives like ours.

I can achieve happiness.

DENMARK

Proponents would talk of the progressiveness and moral obligation of Denmark in relation to the rest of the world. This was the country of frisind—*broad-mindedness, tolerance, and social responsibility in securing real equal opportunity for everyone. By thus being at the front edge of civilization, it had an obligation to lead the way for the rest of the world.*
—*Henning Bech*

On October 1, 1989, registered partnerships, equivalent to marriage, became the law of the land in Denmark. It isn't perfect—the legislation did not give gay couples automatic rights to adopt children nor did it allow clergy to perform legal church "weddings"—but good enough to deserve a gold medal for progress in the world's halting movement toward equity for gay and lesbian people.

Denmark is an extraordinary country. It hasn't fought a war in over a century. (When I was in college there, a big joke was that the entire defense force consisted of a voicemail message saying "We surrender" in Russian.) Sodomy laws were repealed back in 1933. Because it is so small, the Danes are highly aware of their interdependence with the rest of the world. Most high school graduates speak 4 to 6 languages, quality of life is extremely high and it is absolutely impossible to buy an ugly piece of furniture.

Danish tolerance for difference—and more important, the record of action in its defense—is historic. Among all the peoples of the world, only Denmark distinguished itself by absolute refusal to turn its back on those marked for genocide in World War II. With only 3 days' notice, a nationwide underground railroad immediately created itself and over 7000 of Denmark's 8000 Jews were spirited to safety.

This is the Danish commitment to *frisind,* a unique word translated as *free mind* or *free spirit*. In the life of this people it is no vague spiritual concept. Rather it is an indispensable basis for community, mutual respect, action in the face of danger, and for civil policy at the front edge of civilization.

The spirit of freedom is strong in the world.

DEEPENING

The more I come out the better I sing.
—Steve W.

Gayness is much more than the definition of our sexual orientation. And certainly less than a total definition of who we are. At our core, we are spiritual beings. We contain light and we contain song.

It is far too limiting to imagine coming out as a matter of owning our sexuality, of redefining life's possibilities, of personal pride, or of gay pride. People speak of the coming out process as lifelong. It is. But it ceases to be about announcing our homosexuality and becomes a process of singing our song.

"The more I come out the better I sing." It is our range as human beings that grows. More high notes. More low. Richer, purer tones.

I have been given a song.

MAKEUP

One is not born a woman. One becomes one.
—*Simone de Beauvoir*

He shaves close. And a second time, holding the razor backward against the grain. A very light splash of aftershave. His face is smooth to the touch. It is 8:50 p.m. and already dark outside. He is in the bathroom with the door closed. His lover is in the kitchen doing the dishes. He removes mascara, eyeliner, blue eye shadow, and red violet lipstick from a small drawer and arranges them on the washbasin.

He puts on black lace underwear designed for men. In the mirror he is different, shoulders a bit back, upper body more elegant. His center of gravity shifts downward. He starts with the eyes; forefingers in gentle pressure pull color across the soft space above them. His eyelids fall more heavily, are darkened by a thin line above the lashes. He slowly rolls his head on his neck, relaxing.

The lipstick is firm and cool on his lips which gain precise definition, feel full, hold moisture from the tip of his tongue. He sees their imprint in a soft paper tissue. Next, a subtle reddening of the cheeks. He can feel his heart beating at his chest, follow the movement of blood as he grows full below. He brushes black into his eyelashes. Blinking becomes an art. He spots his neck, wrists, and one place on his waistline with scent. He is finished, feels incredibly sexy. He make faces. Joan Collins. Tina Turner. Angelica Houston. Isabel Adjani.

The dishes are done. His lover brings two glasses of wine into the bedroom, lights a candle, and waits.

Getting ready is half the fun.

COURAGE

*I think the great thing is for us all to try to give each other courage.
That's all that matters. And if some of us are timid, so much the more
reason for others of us not to be.*

—Don Bachardy, interviewed by Mark Thompson, Gay Spirit

Courage is connected to truth, which is why it commands
such respect. It is the rare gay man whose truth has not meant
wrestling with demons—some of us for so long and so intensely
that our inner life exhausts us. Some might view us as timid
when it's taking all the courage we've got just to carry on.

Courage is rooted in heart, which is why it inspires others.
What is in our hearts matters greatly. We each have something
precious, something unique to bring out of our deepest selves;
something that is not defined by gayness but may beg to be
expressed through it.

When we tell the truth of our hearts—to ourselves, to a
friend, to a lover, or on national TV—we give the gift of strength.
Such are acts of courage and they are not easy for any man. For
gay men, they are particularly important. With so much of the
world still violently opposed to our existence, every single one of
us—from the most outspoken to the shyest wallflower—needs
truth and heart and encouragement to carry on.

I am a courageous human being.

LEGISLATION

Political courage comes in all shapes and sizes and in all sorts of political arenas. Thursday morning, political courage came in the person of [Senator Dean] Johnson, a Norwegian Lutheran preacher from Willmar, Minn.

—Minneapolis Star Tribune

On Thursday, March 18, 1993, Minnesota became the eighth state in the union to extend civil rights protections under law to gay and lesbian people. God, I felt proud!

There were tidy victories in both houses of the legislature and lots of footage on the evening news of the beaming gay senator and lesbian representative who sponsored the bill. There was the interview with the choked-up gay activist recalling the 20-year battle that culminated this day. But the detail in the news that stopped me in my tracks was the performance of Republican Senator Dean Johnson, who listened to his conscience and gay constituents, defied his caucus, reversed an earlier anti-gay rights stand, and stunned his colleagues with a speech detailing the outcome of a moral fight he "...couldn't avoid anymore."

Credit where credit is due: to the activists and volunteers who fight long and hard, *highest praise for vision and determination*; to eleventh hour converts like Dean Johnson, *highest praise for breaking ranks and showing the route to higher ground;* to everyone who plays a part, *highest praise for moving one step closer to making common decency the law of the land.*

Yes!

EDUCATION

The parents who protest the Rainbow curriculum grew up at a time when gay people were invisible. But their children will live in a different world. A curriculum that ignores homosexuality will no more prepare a child for the year 2010 than a flat-earth curriculum would have prepared a child to become an astronaut.

—Sasha Alyson

It's a pretty standard afternoon. One kid is down with a fever, reading a book, and listening to her Walkman. The other is in the 4th quarter of the Dallas/San Francisco game. A 3D dinosaur jigsaw puzzle got as far as taking the pieces out of the box and there was just a 3M commercial on TV advertising CD ROM which will shortly make an illustrated compendium of all nonclassified human knowledge into something roughly wallet-size. Gay dad is at his lap-top writing a book about it.

There are just a few things in this picture that would have seemed preposterous to our parents. You can't blame them, really. They knew so little by comparison. And you can't blame the people who taught them, or *their* teachers, or even the long ago and far away Hebrews who put the codes of tribal survival into God's mouth in order to ensure group discipline and enough children to work the family plot.

A measure of blame goes to past and present flat-earth crowds who are always running to pound stakes into the heart of new ideas and light bonfires under them. But we know more. There's even signs we might be learning to know better. As for a brighter outlook in 2010, the key to our issues, and to so much else, is education, education, and more education.

I'm a teacher.

THANKSGIVING

And most of all, God, I thank you for my life. It has been one hell of a trek. But I wouldn't have had it any other way. Keep up the good work.
—John E. Fortunato, Embracing the Exile

This peculiar American holiday highlights the striking contrasts between all we should be thankful for and the many things requiring a stretch in terms of giving ole God a pat on the back.

For many Native Americans it is a day to mourn and to observe by fasting. While tables across the land groan with the weight of incredibly constipating foods, the evening news features the homeless and hungry being thankful for at least one decent meal. Whatever meaning exists in a main course of national thanksgiving is ladled with an overwhelming relish for robust retail sales. And this November appetizer ushers in the annual season of stress and angst associated with family gatherings great and small.

The gay perspective serves up contrasts as well. One state bans discrimination while another attempts to legalize it. *Angels in America* is a smash hit on Broadway and real-life PWAs continue to hit the wall physically, emotionally, and financially. Warm families eagerly welcome our partners while other families' dysfunction is so severe we must choose to stay away.

How to stop and give thanks for the mysterious and contradictory gift of life? This may not be the day, but it is a good thing to do at *least* once a year. It's a hell of a trek, but it's what we've got.

I am thankful for my life.

EXTREMISM

If someone took out [the names of two U.S. Senators], I would be the first to stand up and applaud.
> —*Michael Petrelis as quoted by Michael Willrich,*
> *Mother Jones Magazine*

I have nothing but respect for movement radicals. Their tenacity, outrage, creativity, and media savvy occupy a vital place on the spectrum of what is necessary to confront the ignorance, apathy, and intentional evils that plague us all.

My respect comes to an abrupt end when talk turns to threatening other people's lives. I know the other side is threatening ours. I know there are gay men dead who needn't be. I know I wish someone had put a gun to Hitler's head and stopped him cold in 1938.

As bad as they are, these Senators are a far cry from Hitler and everything in me recoils at the idea of Michael Petrelis' alleged words finding their way into some unbalanced gay man's mind and providing him the inspiration to off them. Do we really want to unleash a spiral of vigilante reprisals? Do we want gay men to lose their lives in this way, too?

At the end of World War II, concentration camp survivor Simon Wiesenthal won a debate with his peers who, spitting and choking in the sea of ashes that drowned six million of their people, were desperate to rampage over the land and murder every Nazi in sight. He won on the basis of history: no violent revenge to be written on the same page with the crime; no sinking to their level; bring them to courts of justice instead; full documentation. Out of the madness and horror, taking and holding the highest possible ground.

Let us be extreme in our righteousness.

November 22 ————————————————————————————

MARRIAGE

...the critical measure necessary for full gay equality is something deeper and more emotional. It is equal access to marriage...Marriage is not simply a private contract; it is a social and public recognition of a private commitment. Denying it to gay people is the most public affront possible to their civil equality.

—Andrew Sullivan, The New Republic

Among ourselves it isn't that big a deal. We can get hitched in droves in front of the Lincoln Memorial, pronounced husband and husband in All God's Children Church, throw a rock off a cliff into the Aegean Sea, kiss, and call it a match. We can construct equivalent status through domestic partnerships, airtight wills, and precedent-setting lawsuits brought against hospitals, mortgage companies, and insurance brokers.

None of this is enough. And not because we're all in a dither to get on the Newlywed Game. Unquestioned rights to inherit his stock portfolio aside, marriage is a flawed institution at best. But an institution it is, one unlikely to ever be diminished in its deep civil and emotional resonance and therefore one that must be legally inclusive of gay and lesbian people if we are to have the protections of full membership in society.

"Oh, fuck society," you might say and I don't blame you. But we need this. We need the opportunity to celebrate fully with our families and communities. We need to be at his bedside without a court order. Gay teens, sure it's a black and white world, need a total option package convincing them suicide is not the solution. We need to finish the job of creating widespread public recognition that we're done being viewed as bridesmaids without prospects of being the bride.

Total equality and nothing less.

LIFE PARTNERSHIP

Do you take this man, to love and to cherish, for richer and for poorer, in sickness and in health, until death you do part?
—*Traditional Wedding Vows*

In concept, the idea of gaining a life partner has much appeal. There are souls who simply were made for each other. The whole is so much greater than the sum of its parts as to render further calculation absurd. Gertrude Stein and Alice B. Toklas come to mind. Benjamin Britten and Peter Pears. Heckle and Jeckle.

There are tons of advantages. The gifts, for starters. Nice rings. Not having to date. The opportunity to stage a sweet little affront to the "family values" creeps. And the express commitment of another person to tough it out is a noble thing. It's wonderful to take the long view, plan and build something together, be loved and cherished and remembered.

The downsides are well documented by stand-up comics, divorce courts, and domestic abuse hotlines. You don't have to be a homo to view this primarily heterosexual construct with a jaundiced eye. The destructive notion of any person claiming property rights to another aside, the real problem is the death part. We need to revise the concept to life of the *partnership,* not lives of the partners. Love dies, spirits misplaced wither, the positive reasons to be together evaporate and we may have to let him go. Otherwise, what we thought was a chance at eternal bliss turns out to be a suicide pact.

When it's right, more power to us.

PHONE SEX

There are two types of phone sex. One with someone you know, the other with someone you don't. Type one is vastly under-rated (much to my initial surprise, it really *is* the next best thing to being there). Type two is vastly over-hyped.

I speak from experience, of course. One must conduct research. Which is exactly what I did one 20-degree-below-zero Minnesota night when the idea of a warm disembodied voice didn't actually seem bad. A disclaimer: I just could not bring myself to punch the button to connect me one-on-one with a live, hung, horny stud. I'm sure he gets callers with kinkier notions than mine, but the idea of stammering about this being my first time and did he have any suggestions sent me cuddling up to my space heater instead.

The national ads, in a *tour-de-force* of regional dialects, introduce me to four Daves, two Mikes and one Juan, make me worry about the prospects of fats and femmes, give me a business opportunity if I'd like to be of rousing service to a group of disease-free attorneys, and invite me to have a close look at some boots if I'm ever in Houston. The messages are poignant, friendly, statistical, occasionally raunchy, and the smooth young black body from South Chicago sounds, well, smooth, young, and black. I kind of want to meet the guy in Charleston who's into scenes from the Rocky Horror Picture Show. I screw up my courage and dial into the sleaze party line. "Hello? Hello?" No one there. The XXX cum fantasies come up more expensive and less tailor-made than what I enjoy off the rack. (And no pictures!) Besides, I really *don't* want to get pissed on by Hells Angels at a truck stop. Forty-five minutes colder, I light a cigarette which bears no resemblance in taste whatsoever to those that follow the real thing and marvel at the strangeness of it all. I figure I dropped thirty-five bucks.

Yet for some of us, it's a lifeline.

STRAIGHT-ACTING/STRAIGHT-APPEARING

What we're all trying to do is figure out, How can I take the spirit that is within and allow my spirit to become more important than anything else in my life? It's the spirit that energizes us. It's the spirit that activates us. It's the spirit that defines how we interrelate with other people.
—*Monsignor Thomas Hartman*

The big question I have about gay guys who advertise this feature is, when exactly would they want me to stop appearing straight? Would it be just before or just after we took off our clothes? Should I act like I've never done this before?

Now some queens look straight through no fault of their own and are certainly as attractive as the next girl, but the *desire* to be S-acting/S-appearing betrays something between a little self-consciousness and a lot of self-loathing. We play a pre-programmed mind game:

"I'm not gay, are you?"

"No, I'm not gay."

"Good, then we can do what gay guys do and pretend we're not."

This may get us off, but it doesn't get us far. As long as we leave our sexual attractions in a straitjacket, we drastically limit our ability to be energized and fully alive as gay men. When we tune into the spirit inside, it really doesn't matter if we swagger or swish because we've already slipped the bonds of a narrow frame of mind.

I act and appear like myself.

REAL MEN

Arthur's hands came around quickly, landing one on Kurt's shoulder, one on his butt. "Oooh, man—go slow. Oh, Kurt. God—this takes dedication. Being a homosexual ain't sissy stuff."
—*John Wagenhauser, The Group, "Flesh and The Word"*

It really is most absurd that many gay men got labeled early in life as sissies. So we liked Barbie and Ken. Or just Ken. So what? We were busy developing nerves of steel in response to the abuse. Anyway, I was a Boy Scout and to this day I build a damn good fire. In fact, I experience this rush of being a Real Man every time I go over to the house of a certain woman friend, lug in the logs, and demonstrate mastery over the fireplace.

That's what it is, a sense of mastery. A certain ruggedness. Being willing to subscribe to a "no pain, no gain" approach to at least some aspects of life. In case anyone's wondering how that applies to a number of grown-up Barbie-lovers, just ask any drag queen about the rigors of walking in heels.

More universal is the question of the sphincter muscle. I don't care whether it's considered a natural or unnatural act, getting in the groove with Arthur requires some dedication. This definitely ain't sissy stuff. It takes a real man to learn the art of yielding, to try enough configurations to find the right ones, to deal with hard things head-on and make them good.

I'm a master.

FORMER LOVERS

I could be the poster boy for bad judgment.
—Rob Lowe

A fifty-year-old man at his birthday dinner looks around the table and counts eleven of the twelve men present as current or former lovers. He realizes this is the fact of his life. Many lovers. Ongoing connections. He counts himself blessed.

No judgment problem here. While there are certainly past flames who were *not* invited, by and large he has chosen well. Others of us more easily identify with Rob Lowe.

If we took the trouble to make poster-size blowups of comely past boyfriends, more than one has come in handy as a dartboard. Of course we don't get a chance to forget what they look like. The especially displeasing ones are precisely those that turn up like bad pennies. Don't they have the good grace to leave town? Oh yes, the lack of even a shred of decency was part of the problem. Hopefully we learn from our mistakes.

Mostly they aren't mistakes. They were fun, or served a purpose, or—check your expectations at the door—plenty good, just short. Many are welcome guests at the table of memory and a few in particular would be lovely to have back from the places they disappeared to for a cup of tea or a birthday party or a little uncomplicated reliving of what we hope they would recall as fondly as we do.

Everyone I have loved is a part of me.

WIDOWHOOD

Peace dies when the framework is ripped apart. When there is no longer a place that is yours in the world. When you know no longer where your friend is to be found.

—Saint-Exupéry

Little in life exceeds in pain the loss of a lover to death. There is no way to completely prepare for—and no way to diminish—the tidal wave of grief that overcomes us.

In our most difficult periods, we are displaced, there is no center. Our waking hours have the character of sleepless nights; no position is comfortable, no images lull us. We close our eyes and dream his presence, dream us together, but harsh daylight always intrudes, taking him away. His face appears constantly. It's him crossing the street, he's ducking into a cab...that man in the checkout line. But it never is him.

The framework is gone. So many little things that add up to who we love. Something in his voice. The way the skin felt on the inside of his thigh. The first time we saw him. His smell. The sum of how it felt to be in the place that was ours.

Only with months and years does a new framework assert itself. His memory is a part of it. Our mending heart is a part of it. We go on heavier—and in a strange way lighter—for carrying this lover, this friend inside of us.

With time, there is a slow rebirth of peace.

BEING THERE

The friend who can be silent with us in a moment of despair or confusion, who can stay with us in an hour of grief and bereavement, who can tolerate not-knowing, not-curing, not-healing, and face with us the reality of our powerlessness, that is the friend who cares.

—Henry Nouwen, Out of Solitude

The ability to be present for those enduring pain is an inborn gift for some, a learned discipline for others.

The discipline begins with being present for our own pain. We continue learning in the care of others, schedule time to be instructed by a pastor, teacher, or healer; someone already adept. We take walks in the woods and observe the natural process of decay and regeneration. We care for ourselves.

As we grow stronger, we develop the capacity for self-protection. It becomes a choice whether or not to allow others' feelings in. At times despair crashes through as well it must. We develop the capacity to let suffering run its course.

Finally, the discipline becomes quite simple. We remind ourselves we are safe. We call angels to our side. We tolerate our own powerlessness. We extend ourselves to those who need us.

Care is action of the highest order. The times to touch and soothe are there; the occasions to tell stories, to cry for our friend when he cannot do it himself; the moments to silently take his hand, to hold him asleep, to say nothing, to do nothing, and yet to have done everything.

I am there for you.

AUTHENTICITY

Our feelings are the most genuine paths to knowledge. They are chaotic, sometimes painful, sometimes contradictory, but they come from deep within us. And we must key into those feelings…This is how new visions begin.

—*Audre Lorde*

There is a talented and charismatic man in Minneapolis named Patrick Scully who operates a cabaret out of his street-level loft-style home. During one of his opening monologues he talked about having money problems, quitting his job to become a radical queer performance artist, and the fact that everything has more or less worked out perfectly since.

Before we all rush to our typewriters to whip off letters of resignation and start tie-dyeing jockstraps for our debut, let's be clear that Patrick's success is due to his wonderful ability to be *Patrick*. And based on what he shares through his performances, that appears to go for his sometimes chaotic, painful, and contradictory private life as well as his hour upon the stage.

Living authentically is both a moment by moment reality and a long-term proposition. They feed into each other. By keying into our feelings we develop visions. By living out our visions, we bring forth even greater depth in what we feel. This is not about logic. Like dreams, our feelings speak a language of symbols we must learn to interpret. As we do, our lives begin to unfold more clearly, more strangely, and more singularly *ours* than we ever could have planned.

Deep inside me lies the pathway to my life.

—— December ——

RELEASE

Comfort, comfort my people
—it is the voice of your God;
speak tenderly to Jerusalem
and tell her this,
that she has fulfilled her term of bondage,
and her penalty is paid;

—Isaiah, 40:1-2

We have been overrun, subdued, our spirit and aspiration at the mercy of hostile invaders. We burned for our sins. We were carried off in the night. We hid our worship and offerings in cellars, assumed false identities, wrote our longings into poems of disguised verse.

We have paid our term of suffering, God knows for what reasons, and many of us are in great need of comfort still. We are lonely in the night. Spurned by those who gave birth to us. We are dying of plague. We sell our young bodies for warmth and food.

It is time for release. We have paid enough. *O tenderly hear this voice:* do not forget Jerusalem. She is just ahead, shining on the horizon. She holds the hope and dream that we have long stored, always cherished. We are closer than ever. We are almost home.

I shall be released.

COME

An intense sensation made Moni tremble as if his body were suddenly filled with light. A thought entered his mind: "A god has entered me."
—Alain Danielou, Fools of God

I have twice made love with the intentional result the conception of a child. One of the times we were both quite drunk, but it was the right day of the month so we laughed our way through it. What kind of a child could come of this? A son slightly high on life, it turns out. The other time was different. We knew we were creating something and we trembled with the holiness of it. Our young daughter smolders with spirit.

The seed that spills out of us is imbued with the most extraordinary power in the universe. In great moments of climax we experience the agony of it, a relentless onrushing, the giving in to its force, sudden light, astonishing pleasure. No wonder movie scenes build to it, no wonder we are fascinated, no wonder they go to slow motion.

It is gorgeous. It spurts onto us like an elixir, fiery and dense, smelling rich and earthy and quickly changing as it mixes with air. This we share with other men. It is meant to be loved. It is the very stuff of life.

Come on me, baby. Come on me.

DRAG

Oh, sure, I try and keep a flat-looking crotch, but sometimes my balls shift around like the San Andreas fault! I pray to the computer gods that my hardware will stay software, at least for the duration of a performance...My acting career is really taking off this year. I'm starring in a new soap opera called, "The Hung and The Breastless!"

—*Shaun Derek, Dragazine*

Can't you see it? Little boys across America getting caught putting their mother's makeup on and instead of a slap on the ass and a trip to Confession, mom stoops down on bended knee and says, "That's not quite your color, dear. You know, though, if you work really hard at it, you might grow up and make a million dollars like RuPaul. Who would have thought? My son a famous drag queen! Whaddya say we go for ice cream and then shop for wigs?"

If Ru has her way it might happen. She's playing straight discos (when she isn't *everywhere* with Elton John) because (she says in another *fabulous* Dragazine interview) "...it's a great forum to place new ideas into a lot of young minds that really have a future...and in the new drag movement, I think there is very little about sexuality. It has to do with self-realization and having fun..."

This could rival Bertha VaNation (thank you, Harvey Fierstein) and will undoubtedly unleash a chorus of criticism arranged for mass consumption by Miss Yawanna Bet backed up by Holly Luya and her Holy Rollers. Let 'em whine. Drag is here to stay. And if there's any doubt, be in the audience when a veteran performer in your town leans her entirely man-made tits over your table and with a look of timeless determination burns the lyrics of "It's My Life" deep into your eyes and all the way down to your soul.

Ima Bigfan.

SELF-SUFFICIENCY

Be thine own palace, or the world's thy jail.
—John Donne

How often we go through the day disappointed at some level at what the world sends our way. We wish we had a better job, or boss, or more money, or a lover, or a better apartment, or a better lover. If we're ill or in trouble we are completely entitled to sympathy and support. But sometimes we need to take charge, try harder, and make some changes.

What we may run into are the walls of our own thoughts. We lock ourselves out of the palace and give other people the keys. It's tough to accept that we've got what it takes to make it on our own; that we can provide ourselves the love, nurturing, security, and enjoyment we all crave.

Strangely, when we finally catch on that we're king of our own castle, Prince Charming is more likely to show up after all.

I have everything I need.

RIPENING

In the beginner's mind there are many possibilities, but in the expert's there are few.

—*Shunryu Suzuki*

Ever watched a three-year-old match geometric shapes to places in a puzzle? He works with the utmost concentration, methodically narrows his choices, and claps with delight at his results. Ever talked with a twenty-two year old trying his hand at relationships? He follows up on every lead, endures hardships and fruitless hard-ons, is eager to experiment with most any piece he can manage to pick up. The puzzles grow more difficult for a good long time.

We arrive with beginner's minds into a situation of boggling complexity. The possibilities are astounding, the process of trial and error taxing, and the desire to find our place often heart-rending. Some anonymous soul summed it up like this, "Experience is a hard teacher. She gives the test first and the lesson after."

There is a light at the end of the tunnel. After a few decades of this—if we've kept at fitting all the pieces together—we begin to get in shape, our own specific and unique shape. We develop a wondrous deliberateness that allows us to size up a match without all manner of awkward contortions. Quite simply, we ripen. And we know how to select and bite into other luscious pieces of fruit while avoiding the pits.

Maturity is all it's cracked up to be.

TRUTH

We should stop kidding ourselves. We should let go of things that aren't true. It's always better with the truth.

—R. Buckminster Fuller

Someone should have clued in Richard Nixon. But before we cast the first stone, how many of *us* authorize little Watergates in our own lives?

The consequences are clear enough. Managing cover-ups requires tremendous energy to keep the facade intact. We end up reinforcing a little management of appearances here with an even more elaborate invention there. In the long run, we get found out and impeached. Or we just get spiritually exhausted from all the work of kidding ourselves.

Truth has a power of its own. And not just with the big stuff. Truth-telling carries an underlying quality that gives order and spaciousness to our lives. Not boring, predictable order, but a firmly grounded way of being that is deep, secure, and alive with creative possibility. It is always better. Living and saying what's true exposes the realm of *un*truth for the flimsy and arrogant house of cards it is.

The cost of truth is far outweighed by its rewards.

THE WIZARD OF OZ

What a gay story it is, of a seeker who discovers that dreams are real and reality, dream...

> —Judy Grahn, *Flaming without Burning:*
> *Some of the Roles of Gay People in Society, Gay Spirit*

Toward the end of the first gay men's chorus concert I attended, I found myself wondering, "Isn't there some sort of gay national anthem?" and then, of course, there it was, *Over the Rainbow*.

Now all this adoration gets pretty hard to sort out since millions of non-gay folks also love The Wizard of Oz, Judy Garland herself was a major attraction among gay men, and what drag queen wouldn't, at some point in her career, have killed for those little red shoes? Nonetheless, a collective tingle did go up our spine in the hushed concert hall when those handsome guys in tuxedos softly began to sing "our song."

Call it starry-eyed, call it sentimental, call it anything you want, Dorothy's story strikes a deep chord. How many of us didn't, at one time or another, feel compelled to run away from Kansas? How many of us didn't, at some point, encounter a world we had only dreamt of? How many of us had to learn, often with great difficulty, that "home" was a place you found inside, not a place you went back to? It *is such* a gay story. Brains, courage, heart...and the costumes are fabulous.

Welcome home, Dorothy.

THE CHILD WITHIN

Great is the human who has not lost his childlike heart.
—Mencius

Children are neither sweet blank slates nor uncomprehending innocents. We come with leftover karma—or whatever it is that seems to predetermine how, from the very start, we engage with the world. We then proceed to take in everything around us, react in the moment, and be deeply affected in the long run.

The early years of childhood are often idealized as the garden spot of life. At this point, a vacation there might do us good. We may have forgotten how to play, to be mischievous, learned too well to hold back our emotions. Our childlike heart capable of wonder, of glee and tears, can pull itself closed like an overcoat against the wind.

If you're feeling a little too bundled up, here's some tips:

1. Get some really smelly flowers, put your face in them, and breathe deep.
2. Rent Bette Midler's "Divine Madness," alter your consciousness if you like, and sit on the floor in front of the set.
3. Take a bubble bath.
4. Invite him to join you in the tub and do fun stuff.
5. Skinnydip.
6. Go see "101 Dalmatians" in a movie theatre and buy everything you want to eat.
7. Stomp your feet when you're mad.
8. Cry when you're sad.
9. Do anything that makes you say, "Wow!"
10. Fail to be embarrassed by any of the above.

Want to come out and play?

ALLIES

The resolution envisioned a future with Unitarian Universalist congregations becoming truly welcoming places for all persons. These "welcoming congregations" would:

- *Celebrate the lives of all people and welcome same-gender couples, recognizing their committed relationships and equally affirming displays of caring and affection with regard to sexual orientation.*
- *Advocate for gay, lesbian, and bisexual people, attending to legislative developments and working to promote justice, freedom, and equality in the larger society.*

—Excerpts from the Welcoming Congregation Resolution of the General Assembly of the Unitarian Universalist Association, 1989

It is a challenge to all maturing social and political movements to accept allies. The issue often gives rise to bitter infighting. Separatists and integrationists square off in one corner. Zealots suggest the pragmatists step outside to settle the matter. People with *"victim"* stamped irreparably on their consciousness are so bitter and angry they simply cannot recognize a good thing when they see one.

The rise of allies often threatens longtime activists. A change in personnel may be required. Those that hurled themselves against barricades and forced dialogue in the seats of power may lack talent, effectiveness, or interest when it comes to the compromise-laden task of legislation. On the other hand, those who comfortably don suit-and-tie drag may fail to respect the contributions of those who got them in the door in the first place.

Whether it's progressive churches, Tom Hanks, the ACLU, recovering homophobes, Johnny-come-lately gays, or the NAACP, late is not too little, and with so many enemies lining us up in their sights, we do well to welcome all who volunteer to stand with us in the cause.

Thank you for joining us.

GAY CULTURE

Culture is the sum of all the forms of art, of love and of thought, which, in the course of centuries, have enabled man to be less enslaved.
        —André Malraux, *New York Times*

When I hear the word "Culture" I slip back the safety catch of my revolver.

—Hanns Johst

If you happen to be on the lookout for a Ph.D. topic, stop right here. And start developing your self-defense strategy. Anything you say will arouse opposition and anyone from the deconstructionist debate team to the Kulture Police may come crashing through your door.

Ah, the questions are deep and ripe for academic plumbing. If a gay artist paints something, does that automatically make it "gay art"? Are we talking a history-based Culture that hangs together across generations or pop culture that celebrates its icon-du-jour? Is "camp" culture? Is getting the joke? Who's in and who's out? Transsexuals? Transvestites? The guys with the little dairy farm in Vermont? Is sexuality a basis for culture? Is sexuality the basis of being gay? Is the gay contribution unique? Does any of it matter as long as we're having fun?

Some argue culture. Some create it. The definitions are always faulty. We live, we love, we work, we partake of and con-tribute to what is there. We can trace a lineage of how we got here, but care should be taken before drawing boundaries around it. The point is enrichment. And not to be enslaved.

I'm transcultural.

DIVORCE

Some pink and blue evening, we shall exchange a single impulse, a kind of long sob, heavy with farewells.

—*Baudelaire*

It's over. An ashtray sings past our head and crashes against the wall; the perfect symbol of where we have come. It's over. We see it through a blur of tears in the therapist's office. It's over. In stunned silence we place our toothbrush and body lotion into a shaving bag. It's over. With heavy fingers we dial the number of our attorney and make an appointment to start going over what to do about the house.

It's really just the beginning. We've got a lot of untangling to do and dividing up the dishes is the least of it. It's a grief process. A long one. Somewhere along the line, past the fury, past the list of what we each did wrong, past the failed attempts at reconciliation, past the depression; at the end of it, we do what is actually the very hardest thing. We finish it and say good-bye.

We look at the sky, across the emptiness that has fallen between us, into the pink and blue moment as the sun signals it's setting, and no matter how bad or ugly it may have gotten, we touch souls with this person we loved enough to want to love forever and—a final opening of the heart—we bid farewell.

We must see all the shades to let it go.

HETEROSEXISM

No one can make you feel inferior without your consent.
—*Eleanor Roosevelt*

It is inordinately pleasing to walk the streets of New York City and take in the lesbian chic/pretty boy fad in advertising. My attitude toward advertising is generally hostile—the whole *point* is to make you feel inferior—but it's still pleasing because the use of models in frankly lesbian and gay relationships is a significant hole in the heterosexist dike.

Oh, the little Dutch Boys are out in force crying danger to the town and trying to stick their finger in it. The bad news is the entire dam is not currently predicted to give way. It's too big, too convinced of its superiority, and the pilings run too deep.

The assumptions are everywhere. You cannot turn around without walking into yet another homosexual-free environment. Twelve movies at the multiplex and not a gay or lesbian character to be seen. (Actors, yes. Characters, no.) Mass mail dating service ploys asking, "Are you single and alone? Is it hard to meet attractive members of the opposite sex?" Jewish people who want to keep the Holocaust all to themselves.

So hear-hear for the ads. And for *thirtysomething*, Roseanne, and Sassy Magazine running a story called, "My Brother is Gay. Big Whoop." With their power over an entire generation, advertising, TV, and teen rags may prove some salvation yet.

We are everywhere.

FEET

Most of the time I had dreamed of an English lord who'd kidnap me and take me away forever; someone who'd save me and whom I'd rule. But now it seemed that Kevin and I didn't need anyone older, we could run away together, I would be our protector. We were already sleeping in a field under a sheet of breezes and taking turns feeding on each other's bodies, wet from the dew.

—Edmund White, A Boy's Own Story

It is morning. We have come from our bed where we made love again at dawn, then showered, and now sit in robes in low living room chairs drinking coffee.

You have kidnapped me. We have run away together. I am already yours. Your face is extraordinary to me, I feel I have been looking into faces searching for this one all my life. Concealed beneath terry cloth is your body. It is still on top of me like a sheet of breezes.

I look down to your feet. They are so purposeful. I have not yet heard the history of where they have walked. Here is where your body tapers and connects with the earth. Here you have been filthy and tired from work. Here is where you have known the feeling of sand and grass and pavement and broken glass. And here is where, as my heart bends toward yours, I am about to kiss you and have your feet know the touch of my lips.

Let us be one another's protectors.

THE UNITED STATES

I welcome all of you who have come here as old souls, returning to restore to this land the gayness it once had.
—*Paula Gunn Allen, 1979 March on Washington*

The nation and land we now call America must face her history if she is to reclaim her soul. The invaders of five hundred years ago brought the inevitable expansion of White Europeans to the continent and with them came colossal crimes. These United States were built on the bones of the tribal nations, the backs of black slaves, with the sweat of all manner of "minorities" who were systematically excluded from written history and our fair share of what came to be envisioned as The American Dream.

There are redeeming accomplishments: the Constitution is a striking document; the abolitionist movement; suffragettes; Mount Rushmore; our troops landing at Normandy; the Museum of Modern Art. And the largest, most creative, active, and aggressive gay community in the world today.

We have it all here: our poets, historians and storytellers; our martyrs; our gathering places; our shamans, rabbis, and priests; our holidays; our families, friends, and tribes; our elected officials; our culture; our vibrant vision of the future. We have work to do here. We are in a land that is reaching up and asking our help to restore its spirit.

Welcome, old soul.

SEASONS

All changes, even the most longed for, have their melancholy; for what we leave behind us is a part of ourselves; we must die to one life before we can enter another...

> —Anatole France, *The Crime of Sylvester Bonnard*

Living in a climate of dramatic contrast, one experiences the melancholy of change at least four times each year. Even the abatement of a bitter winter gives pause. In the last days of indoor imprisonment, there is the sharp sense of time's turning. The bittersweet taste of hot chocolate passes from our lips, the elegance of bare trees is about to be swept up in a flush of green, the deep silence of frozen night interrupted by insect songs and the lapping of waves. *To everything there is a season. A time to sow and reap. To be born and to die.* Ancient lyrics gently set to the rhythm of life.

Today, time is tripping over itself. Change is so radical and so fast it's a wonder we recognize ourselves one day to the next. We're thrilled to get on an airplane for the chance to sit down.

We must make room for our own lives. If all we do is leave parts behind, what do we end up with? Change is inevitable, but its original pace allowed time for mountain ranges to rise; for green shoots to grow from dust, flower, and become dust again. Properly dying to even small ways of life allows rebirth to take place.

There are seasons to my life.

FIRST LOVE

I saw Alexis walking in the road at noontide, at the season when the summer was just being shorn of the tresses of her fruits; and double rays burnt me, the rays of love from the boy's eyes and others from the sun. The sun's night laid to rest again, but love's were kindled more in my dreams by the phantom of beauty.

—Meleager of Gadara in Coelo-Syria

I was eighteen, he was nineteen. He painted, danced, made music. I went off to college with a small watercolor of a rainbow that stayed taped above my pillow all year. We made love only three times. I remember what it felt like the first time when he finally convinced me to take off my underwear in bed. It was so warm, like the sun had come under the covers. I shook uncontrollably. I didn't know I was in love with him. The second time a little kitten named Skyler walked back and forth across our ankles.

He became a phantom. I couldn't find him any more. Double rays were burning me and I turned to follow a different sun. The dreams never stopped.

We always have the fruits of first love. We know what we felt. Night may fall over us, but what was kindled then remains alive and may come again, in another summer, bright and beautiful in our eyes.

Every day, the sun rises.

SELF-PITY

There is no Santa Claus. I'm Santa Claus.
—Josephine Baker

Honey, ain't no one goes through what I do. I've been beaten up, beaten down, lied to, cheated on, and dropped off at the cleaners. I've got overdue bills, overdue books, a wicked case of hemorrhoids, and my cleaning lady isn't returning my calls. Man, if I could find a pen, I'd write a book.

Oh, really? Who'd read it? Self-pity has its place, but fails in the open market. Better to take two aspirins, drink plenty of liquids, and call me in the morning. Feeling good and sorry for ourselves is a fine thing in moderate doses; if we can't complain to the person we know best, who can we complain to? For that matter, close friends should indulge a little whining from time to time, too.

That's it, though. Break's over. Let's get going. If somewhere along the way we've been suckered by the line that living well—or dying the goddamn best we can—isn't worth the effort, then we've bought into the most boring load of crap there is. The slightest effort on our own behalf builds a head of steam behind it. And if we want to find presents under the tree on Christmas morning, then we'd best get our butts in gear and get shopping.

I believe in Santa Claus.

SURRENDER

And then I asked him with my eyes to ask again yes
and then he asked me would I yes...
and his heart was going like mad
and yes I said yes I will yes.

—James Joyce, *Ulysses*

Long after love's first flush has passed, after we have again become separate beings, after we have fought and hurt one another, lifted and carried one another, after we have made love countless times in countless ways, after we have shown each other the very best and very worst of our humanity; after all of this we arrive at a place where love once more waits flush and breathless.

Please ask me again; the answer is yes. Yes, I will accept you. You have proven yourself against the tests of time and you have won my faith. I am ready to give in to you, to lie down before you. I want you to have your way with me; you have my trust. I believe no harm will come to me.

Ask again yes, our hearts are going like mad, we are ready for surrender. Let me show you now how I will let you kiss me. Let me show you how I put my lips to yours. I will give myself to you completely. Yes I say yes I will yes.

At last, we lay down our armor.

EQUALITY

My affection, my love that I share with my boyfriend is just as pro-
found and strong and I'm just as protective and loving as anyone else
that loves someone of the opposite sex. I'll tell ya, I would never change
if I had the opportunity. If somebody said there was a pill that I could
take to be straight, I'd never want it.
   —Sgt. Edgar Rodriguez, New York Police Gay Officer's Action

There's a good long way to go, maybe more than a hundred years, before all the legalities are in place, all the systems changed, all the scientists and sham healers finished with cures, the whole package of "not as good as" assumptions dead and gone.

In the meantime, things are already better. We used to only look at cops as guys who beat us up. Now they beat us off. And are just as public and proud of their new behavior as they used to be of their old. Not all of them, of course, but this isn't about quantity. It's about equality.

The truth is we were always equal. Our affections and relationships have always been as strong and protective and loving as any between a man and woman; our spirits just as alive, necessary, and worthy as any human being's. There never has been and never will be anything second class about us.

All men are created equal.

DEPRESSION

Death keeps happening, friends keep dying. Some days I don't feel like standing before a group of people and trying to pump them up. Some days I want to not get out of bed, I want to stay under the covers and cry all day long.

—Reggie Williams

I hope you do, Reggie, I hope you stay there and cry all day. Then I hope you get up and eat a whole bowl of your favorite ice cream and go outside and let the wind kiss your burning eyes. I hope you do this as often as you have to and remember all your friends and what you loved about them. I hope you get good and angry and throw stuff around the room and even break things if it makes you feel any better.

Our depressions are immobilizing because they've got something they want us to know. They're lead weights attached to the tremendous anger and sadness we carry around inside. The longer we bravely go, the heavier it gets. Most depression is caused by life, but some is caused by chemistry. If it goes on day after day, month after month, there is medical help. We may have to intervene with a friend; untreated, depression can take his life.

Reggie? Reggie, are you okay? I know there's nothing I can do, but I want you to know I'm thinking about you. The emptying out is so hard; it feels so bottomless. I hope you ask for help, for guides and strong forces to be with you and show you some light. Your energy will come back, it really will. You'll be standing in front of a group and pumping them up and you won't be depressed at all because you'll remember how fresh and good the wind felt and you'll be bolstered by your sense of purpose in helping all of us find the strength to get through.

Sometimes I just stay under the covers and cry all day.

DEATH

In the feeble light of the lone flame the face of Meir was transfixed. He pushed abruptly into the children's chamber. For a moment there was only silence behind the swaying curtains. Then through it there cut the horrible rasp of rending cloth. Elisha covered his face. He knew that sound. It was the tearing of a garment in the presence of death.
—*Milton Steinberg, As A Driven Leaf*

There is a hierarchy to the impact of death. At the top is the loss of a child or grandchild. Next come lovers, husbands, and wives. Next parents and closest friends, then the parting of dear elders, our teachers, aunts and uncles, grandparents. Any loss of a human being we love is painfully sharp at the start. We recover slowly but surely from some. From others, we may never recover.

It's finished for those who die. They are snatched away suddenly or pass on gracefully or endure unspeakable mental and physical torture. In the end they are gone. Stories from near-death experiences and what many of us hear from the other side describe the peace there. Once death has happened, it appears it is roughest on the living.

During Grandma Sophie's last hospital stay, I asked her if she believed in an afterlife. She said, "Don't you think I'm depressed enough without talking about things like *that*?" I guess she wasn't ready. Nor are most of us. We are furious if it comes too soon.

Adages abound of how death teaches us we should live our lives. What I have learned is that time is not a luxury. It will matter very much how we have spent it.

Death's power is always near.

DEVOTION

On the way to one's beloved, there are no hills.
—Kenyan Proverb

Many of us are called to greater devotion than we ever imagined would be required of us. We tend our lovers and friends as they decline and die. Few of them go without anguish. Their setbacks and hospitalizations and bouts of dementia bid us come running and nothing stands between us and the person we have sworn to protect and swaddle and bathe and whose weakening hand we hold to our heart.

Devotion is a religious term. Those who light candles on these darkest days of the year honor the legends of spirit people and heroes who entered the devil's realm to preserve their people and help the earth make its turn back toward the sun. When everything is at stake, we rise up against armies of darkness.

In peacetime, we are likely to forget. So much can so easily be taken for granted. We may not remember we are on the way to our beloved. We may fail to prepare ourselves. We may become slack and assume the little things don't matter. We may lie back and settle, see hills looming before us that look too exhausting to climb. But we are needed. Everything we have to give is necessary. Our devotion is vital: to care for him, to care for ourselves, to strike the match and bring light.

I am running to you.

FAMILY EVENTS

When you deal with your brother, be pleasant, but get a witness.
—Hesiod, Works and Days

There we are out in the world living our lives like real adults—jobs, friends, interests, at least an occasional sense of being on top of things—and then *presto-changeo* we're the incredible shrinking man, reduced to an assigned seat at the dinner table where, amazed at the transformation, we find ourselves once again fifteen or even five and any minute in need of a high chair and bib.

How does this happen? It helps to bring a witness. Once it's all over he can give us a play-by-play. We have to be prepared, though. He might go on about how nice and interesting and warm everyone is. Perhaps they are. They just don't seem to have noticed that we're out of short pants.

Not all family gatherings are like this. Just most. It takes intestinal fortitude to withstand the blast from the past, to break ingrained patterns, to get our expectations in line with reality, to stop being angry, to be out and show up the person we are today.

The thing to do is be pleasant, count to ten before flying off the handle, and realize no matter how weird or caught in a time warp or in favor of changing the subject they may be, that they're probably doing—just as they've always done—the best they know how.

The person I have to trust is myself.

BODY OF CHRIST

Amazingly I felt I now knew from the inside what "this is my body and blood for you" means. You see, this is what I experienced when I laid my head on his chest, and when we kissed each other. Deep down in my soul I felt claimed and healed.

—Paul F. Morrissey, OSA

Being raised a Jew and the concept of Christ being a *complete* mystery to me, I finally got my consciousness raised when I had the opportunity to spend a weekend facilitating a planning retreat for Communication Ministry, Inc., a sort of above ground underground of gay Catholic Priests and Religious.

The part about Jesus of Nazareth that a lot of folks neglect is the *human* part. Chances are he even made some mistakes. And he came with a body for a reason. Clearly if Christ was completely holy, that went for all the bodily functions, everywhere the blood ran. And I don't recall any big claims that *he* was a virgin.

So encountering the Body of Christ is not so forbidding after all. From the mind emanates a fierce moral stance, the brooking of no hypocrisy. From the heart there is the message of forgiveness; love thy enemy. And from his loins springs the life-giving spirit of human connection.

Christ was a man who loved all men. The body shuddered on a cross of wood. The promise was that through him, through *all* of him, a higher power might claim and heal.

I may enter into his body.

GIFTS

I think that people who are gay verge on being angels, or wayward angels. Gayness is a gift. I know a lot of people who feel that gay men, in particular, can be the most powerful force for transformation within our society.
—Hibiscus, a.k.a. George Harris as quoted by Mark Thompson,
Children of Paradise: A Brief History of Queens, Gay Spirit

What do angels do all day, anyway? We know they spend a certain amount of time with their heads in the clouds, sometimes make mischief, often provide guidance or illumination, and have the job of showing up to announce miracles to a target market of virgins, the barren, and a range of others who weren't necessarily expecting such versatile guests.

As for being wayward, I never did like the beaten path, so I think I'll hang here with the other flyboys. I don't recall going down to the recruitment office or angel headquarters or putting "make me gay" on my list of what I wanted for Christmas. In fact, I was rather put off when I opened the box. It hasn't happened overnight, but it's been quite a transformation—kind of makes me believe in miracles—because nothing I had ever been taught led me to imagine the gift of my gayness would bring such profound human happiness.

Let's help everyone earn their wings.

INTERIOR DESIGN

We'll take almost anything. I am waiting for some leatherman to send us a motorcycle with a used slave on it.
                                    —John Hammond, co-founder of the
                                    International Gay and Lesbian Archives

*Careful! Careful! It's one of a kind. No, no, a little to the left. A hair more. That's good. Yes, center it right in front of the palm. Now move the slave a little further up on the seat. Perfect! Oh, it's **fabulous!***

Goodness, indulging in stereotypes so late in the year! Shame on us. But there is some truth to it. And as long as we're talking truth, there are one or two gay boys out there who really *don't* know what to do with an apartment. Which doesn't necessarily indicate a lack of ability to perform *in* it. But let's not be tacky.

There are three good reasons we got into this racket in the first place. Number one, people who are rich enough to hire decorators, get their hair done regularly, and purchase other niceties gay men are known to purvey, are generally of the class that forgives a number of "eccentricities." Some of these folks are equal opportunity employers. Some enjoy keeping pets. Number two, it's that outsider vantage point again. We value things others discard and have lived slightly apart from the world for so long we've developed an eye for rearranging it. Number three, it's just one of those queenie things. We were *born* to decorate.

I'm having second thoughts about the motorcycle, though. It might clash with the priceless Toussaud wax figure of Bette Davis, which simply *must* remain the focal point of my overall scheme.

We have *such* refined tastes.

MAKING LOVE

*One cannot be strong without love. For love is not an irrelevant emo-
tion; it is the blood of life, the power of reunion of the separated.*
                                        —*Paul Tillich, The Eternal Now*

It's all there. It was waiting for us before we started, incredibly vital in the moment. We are compelled to exploration, tan-
talized not just by his flesh, but by a sense of something long
buried that waits to be discovered just over the edge.

Oh, God, how much I want this, want you. The first full body
touch brings deep sighs, the first kiss unleashes a flood of emotion. Thoughts race and dissolve, we find we are acting out fantasies we didn't even know we had. Remarkably, there is a complete absence of fear. We press forward. Nothing seems as important. We want to go on and on.

There is a pause. We sit back from him on our haunches,
watch each other. *You are a whole world.* We bend over him slowly, tasting the part of his body that next asks for our hands, our
lips, our tongue. Strength pours out between us and we draw
closer; there is no leader or follower, we are no longer separate.

It is more than emotion, more than body. The blood beats
though our hearts, we sweat, dig in our nails, throb mightily. *I
love you. Oh, my darling, how I love you.*

We reach together for a place beyond.

SPIRITUAL UNION

"I want to breathe my Self into you. And I want to explore the mysteries in your body, the whole history of your body."
"And I want to smell the hair that drops across your forehead that way. I want to take all of that rich human perfume into myself. I want to take you into myself. I want you."
"You have me."
"We have each other."

—John Gilgun, Music I Never Dreamed Of

Underlying deep love relationships is a vision. There are stages to move through to get there; times we draw closer, times we must pull apart. There are lessons to learn of each other, of boundaries, compromise and change, of sacrifice, ecstasy, and surrender.

The vision is of union. Two people, mature and whole, deliberately choosing to place themselves fully into one another's hands. We try this as we go and sometimes the experiments fail. We may sustain the vision and apply our lessons to a future together or we may realize limits and either live with them or take our leave.

If it is union of spirit we want and in the cards for us to have it, the fullness of time arrives when promises can be made.

I want to take you into myself. And breathe my Self into you.
I offer the unconditional holding of your heart as if it were my own.
You have me.
I will be a sanctuary to you.
A light to your spirit.

And I your sacred trust.

SWEAT

"You want it?"
"Yeah."
"Say you want it. Arthur—say you want it."
"Fuck me, Kurt. I want you to fuck me."
                    —*John Wagenhauser, The Group, Flesh and the World*

They meet at the beach on the river. It is summer, ninety-six degrees. Ritualistically they choose each other, go to a secluded place, strip down but do not cool off.

There is sweat at the very beginning. The strange bodies slip against each other, human smells mixing with sand and dirt and steaming leaves. The salt sweetness is in their mouths—they remember the taste long after—it is nice and fine when it is fresh.

At the end, they break the rules. They talk. They acknowledge something more than body lust, say a little of what they want, exchange phone numbers. They wash in the river and leave wondering.

Now it is winter and for the past six months they are lovers. They go to the gym and steam room together. They meet on cool sheets and strip down and bring the temperature back up to where they like it. They use strength and time and intimacy to their advantage. They lick the sweat from each other's bodies, ask each other to say things, ask to be fucked, to be loved, and they move hot and hard and fast on sheets now wet from what they have made and fall into them for darkness and sleep and the feeling of being together deep inside.

Oh, *yeah...*

LIBERATION

Any action or activities that do not create a problem for others, and even for the temporary satisfaction of the individual, if it does not create suffering in others, then that kind of action is all right.

—Tenzin Gyato, The 14th Dalai Lama

Shortly after I came out I went to see a Rabbi, who happens to be a lesbian, to tell my story and ask for advice. It was just sbefore Passover, the Jewish holiday that commemorates the liberation of the Children of Israel from bondage in Egypt. The Rabbi listened warmly and gave this counsel: like the wandering Israelites I was to remember that with freedom comes the need for discipline.

I suppose her comments were a bit of a safe sex allegory, but they also went further. I was starting out in a new life, freed from the effort of building something that was not to be mine, and how the story went from here was completely up to me.

The Dalai Lama's short meditation is in response to the question of homosexuality. He is also describing self-discipline. Liberation, won at the cost of blood and sweat and many tears, does not give license to harm ourselves nor to create suffering for others. Once we are free, we are our own masters. We must reach deeply to know—moment to moment—what we wish to bring to the world.

Every day, I strive to do what is right.

THE NEW YEAR

The present contains all that there is. It is holy ground; for it is the past, and it is the future.

—*Alfred North Whitehead*

New Year's Eve—night of false promise, drunken revelry, prelude to morning-after resolutions. The past and future converge on this day that marks the turn of millennia by a countdown of the second hand. Accomplishments are counted, predictions and goals set. A mad rush to forget ourselves for once in the present. It has never been quite clear to me what all the celebration is about.

Somewhere in the midst of the mayhem, nearly all of us pause to take stock. We do reflect on where we've been. We dare to hope a little on what's to come.

Mystics tell us the past and future are illusions. The present is where infinity lies and the small shell of *self* is what prevents us from seeing it. This *self* has no inbred desire to give up its turf. It is the intense flare of our lives that has the capacity to burn away its edges from within.

When we emerge from illusion, denial and judgment, from any shrinking away from our full humanness, then the ground beneath us becomes our holy anchor and we are allowed to grow, faces to the sun, into the expanse of all that there is.

Happy New Year.

Index

photo by Kel Keller

About the Author

Gary J. Stern is a nationally known organization and human development consultant, trainer, and keynote speaker and is author of the *Marketing Workbook for Nonprofit Organizations*. He lives in Minneapolis and New York, is an active father and community volunteer, and is a great cook.